PUBLICATIONS OF THE
DEPARTMENT OF SOCIAL AND ECONOMIC RESEARCH
UNIVERSITY OF GLASGOW

GENERAL EDITOR: A. K. CAIRNCROSS

SOCIAL AND ECONOMIC STUDIES

6

THE ECONOMICS OF SHIPBUILDING IN THE UNITED KINGDOM

T0300466

THE
ECONOMICS OF SHIPBUILDING
IN THE UNITED KINGDOM

BY

J. R. PARKINSON

CAMBRIDGE
AT THE UNIVERSITY PRESS
1960

CAMBRIDGE UNIVERSITY PRESS
Cambridge, New York, Melbourne, Madrid, Cape Town,
Singapore, São Paulo, Delhi, Tokyo, Mexico City

Cambridge University Press
The Edinburgh Building, Cambridge CB2 8RU, UK

Published in the United States of America by Cambridge University Press, New York

www.cambridge.org
Information on this title: www.cambridge.org/9781107601420

© Cambridge University Press 1960

This publication is in copyright. Subject to statutory exception
and to the provisions of relevant collective licensing agreements,
no reproduction of any part may take place without the written
permission of Cambridge University Press.

First published 1960
First paperback edition 2011

A catalogue record for this publication is available from the British Library

ISBN 978-1-107-60142-0 Paperback

Cambridge University Press has no responsibility for the persistence or
accuracy of URLs for external or third-party internet websites referred to in
this publication, and does not guarantee that any content on such websites is,
or will remain, accurate or appropriate.

CONTENTS

V CONCLUSIONS

LIST OF PLATES

LIST OF FIGURES

LIST OF TABLES

PREFACE

The writing of this book has raised two major problems: the choice of audience to which it should be addressed, and the analytical methods that should be followed in treating the economics of an industry. So far as the first is concerned, the book is addressed largely to economists; but it is hoped also that in the give and take of opinion it will be of interest to ship-builders, particularly to those younger members of the fraternity who are concerned at present largely with technical matters and day-to-day administration but would welcome a wider view of the industry taken from a different standpoint. They at least will find no difficulty in filling in the details of shipbuilding processes, visualising the localities or sensing the ships in course of construction—in short, in providing the shipyard atmosphere which is of consequence to the general reader but falls largely on the periphery of economic analysis.

It is one of the main purposes of economic analysis to circumscribe attention and to concentrate on a certain limited approach to everyday affairs. But as the examination of mankind in the ordinary business of life is directed to the industry or the firm rather than to the national economy, its scope, narrowed in one way, broadens in another: the academic economist engaged in the examination of an industry is likely to find that other, perhaps allied, disciplines are of as much assistance to him as the content of economic analysis on a grander scale, and that in consequence his approach should be more that of an historian than an economic logician.

The central core of the examination of an industry from an economist's standpoint lies in the assessment of economic efficiency and the factors governing it. In some cases it may be thought sufficient to examine whether the industry is competitive or not and the factors making for competition; but the term competitive is not an unambiguous one and it often happens that the conditions in which the industry is operating approximate to monopolistic competition or even monopoly; consequently other tests of efficiency require to be developed. Some of these will be of simple outline approximating to the comparison of output per man-hour or similar measures of greater refinement. Such tests are not always easy to perform, but even in those conditions when they can be made to apply they do little more than present an instantaneous photograph of a limited aspect of complicated evolutionary processes, and a wider basis of assessment is indispensable. This involves the detailed examinations of the structure of the industry; its capital equipment; the techniques it uses; the quality of management; the labour force available, as well as many other matters of current moment: but no less the historical trends (and not always those most closely concerned with economics) need to be established, in the hope that they can be projected forwards as a guide to the probable evolution of events, and (though this is doubtful, but more rewarding) to serve as pointers to the kind of factors which need to be considered in judging industrial matters. An historical examination of any industry is thus an indispensable tool of analysis for the contemporary industrial economist and not least for the shipbuilding industry; in this connection Dr S. Pollard's study[1] of the period from 1850 to 1914 is particularly valuable.

In this study, however, history is used only as a selected tool, and apart from the brief introductory sketch of the evolution of the industry the emphasis has been placed on the current position of the industry as revealed by an examination of current facts. When the course of history has appeared to throw useful light on the present position, or to bring out the kind of forces at work, some digression from the present has seemed desirable, as, for example, to demonstrate how near an industry can come to unified control, or to illustrate some of the supposed merits and demerits of standardisation, or to bring home the role of technical progress in the past and so to infer its likely importance in the future.

For the rest current documents and current conversations have been the source of information. Many shipbuilders, on the Clyde, in other parts of the country and abroad, as well as others who are not actively engaged in the building of ships, have helped me in this way, and while preserving their anonymity I should like to thank them warmly for their assistance, and particularly to thank those in other countries for their kindness in receiving me. In these meetings there was sometimes the lesson that the recorded word can convey a false impression to its readers and that the impression formed on the ground, though lacking in depth and perspective, is likely to be rather different from, and generally more accurate than, that formed from reading contemporary accounts. It should not, however, be thought from this that there is any marked consensus of opinion amongst shipbuilders as to the happenings of their industry. Indeed, one of the difficulties experienced in obtaining first-hand information is that it so often is in conflict with other information. When this happens the observer is forced to make up his own mind on the issues in question, or if they are too intractable, to note that judgment must be withheld. Inevitably, therefore, there is a great deal with which some shipbuilders may be expected to disagree, and, no doubt, some conclusions suggested by an economic training that will command

---

[1] 'The economic history of British shipbuilding, 1870–1914,' University of London Ph.D. thesis, 1951.

little support amongst those engaged in the industry. But that is largely to be expected.

There, is however, one important and by no means obvious conclusion that emerges from an economic study, and this is that organisation, particularly managerial skill, can go a long way to nullify advantages and disadvantages of a more strictly economic kind; so that perhaps more generally the industrial economist is likely to find his attention directed less to the market-place and more to problems of industrial administration as time goes on. But from whatever point of view an industry is examined it would be a mistake to think that everything of importance about an industry can be distilled from an examination restricted to its own affairs. The knowledge that standardisation is a means to more economical production in a variety of industries, and that the benefits that accrue from pursuing standardisation in any one industry are frequently widely dispersed among other industries, may well be a more useful tool of analysis than an attempt to measure the likely effect of standardisation within any one industry on that industry itself. It is in generalisation and the application of generalisations that the strength of economic analysis lies, and because of this that the economist's approach may sometimes show a new aspect of industrial problems.

I gratefully acknowledge the courtesy of Messrs John Brown & Co. in placing photographs of their yard at my disposal. I should like also to thank my colleagues for help given in various ways and particularly Mr A. I. MacBean for preparing the index and Miss Macdonald, who typed the various drafts of the book as they emerged. Finally, it is difficult to express the measure of my thanks to Professor A. K. Cairncross for the help and encouragement he has given and not least for the many suggestions and criticisms he offered as the work developed. The faults that remain are, of course, my own.

The publication of this book has been made possible by a guarantee from the Carnegie Trust for the Universities of Scotland to which I gladly express my indebtedness.

I

INTRODUCTION

CHAPTER 1

The Growth of the Industry

In the second half of the nineteenth century the British shipbuilding industry eclipsed all others in its rate of growth and, in the fullness of its competitive power, overwhelmed all markets until it produced for a time over 80 per cent of the world's ships. The triumph of the industry, though complete, was short-lived; what it had learned was used elsewhere and improved upon, so that by 1958 it produced less than 20 per cent of the tonnage of ships launched outside the communist bloc, and could no longer justly claim to be the shipyard of the world.

Before 1850 it was the Americans who were supreme—but only in the building of sailing ships. With 'a high level of intelligence and initiative . . . freedom from the complex of prejudice and tradition which governed the thoughts and activities of the old world . . . and unbounded resources . . . in fifty years they contributed as much to the development of the sailing ship as the whole maritime world had contributed in three hundred'.[1] The United Kingdom industry, handicapped by difficulties in timber supplies and putting longevity and solidity of the ships built against speed and quick results, could not compete in price with either Dantzig or the United States, where well-found ships could be had for £11 and £12 a ton[2] against the £15 needed in the United Kingdom.[3] Small wonder that the repeal of the Navigation Acts in 1849 seemed to threaten the previously assured home market for United Kingdom shipbuilders and strike at the roots of the industry.

But a new era was advancing which would free the United Kingdom shipbuilding industry from the need to rest on protective props and change so much so radically that prejudice and tradition would drop away before the experimental temper of the day. It was the building of iron and steel ships propelled by steam that worked the change and gave the United Kingdom, for a time, overwhelming advantage.

The ascendancy of the United Kingdom was no foregone conclusion. Early experiments in steam propulsion had been at least as advanced in America as they were on the Clyde, and plagiarism enabled Mr Robert Fulton (of Napoleonic fame) to establish the paddle-steamer *Clermont* in

[1] R. H. Thornton, *British Shipping* (Cambridge University Press, 1939), p. 5.

[2] Evidence placed before Parliament when the repeal of the Navigation Laws was under consideration; quoted in *Survey of Metal Industries*, pt. IV (Committee of Industry and Trade, 1928), p. 363.

[3] The following abbreviations are used in this book: t.—ton; g.—gross; n.—nett; r.—registered; d.w.t.—deadweight ton.

regular service between New York and Albany before Henry Bell offered his *Comet* as a means of transport between Glasgow, Greenock and Helensburgh. The Americans, like the British, also commanded the materials for iron and steel, if not the means to exploit them. But the Civil War and the preoccupations of the Americans in other fields of economic endeavour gave an opportunity for the British industry to get ahead and to develop in unrivalled fashion its cheap supplies of coal and iron and budding engineering skill. When the American industry re-emerged in modern form towards the end of the century it was too late to compete economically with the main sector of the British industry, where lower wages for skilled men and simple but highly effective organisation, without frills or excessive capital expenditure, kept costs at minimum levels.

TECHNICAL CHANGE AND EDUCATION

The final refinements in sailing ships which the Americans had so skilfully introduced paled beside the growing technical revolution that affected every aspect of naval architecture and constructional technique. But sail died hard and for a time the old and the new intermingled in uneasy compromise. Sails were fitted to vessels made of iron, steam engines were installed in hulls of wood, and wood and iron combined in composite vessels of iron frames and wooden sides. It took time also to appreciate that the new materials should be used in new ways and their different properties properly exploited. In early ships 'the copy of wood frames was carried so far that the frames were made in separate bits of angle iron, and scarphed and spliced just like timber frames'.[1]

Wooden ships were small in size, averaging 200–300 t. in the early nineteenth century, and they were seldom more than 100 ft. in length. In consequence there was little need of longitudinal strength, and the main support of the ship could be provided by transverse frames. Ships in iron and steel were much larger and of greater length, and longitudinal strength was necessary in order to enable them to withstand the buffetings of the sea. Technically, the answer lay in longitudinal framing which could provide increased strength while at the same time making possible a reduction in the weight of steel required, thus lightening the ship. Early attempts to devise suitable systems proved unsatisfactory, largely because the arrangements proposed were too complicated, making construction difficult and requiring the use of supports, such as pillars, which impeded the stowage of cargo in the holds. In 1908, J. W. Isherwood (later Sir Joseph), an outstanding naval architect, developed a new system which overcame some of the con-

[1] Scott Russell, quoted by Sir Westcott Abell in *The Shipwright's Trade* (Cambridge University Press, 1948), p. 111.

structional difficulties previously experienced, and this was destined to achieve considerable success, particularly in the construction of oil tankers where structural strength was of prime importance and projections in the hold no obstacle to the carriage of oil.

One of the impediments to the adoption of new methods of construction was the lack of fundamental knowledge and the means to disseminate it. Outstanding researches on the form and rolling of ships were carried out by William Froude, who remained at Oxford after taking his degree in mathematics to study the motion of the ship. After assisting Brunel for a time with the Great Western Railway and with studies of the rolling of the *Great Eastern*, he devoted himself, from 1846 onward, to experiments on towing model ships in tanks. Experiments on a small scale led to a grant from the Admiralty, and this enabled him to complete the construction of a larger tank in 1871.[1] Froude's law of comparison between the performance of model ships and those of full size, developed from his experiments, paved the way for extended studies of the form of ships and the transmission of engine power into useful propulsive forces.

This was not the only way in which the Admiralty, albeit on occasions reluctantly, was able to encourage the development of a scientific approach to the construction of ships. The first School of Naval Architecture was founded at Portsmouth in 1811, for the training of apprentices. It was short-lived, being closed in 1832 by Sir James Graham, First Lord of the Admiralty, and the Central School of Mathematics and Naval Construction established in 1848 suffered the same fate five years after it started instruction, when Sir James again turned against the theoretical approach. A paper read by Scott Russell before the Institution of Naval Architects, newly founded in 1860, was instrumental in the establishment of a third school started at South Kensington by the joint action of the Admiralty and the Science and Art Department. Known as the Royal School of Naval Architecture it was moved to the Royal Naval College at Greenwich, where it still exists for the training of naval and private students.[2] At the universities, Chairs in naval architecture were founded by Glasgow in 1883 and at King's College, Newcastle, in 1886.

These and other developments in education provided an opportunity for the teaching of naval architecture and the assembly of a systematic body of knowledge. But practice was strongly blended with theory in the British shipyards, where an ounce of practice was thought to be worth a pound of theory. In this the British-trained shipbuilder may have been at an advantage over his foreign colleagues, whose lengthy theoretical training did not necessarily fit them any better for the task of building ships.

---

[1] Sir Westcott Abell, *op. cit.* p. 154.   [2] Sir Westcott Abell, *op. cit.* p. 152.

For all the progress which has been made in the construction and form of ships, it is to the development of prime movers that pride of place in technical innovation must be given. The early steam engines were adopted only slowly, largely because they were inefficient converters of heat into propulsive energy. Improvement was gradual and sometimes imperceptible, and it was over a century before it could be said that the steam engine had finally put an end to the days of sail, and by this time newer engines of different principles were going into service. So long as the steam engine was a heavy consumer of coal its use was restricted to short and coastal journeys keeping it in touch with its fuel supplies. Economy was the prerequisite of longer hauls and no less of the establishment of bunkering stations overseas. On long runs it was not unusual for steamships to be bunkered for the return voyage with coal carried out by sail. The opening of the Suez Canal in 1869 encouraged the use of steam by shortening the routes to the East and easing the problem of bunkering.

A long series of small improvements in many aspects of steam propulsion brought ultimate success. These improvements were not the fruit of progress in marine engineering alone: they depended on progress in the sciences and in the many kindred arts and technologies which must advance in step. Steel, for example, enabled boiler pressures to be raised, as did the change from boilers of square to those of cylindrical design and the use of water-tubes round which the furnace played instead of the hot gases being led by tubes through the water. Scientific calculation enabled the shape and speed of revolution of propellers to be decided in order to get the maximum propulsive effect, and new metallurgical processes enabled tougher materials to be used. It was possible to discard the paddle wheel, so vulnerable in the Crimean War to passing shot and dependent on the weight of coal in the bunkers for optimum depth of immersion, and to substitute the propeller.

Some of the biggest improvements were made in the steam engine itself. The use of superheated steam, which, like the hot jacket used to surround the cylinder, prevented condensation, paved the way for the compound engine and triple, quadruple and even quintuple expansion, with a considerable gain in economy at the expense of further complication of action. For the steam engine as for other prime movers, high temperatures and high pressures were the prerequisite for efficiency, and progress could be measured in terms of these physical characteristics. By the late nineties boiler pressures were up to 220 lb. and twin, triple and later quadruple screws were being used to obtain the power necessary for the larger and faster ships that were being built, with the result that the coal required per h.p. developed was reduced to one-third of that needed in 1860.

Quadruple expansion appeared to represent the ultimate in the practical development of the steam piston engine, and innovation took a new turn when the Parsons' steam turbine was perfected and demonstrated in the *Turbinia* at the Spithead Naval Review in 1897.

The steam turbine was the last of the developments pioneered by British shipbuilders in the nineteenth century. It was suitable only for the largest vessels and those requiring high speeds, but for these types it gained ready acceptance. The new machinery was adopted in warships and in the *Lusitania* and the *Mauretania*, both completed in 1907, and it was improved in 1910 when geared turbines came into use. At that time about 5 million h.p. was being installed or used on board ships.[1]

It was left to the Danish company of Burmeister & Wain to lead the way in adapting the invention of Rudolph Diesel to marine propulsion; between 1897, when they first acquired a production licence, and 1910, when Diesel visited Ivor Knudsen, who had been responsible for the development work at Burmeister & Wain's, the diesel engine was revolutionised for marine purposes and assured of instantaneous success. With this passing of technical genius in the shipbuilding world to another country there went something of the brilliance, adaptability and experimental attack of the industry which had come to the fore when, with steam and steel in the ascendancy, shipbuilding centred itself in the industrial centres of the north.

LOCATION

Before the coming of iron, steam and steel, the industry was widely scattered on many river banks as well as being strongly represented on the Thames, the centre of high-quality work, and on the Wear. It is difficult to ascertain what proportion of the tonnage of ships built in the United Kingdom in the early nineteenth century was constructed on the Thames. An analysis of the place of build of vessels constructed for the United Kingdom flag included in *Lloyd's Register*, conducted by Mr H. A. Moisley, suggests that in 1834 and 1835, and in 1847 and 1848, little more than 5 per cent of the tonnage constructed was Thames-built. These figures do not, however, reveal the full importance of the Thames as a shipbuilding centre. Naval orders placed·in private yards and work carried out in the naval dockyards were an important source of employment for the shipyards on the river, and it appears that in 1841 more than one-third of the men employed in shipbuilding and repairing on the Thames were engaged in the naval dockyards. Employment in the Thames shipyards was very variable. There appears to have been, for example, an increase in activity on the Thames between 1831 and 1851, followed by a steep rise when orders, in part spilling over into the Thames yards at the times of the Crimean War and the Civil War in America, boosted employment to unprecedented levels. The 117,000

---

[1] Sir Westcott Abell, *op. cit.* p. 166.

g.r.t. of iron merchant ships said to have been produced on the Thames in 1865 must have far exceeded any previous output levels.[1] It is at least as true that the Thames profited from building early iron ships as that output declined precipitately after 1865.

In addition to warship work the reputation of the Thames was founded on the production of high-quality vessels, particularly the East Indiamen, which were constructed and refitted after every voyage regardless of expense. Construction for the East India Company came to an end in 1832 when its charter was withdrawn, and although, as we have seen, this did not prevent a rise in output in later years, it became more difficult for the Thames to maintain its position in an increasingly commercial age when a reputation for quality was small substitute for the lowest price, and quantity a surer foothold to success than a single special ship. Higher wages for labour and its independent attitude, higher costs for materials and for coal, and the attraction of London for other industries and the growing demands of its port facilities combined to make competition difficult with the northern centres; but modern parallels would suggest that none of these factors, either singly or in combination, would be decisive of themselves; the energy and initiative that had led Brunel to construct the ill-fated *Great Eastern* on the Thames flowed more readily in the other centres, where managerial skill was a vital factor in the expansion of the industry's production. Thus it was that Thorneycroft moved to Southampton and Yarrow to the Clyde.

In the 1830's, when employment and output on the Thames appear to have been at a low level, about one-third of the nation's merchant ships were produced on the Wear. The growth of output, striking as it was in subsequent years, was no more perhaps than might have been expected in a firmly established shipbuilding centre faced with an expanding market. The Clyde also was established as a shipbuilding river in the early nineteenth century but not on the scale of the Wear. The growth of the industry on the Clyde rested very largely on its engineering skills. 'Steam engines had been built in the City of Glasgow since 1800 and in 1835, before marine engineering had reached more than modest proportions, there were already 14 Glasgow firms engaged in their construction.'[2] But great enterprise was shown by local builders in their experiments with marine engines, and they were willing to change from wood to iron and, later, steel vessels ahead of other shipbuilders.[3] Moreover, proximity to the transatlantic routes led to the

[1] See the Appendix to S. Pollard's 'The decline of shipbuilding on the Thames', *Economic History Review*, vol. III, no. 1, 1950, for the available statistical evidence.

[2] A. K. Cairncross, 'The economy of Glasgow' in *The Glasgow Region*, p.223 (prepared for the British Association, 1958).

[3] Note, that as output on the Clyde increased, a greater tonnage of sailing ships as well as of steamships was constructed. As late even as 1892, over 100,000 g.r.t. of sailing ships were launched, roughly half the total constructed.

building of many vessels on the Clyde for this exacting service and encouraged technical development and the construction of the better class of ship, while Glasgow merchants and shipowners provided an increasing market for ships of all kinds.

The Clyde was also at an advantage in its ready access to iron and steel supplies, but, like so many other shipbuilding centres, without the deep-water channels needed to launch its ships. Only extensive dredging and river works made it possible for the Clyde to scour its bed and for the shipbuilding industry to develop upstream from Greenock and Port Glasgow, close to the larger centres of population.

The new labour needed to work iron and, later, steel was found with surprising ease. Outside the naval dockyards, the woodworking shipwrights were generally reluctant to desert their accustomed material and change their craft, but the boilermakers and new generations of skilled men trained in the yards took over. When housing was inadequate to accommodate the numbers needed, new streets or towns were built by the shipbuilding companies themselves so that the output of ships could continue to grow. The shipyard labour forces were highly mobile and did not hestitate to set out in search of work if a yard worked through its orders. Thus it was possible to furnish the Belfast yard of Harland and Wolff with its complement of workers from the Clyde, and from the Tyne,[1] and there was no shortage of men even in junior ranks to go overseas to supervise the foreign shipyards that British interests established or financed.

THE GROWTH OF OUTPUT AT HOME AND ABROAD

In the absence of complete figures of output or employment it is difficult to give a detailed picture of the increase in the tonnage of ships constructed during the nineteenth century. Output on the Wear, for which a continuous series of figures of the tonnage launched is available,[2] shows no marked increase between 1840, when 64,000 t. were launched, and 1870, when the figure was 70,000 t. Thereafter, the signs of growth are more spectacular—135,000 t. in 1872, 212,000 t. in 1883, 295,000 t. in 1901 and 366,000 t. in 1906, all, of course, exceptionally good years. Expansion was more rapid for the country as a whole, mainly because the Clyde developed its shipbuilding potential rapidly. Output increased from a few thousand tons at the beginning of the nineteenth century to 178,000 t. in 1864,[3] considerably more than was

[1] See S. Pollard, 'The economic history of British shipbuilding, 1870–1914', University of London Ph.D. thesis, 1951, p. 231.

[2] J. W. Smith and T. S. Holden, *Where Ships are Born: Sunderland, 1346–1946*. (Thomas Reed, 1946.)

[3] See A. K. Cairncross, *Home and Foreign Investment, 1870–1913* (Cambridge University Press, 1953), table 24, p. 129.

produced on the Wear at that time, and by 1901 over 500,000 g.r.t. of shipping were being produced. From 1886, *Lloyd's Register* published a continuous series of figures of total output of the industry, and it will be seen from fig. 1 that output had reached 1½ million g.r.t. in 1901 and nearly 2 million g.r.t. by 1913.

The strength of British shipbuilding rested as much on the economical production of tramps on the north-east coast as it did on the more highly finished and specialised output of the Clyde. The United Kingdom produced ships for the world at the end of the nineteenth century because she produced them cheaply. Her competitive advantage at this stage of evolution of the

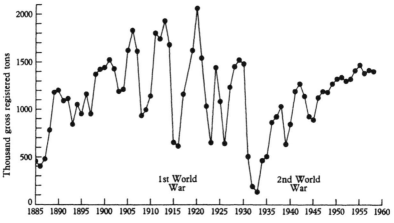

Fig. 1.—United Kingdom Shipbuilding Output (100 gross tons and over)

industry rested heavily on the highly-skilled labour force which had been assembled by the shipyards. The British shipyards producing tramps were sparsely equipped, indeed under-equipped in relation to those of her competitors; but for the production of small and simple vessels it is not always the large yard with new and costly equipment that has the advantage. The British production of tramp ships was akin to the production of coasters on the canal banks at Groningen in Holland which continues competitively today; the lightness of overheads was a source of strength in a speculative industry in which over-equipment and heavy standing charges could lead to loss and ultimate failure. But if simplicity characterised the organisation of the shipyards, it was made good by specialisation and the production year in and year out of near-standard vessels assured of a market whenever freights boomed and trade expanded. There appears little doubt that productivity was high by the standards of the time.

10

Calculations made by Pollard[1] on the basis of figures of employment in shipbuilding compiled by the Board of Trade,[2] and the output of merchant vessels, suggest that output per head in the United Kingdom about 1900 may have been almost double that of her nearest rival, the United States, and many times more than that in other countries. It is difficult to believe that the United Kingdom was as much in advance of other countries as the figures suggest[3] but it is clear she was ahead, and far enough ahead to more than offset any differences in wages between herself and her competitors.

In the face of such established supremacy there might have appeared to be little hope for the United Kingdom's competitors to overtake her lead. But a merchant marine as well as a modern navy is an essential feature of a sea-going power, and what could not be achieved by competitive power could be achieved with subsidies and government aid. With naval orders and an expanding steel industry, the German industry developed so that it became more closely competitive with the United Kingdom. In France and Italy government assistance helped their shipbuilding industries without, however, putting them on a competitive basis, and Japanese shipyards were also assisted by similar means. This was to the disadvantage of the United Kingdom shipbuilding industry, but the mail subsidies paid to the first Cunard liners built upon the Clyde many years before had also played a part in the development of shipbuilding at home.

After the First World War expansion was succeeded by contraction. The tonnage of ships launched by the United Kingdom in 1913 was exceeded in 1920, when, in the first flush of reconstruction and over-optimistic expectations about the course of trade, 2 million g.r.t. were launched, but such a figure has not been attained since by the United Kingdom shipbuilding industry. In the remainder of the inter-war period, in good years as well as bad, the shipbuilding industry operated far below its capacity and could not offer employment to many of the workers who, in more prosperous days, had been drawn to the shipbuilding areas. Unemployment averaged 30 per cent of the labour force in the 1920's and over 40 per cent in the 1930's.

THE YEARS OF DEPRESSION

The United Kingdom's difficulties stemmed only partly from the failure of world trade to regain pre-war levels. The large amounts of laid-up tonnage, which only in 1929 and 1937 fell to negligible amounts, were a constant

---

[1] 'British and World Shipbuilding', *Journal of Economic History*, No. 3, 1957, p. 438.
[2] *Second Series of Memoranda*, 1904 (Cd. 2337), pt. xvii, p. 475 *et. seq.*
[3] Some of the more obvious statistical difficulties are the extent to which shipbuilding employment covers repair work and warship construction, and the number of small boats and barges produced, which are not recorded in the tonnage of vessels of over 100 g.r.t.

drag on orders, and since much of the world's fleet had been constructed recently, there were relatively few old and obsolete vessels that needed to be scrapped. But the United Kingdom was also affected by the growth in the output of her shipbuilding competitors overseas. Her share in the world market slowly declined from 80 per cent in 1892–4 to 70 per cent in 1895–9 and 60 per cent in 1910–4, and continued to fall with ups and downs in the inter-war period.

During this period the Germans, the Dutch, the Swedes and, in particular, the Japanese emerged as Britain's main competitors; the United States and other countries also contributed to the world's output of merchant ships. It was not so much the check to world output that spelled a warning for the United Kingdom industry, as the gradual encroachment of its overseas competitors into what once had been a United Kingdom preserve. There were a number of contributing factors: the state aid afforded to many continental producers and other protective devices; over-expanded capacity which spread orders too thinly amongst the United Kingdom yards; difficult labour relations in the United Kingdom and lower wages elsewhere; and the failure to expand itself, which discouraged investment and innovation. But the fact remains that the initiative the United Kingdom had enjoyed in the nineteenth century in introducing new designs of vessels, developing new engines, using new materials and adopting new methods of working had passed for a time to other centres of production. Most important of these factors, perhaps, was that the major technical innovation exploited in the inter-war period—the oil-burning diesel engine—proved to be of particular advantage to many continental shipowners, and they and their suppliers were quick to adopt it. And since output in these countries was small in relation to the capacity of the United Kingdom, it was possible for them to increase the number of ships they built and the number of berths in use, even in a depressed market, at a rate sufficient to stimulate progress and promote efficiency.

For the United Kingdom, retrenchment was the order of the day. The Continental threat was publicised in 1924 by the placing of an order for five motorships, required by Furness Withy, with the German shipyard of Deutsche Werft. The placing of such an order with a foreign shipyard was unheard of, and the margin between the German price and the nearest British tender was a cause for alarm which could not be wholly set aside when it was learned later that the motorships had been built at a loss. It is understandable perhaps that the industry attributed its misfortunes largely to a difficult and overpaid labour force and sought a solution to its problems in the contraction of capacity more into line with current demand. What were needed at least as much, however, were modern shipyards, new methods of working and more advanced ships, but these things could not be provided

12

when orders shrank to negligible proportions in the 1930's and when some of the best yards were closed sometimes for years on end for want of work, and others failed to keep afloat. In 1933, the depth of the depression, little more was built in the whole of the United Kingdom than on the Thames alone in 1865.

It is possible that United Kingdom output would have contracted even if the world economic outlook had been one of expansion rather than contraction or stagnation in the 1930's, but the severity of the slump seemed to put an end to any hopes of renewed expansion. Fluctuations in output were, of course, nothing new; the whole philosophy of the industry must have been couched in terms of recurrent slump and boom. In earlier years, however, output rose after every major fall to new peaks each greater than the last, and the need for any contraction in the industry other than that effected by economic forces was never felt.

In the changed atmosphere of the 1930's, the primary need was felt to be an orderly contraction in the capacity of the industry. Estimates of the potential output of the industry in the most favourable conditions showed that plant was available to produce the equivalent of $3\frac{1}{2}$ million t. of merchant shipping[1] compared with 3 million g.r.t. in 1914, although, in the absence of warship orders on the pre-war scale and with the decline in the demand for new merchant shipping, output had not exceeded the equivalent of $1\frac{3}{4}$ million t. of shipping since 1920.

Some reduction in capacity was felt to be necessary if shipbuilding was to be put on an economical basis, and arrangements were made to facilitate the withdrawal of shipyards from the industry. For this purpose, the major firms in the shipbuilding industry banded together to set up a new company, National Shipbuilders' Security Ltd., with the object of purchasing and dismantling redundant and obsolete shipyards and preventing their being used for shipbuilding in the future. Support was forthcoming for the venture from the Bank of England, and this made it possible to make an issue of debentures, sponsored by the Bankers' Industrial Development Company. Security for the issue was given by the promise of a levy of 1 per cent on the value of new tonnage to be constructed in the future by those shipbuilders supporting National Shipbuilders' Security. The money raised was used to purchase and dismantle existing shipyards or to induce companies to agree that their yards should not be used for shipbuilding purposes in the future. It is impossible to say how far the reduction in capacity effected by this means would have been brought about by natural processes, or whether it would

---

[1] Counting naval work as equivalent gross tonnage on the basis of the respective manpower requirements of merchant and naval work. The estimates are those of Sir Amos Ayre contained in a reprint of a paper entitled 'Some statistical consideration of the shipbuilding industry', read before the Greenock Philosophical Society on 17 January 1947.

have been longer drawn out. Many of the firms that took advantage of the arrangements proposed by National Shipbuilders' Security were in no position to withstand the deterioration in trading conditions that took place in the early thirties, and to this extent the effect of the intervention of the company in the affairs of the industry was of less importance than might at first appear.

The action of National Shipbuilders' Security was significant in two other ways. In the first place it was open recognition that industrial as well as individual action was needed to regulate the affairs of the industry, and secondly it was a recognition of the difficulties that the United Kingdom shipbuilding industry would experience in the future, in the face of foreign competition, in maintaining its absolute and even more its relative place in the output of ships.

An increase in shipping requirements towards the end of the 1930's resulted in the launching of 1 million t. of merchant shipping in 1938, but United Kingdom costs were high and the demand for merchant ships fell off sharply in 1939. Demand for naval vessels was increasing in that year, but even so the industry was still employed well below capacity, and, although there were complaints of a shortage of skilled workers, 20 per cent of shipyard workers continued to be unemployed until the summer of 1939.

The experience of the industry in the 1930's left its mark on post-war years; fears of over-capacity and over-expansion still lingered. In spite of some wartime re-equipment, the facilities of most yards urgently needed modernisation, both to overcome the neglect of earlier years and to make possible the adoption of new techniques for constructing ships. Supplies of steel and labour seldom appeared simultaneously to be adequate for shipbuilders' needs. And it proved as difficult to increase output in peacetime as at the height of the war. At the end of the First World War production rapidly caught up with demand—too rapidly it may appear—but it had failed to do so even ten years after the Second World War. As early as 1948 demand was seen to be hesitating, and again in 1955 order books of some shipbuilders were unsatisfactory, but it was not until 1958 that it was possible to visualise again a prolonged period in which new orders might be very difficult to get and output shrink below capacity.

It may be that 1958 will mark the dividing line between a period when the main emphasis of the industry needed to be directed towards expanding output, in order both to meet demand for ships and to discourage the challenge of its competitors in other countries, and a period in which the emphasis will have to be directed mainly to increasing efficiency, in order to meet foreign competition and maintain output at existing levels. The two are not of course unrelated. Increased efficiency requires an increase in output per man and per unit of capital employed, and this is the means in conditions of full employment of increasing output and of resisting competition. All this requires the application of suitable managerial techniques as much as the manipulation of economic forces, and it challenges the industry to continue to adapt itself to the changing economic scene.

Shipbuilding will never hold again the key position that it secured in the nineteenth century, either in the world or in the United Kingdom economy, and even in the centres where it is concentrated it is more likely to decline than to increase in comparative importance. New construction is less than in favourable years half a century ago; but other industries have continued to grow, new industries have been established and services have increased in importance. Between them shipbuilding, ship-repairing and marine engineering employ directly about 300,000 people compared with over 1 million in agriculture, over 700,000 in mining and more than 1 million in vehicles. The value of the net output of ships, engines and repairs is about £200 million per annum, or rather more than 1 per cent of the national income.

It is not, however, so much in its contribution to the national income that shipbuilding should be assessed, but in its key position as a supplier of one of the arms of the fighting services, as an export industry, both directly and indirectly in its contribution to shipping earnings, and as the mainstay of the communities in those districts where the industry is highly concentrated. In 1956 the value of ships exported amounted to about £90 million and in the post-war period about one-third of production has been sold abroad, often for hard currencies. Nor can the shipbuilding industry be neglected as a training centre for highly skilled labour, or as a contributor to technical innovation. Its potentialities for growth are probably less than those of some other industries, but in the areas where it is established it is likely to continue to be a major contributor to the welfare of the community.

II

THE ORGANISATION OF THE INDUSTRY

CHAPTER 2

The Firms in the Industry

I

The location of shipbuilding in the United Kingdom was broadly settled by the end of the nineteenth century. The entry of new firms into the industry, particularly characteristic of the 1860's and 1870's, had subsided, and only a handful of successful new companies was founded in the next half-century. Failures and withdrawals from the industry were frequent—in the mushroom growth of the nineteenth-century expansion and in the years of depression following the expansion of shipbuilding capacity after the First World War—but they were fairly evenly spread in their geographical impact and made no lasting impression on the distribution of output; at the same time a nucleus of firms, or sometimes shipyard sites, in the main shipbuilding areas survived the vicissitudes of the industry and provided an element of continuity in the location of output.

Thus the industry has continued to be located on the Clyde, Tyne, Wear and Tees; while Cammell Laird on the Mersey, Vickers-Armstrongs at Barrow and Harland & Wolff at Belfast are large but isolated companies in other places. In addition, there are a number of smaller companies in other parts of the country, for example, on the Forth, Tay and Dee, on the Humber, on the Thames, at Southampton and on the Bristol Channel.

Table 1 records some details of the larger shipbuilding and marine-engineering firms catering largely for ocean-going ships. On the Clyde a dozen fairly large shipyards, some of which are under the same control, produce over 90 per cent of output; they include John Brown & Co., Lithgows, Fairfield Shipbuilding & Engineering Co., Blythswood Shipbuilding Co., William Hamilton & Co., Harland & Wolff, Alexander Stephen & Sons, Scotts' Shipbuilding & Engineering Co., Barclay Curle & Co., Charles Connell & Co., Greenock Dockyard and William Denny & Brothers. On the Tyne there are five large companies: Swan, Hunter & Wigham Richardson, Vickers-Armstrongs, Hawthorn Leslie & Co., J. Readhead & Sons and Blyth Dry Docks & Shipbuilding Co. On the Wear there are seven shipyards with substantial output: Wm. Doxford & Sons, J. L. Thompson & Sons, Sir James Laing & Sons, Bartram & Sons, Austin & Pickersgill (two yards) and Short Brothers. On the Tees there are the Furness Shipbuilding Co., Smith's Dock Co. and Wm. Gray & Co.

In recent years the Clyde has produced about one-third of the total gross tonnage built, the Wear and Tees about one-quarter, the Tyne about one-sixth and the remaining centres of output, mainly Belfast, the Mersey and Barrow, about one-quarter of total output. Over the years there has probably been some decline in the share of the north-east coast in the total gross tonnage built, from about 50 per cent before the First World War to about 40–45 per cent at the present time—a trend examined in the *Industrial Survey of the North-east Coast Area*[1] at some length and regarded as being largely fortuitous.

It is something of a paradox that the forces in the nineteenth century—particularly the change to steel and steam—which exercised such a compelling influence on the location of industry as to stimulate the growth of shipbuilding in the United Kingdom and depress it in America and to favour the northern rivers at the expense of the Thames—have so far exhausted their influence that at one and the same time there has been no move to change the location of the industry in the United Kingdom and a marked trend for world shipbuilding to grow in other countries overseas.

In present conditions natural factors play only a small part in determining the location of shipbuilding. The industry is favoured by a climate which is neither too hot nor too cold, but it can be carried out in a variety of temperature and weather conditions, particularly now that with modern methods much of it can be done under cover. Suitable rivers and deep-water sites with access to the sea are available in many countries, and in the past, when depth of channel has proved to be a difficulty, artificial means have been used to clear a way in preference to moving the industry elsewhere, as for example, in the deepening of the Clyde or Tyne, or the construction of artificial docks at Barrow. The basic raw material, that of steel, once so much more plentiful on the northerly rivers of the United Kingdom than in other places, is now available in many countries at prices relatively little affected by transport costs, while at the same time the technical monopoly, once peculiar to the United Kingdom and the engineering centres of the north, is now widely spread.

A large variety of locations are thus suitable for shipbuilding; wherever engineering skill, labour and capital can be assembled close to the seaways, shipbuilding can be carried on and the final product sent on its way to the markets of the world. It is the skill of management, availability of labour and the application of technical progress that determine where shipbuilding can take place, and, since these can be found both in the old centres and the new, there has been no incompatability in the old centres of production continuing to benefit from advantages acquired over the years and the establishment of new centres of production in other parts of the world.

[1] *An Industrial Survey of the North East Coast Area* (H.M.S.O., 1932), pp. 228–32.

In the United Kingdom there has been little pressure to establish new shipyards. In the inter-war period there was over-capacity and, after the Second World War, investment control, steel and labour shortages militated against new enterprise establishing itself in new or old centres. In the whole of the post-war period there has been only one new shipyard established, for building large vessels, that of the Atlantic Shipbuilding Co. at Newport, and there has been little opportunity to test the locational advantages of other possible centres for shipbuilding.

The location of marine engineering broadly follows that of shipbuilding. The Clyde is largely self-supporting in marine-engineering capacity, producing roughly 1 h.p. for each ton of new shipping; marine engineering is rather over-represented on the Tyne by this standard and rather under-represented on the Wear and Tees, while Belfast, Barrow and the Mersey are at least self-sufficient in engine capacity. There is obvious convenience in having engine-building capacity close to the centres of new construction, but no immutable rules have to be observed, since engines can be transported to the ships they power and hulls to the sites of engine works,[1] and there is an element of historical accident in the present distribution of marine engineering.

In contrast to marine engineering, ship-repairing is more widely dispersed than shipbuilding. Minor and running-repair facilities are centred round the main ports in order to cause the minimum disruption to the sailing of vessels. For extensive repairs, overhauls, substantial alterations and conversions, the shipbuilding centres are more likely to come into their own (although this is not always the case, since, for example, the annual overhaul of the 'Queens' must take place in Southampton, the only locality with a dock big enough to receive them) and the major ship-repairers are well equipped and highly experienced.

The preponderance of repair work relative to construction is less on the north-east coast, in Scotland and in Northern Ireland than in other parts of the country. Dr C. E. V. Leser[2] has concluded, mainly on the basis of the inter-war period, that 'whilst Scotland was responsible for about 40 per cent of the output of new ships it only undertook somewhat above 10 per cent of all repair work, a percentage which is much lower than that for the industry as a whole'. He also found that the amount of repair work undertaken in Northern Ireland was small in relation to new construction, and that there had been a tendency for the Scottish share of repair work to decline. Mr N. S. Ross[3] has observed, on the basis of employment figures,

---

[1] The hull of the *Braemar*, for example, was launched at Southampton in 1952 and towed to Oslo, where the engines were fitted and the vessel completed.

[2] 'The shipbuilding trades in the Census of Production', an unpublished paper.

[3] N. S. Ross, 'Employment in shipbuilding and ship-repairing in Great Britain' *Journal of the Royal Statistical Society*, 1952, Series A (General), vol. CIV, pt. IV, pp. 524–33.

Table 1.—*British shipbuilding and ship-repairing, 1955–7*

LEADING SHIPYARDS

	Average annual output of merchant vessels (thousand g.t.)	Average engine output (thousand h.p.)	Types of vessel built and repairs	Types of engine built	Largest vessel accommodated or built, 1957 (ft.)	No. of berths, 1957	Remarks
IN SCOTLAND							
(a) On the Clyde and West Coast							
John Brown & Co. Ltd.	69	59	All types and repairs	Diesel & turbines	Over 1000	7	See also other members of Lithgow group
Lithgows Ltd.	65	—	Tankers, cargo and passenger vessels and repairs		650	1	Member of Lithgow group
The Fairfield Shipbuilding and Engineering Co. Ltd.	44	39	All types and repairs	Diesel & turbines, incl. free-piston gas turbine	1000	5	
Blythswood Shipbuilding Co. Ltd.	36	—	Tankers & cargo vessels		600	5	
Wm. Hamilton & Co. Ltd.	30	—	Tankers & cargo vessels	—	550	4	Member of Lithgow group
Scotts' Shipbuilding & Engineering Co. Ltd.	26	32	All types and repairs	Diesel & turbine	600	6	
Harland & Wolff Ltd.	25	23	Tankers & cargo vessels and repairs	Diesel engines	750	7	A branch of Harland & Wolff, Belfast
Alexander Stephen & Sons Ltd.	25	22	Warships, special type vessels and repairs	Diesel & turbine, incl. free-piston gas turbine	700	6	
Charles Connell & Co. Ltd.	24	—	Tankers and cargo vessels	Diesel & turbine	580	4	
Barclay Curle & Co. Ltd.	21	46	Tankers, cargo and passenger vessels and repairs		700	5	A subsidiary of Swan, Hunter & Wigham Richardson
The Greenock Dockyard Co. Ltd.	19	—	Tankers & cargo vessels and repairs	—	560	3	Owned by the British & Commonwealth Shipping Co.
Wm. Denny & Bros. Ltd.	12	17	Passenger & cargo vessels	Diesel & turbine	540	7	
(b) On the east coast							
Burntisland Shipbuilding Co. Ltd.	30	—	Cargo vessels	—	450	4	Two other yards (one small) are included in the Burntisland group
Caledon Shipbuilding & Engineering Co. Ltd.	22	—	Cargo vessels and repairs	—	560	5	
Hall, Russell & Co. Ltd.	16	1	Cargo, colliers, coasting vessels and repairs	Steam-reciprocating	400	4	One of the Burntisland group of shipyards
IN ENGLAND							
(a) On the Tyne							
Swan, Hunter & Wigham Richardson Ltd.	107	26	All types and repairs	Diesel & turbine	Nearly 1000	10	Barclay Curle is a subsidiary
Vickers-Armstrongs Ltd.	60	106	All types and repairs	—	1100	7	See also under Barrow
R. & W. Hawthorn Leslie & Co. Ltd.	46	—	All types (except battleships) and repairs	Diesel & turbine	700	7	
J. Readhead & Sons Ltd.	29	9	Cargo vessels & repairs	Steam-reciprocating	500	3	
Blyth Dry Docks & Shipbuilding Co. Ltd.	21	—	Tankers & cargo vessels and repairs		550	4	

(b) On the Wear

Company			Types of vessels built	Types of engine built	h.p.	No.	Remarks
Wm. Doxford & Sons Ltd.	47	72	Tankers & cargo vessels	Diesel	600	3	The two companies are amalgamated
Joseph L. Thompson & Sons Ltd.	46	—	Tankers & cargo vessels, warships and repairs	—	600	3	
Sir James Laing & Sons, Ltd.	38	—	Tankers & cargo vessels and repairs	—	650	3	
Bartram & Sons Ltd.	38	—	Tankers & cargo vessels and repairs	—	525	3	
Austin & Pickersgill Ltd.	29	—	Cargo vessels, coasters and colliers & repairs	—	500	8	
Short Bros.	19	—	Tankers & cargo vessels and repairs	—	500	4	

(c) On the Tees

Company			Types of vessels built	Types of engine built	h.p.	No.	Remarks
Furness Shipbuilding Co. Ltd.	88	—	Tankers, also cargo vessels, floating docks, etc.	—	700	8	
Smith's Dock Co. Ltd	39	1	Tankers, cargo vessels, whalers, colliers, trawlers, extensive repairing facilities	Steam-reciprocating & free-piston machinery	520	4	
William Gray & Co. Ltd.	36	16	Cargo vessels and repairs	Diesel, steam-reciprocating, turbine	480	6	

(d) On the Mersey

Company			Types of vessels built	Types of engine built	h.p.	No.	Remarks
Cammell Laird & Co. Ltd.	86	66	All types and repairs	—	1000	10	

(e) At Barrow

Company			Types of vessels built	Types of engine built	h.p.	No.	Remarks
Vickers-Armstrongs Ltd.	50	83	All types and repairs	Diesel & turbine	1000	8	See also on the Tyne

(f) At Belfast

Company			Types of vessels built	Types of engine built	h.p.	No.	Remarks
Harland & Wolff Ltd.	123	144	All types and repairs	Diesel, steam-reciprocating turbine	1000	18	See also on the Clyde

LEADING MARINE-ENGINEERING ESTABLISHMENTS

Company	Average annual output (thousand h.p.)	Types of engine built	Remarks
On the Clyde			
David Rowan & Co. Ltd.	78	Steam turbine and diesel	
John G. Kincaid & Co. Ltd.	66	Steam-reciprocating, diesel	A subsidiary of Lithgows
British Polar Engines Ltd.	35	British Polar diesel	
On the Tyne			
Wallsend Slipway & Engineering Co. Ltd.	80	Steam-reciprocating & turbine & diesel	Part of Swan, Hunter & Wigham Richardson
Parsons Marine Turbine Co. Ltd.	52	Turbine	
North Eastern Marine Engineering Co. Ltd.	52	Diesel & steam-reciprocating	
On the Wear			
Richardsons Westgarth (Hartlepool) Ltd.	26	Steam-reciprocating & diesel	Associated companies of Richardsons Westgarth & Co. Ltd.
George Clark & North Eastern Marine (Sunderland) Ltd.	44	Turbine	

that there is a tendency for employment in shipbuilding and ship-repairing to become somewhat less concentrated in the main shipbuilding centres. Since shipbuilding has continued to be concentrated in the northern regions, the reason for the shift must largely be attributed to a relative growth of repair elsewhere. An apparent increase in the share of the north-western region can be attributed to the same factor, since in this region, unlike the other shipbuilding centres, ship-repairing was a more important source of employment than the construction of new ships.

The moderate importance of repair work, in relation to construction, in the main shipbuilding regions is in some ways unfortunate. Repair is the more stable element in employment in the shipbuilding and ship-repairing industry, and the fact that it is comparatively weakly represented in the shipbuilding centres means that employment in these regions is more open to fluctuation. Moreover, repair work is thought by some shipbuilders to benefit from the experience gained, and the wide range of skills assembled, in construction. In many of the European centres, shipbuilding and ship-repair can go on side by side because both industries are combined in the major ports, and not, as in the United Kingdom on the whole, in ports of less than the first importance. It is interesting in this context that the Atlantic Shipbuilding Co. has sought, in branching out in a new location, to fit itself for repair by building new vessels in a dry dock rather than on the more conventional slipway.

II

The Census of Production for 1954 lists some 676 establishments engaged in shipbuilding and ship-repairing and some 104 establishments engaged in marine engineering. But this is a far-flung net since it includes all establishments employing more than 10 workers, many of which are concerned with the repair and building of small craft, the supply of special components such as oars, rigging or other tackle besides a number of specialised repair companies, and it should not be concluded from the figures that small-scale organisation is typical of the industry. Repair establishments are, in general, on a smaller scale than those engaged in new construction. Exceptionally, a large repair establishment may employ as many as 2000 men at any one time, but for the most part employment is likely to be measured in hundreds rather than thousands of men. On the other hand, establishments building new ocean-going ships must generally employ workers by the thousand rather than by the hundred. On the average each shipyard worker turns out the equivalent of 20 g.r.t. of shipping per annum. Thus a shipyard producing 20,000 g.r.t. of shipping per annum (the equivalent of three fairly small vessels by present standards) would need to employ about 1000 men if its productivity were no more than average; and one producing up to 100,000 g.r.t. per annum might need to employ as many as 5000 men.

In 1954, in shipbuilding and ship-repairing, there were 18 establishments employing between 1000 and 1500 men, some of which may have been engaged wholly on repair work, and 29 employing more than 1500 men, which would be largely employed on the construction of new tonnage. The output of these groups together amounted to about 63 per cent of the gross output, including repairs, of the industries as defined in the Censuses of Production.

The number of independent companies (as opposed to establishments) launching ocean-going tonnage amounts to about 30 at the present time. The apparent increase in the number of establishments enumerated in the Censuses of Production from about 400–500 in 1930 and 1935 to some 600–700 in 1948–54 (precise comparison is impossible because of changes in the various censuses) is not mirrored in the number of companies launching ocean-going tonnage. Before the First World War there were 60 such producers,[1] but their numbers were much reduced through failure in the twenties and closure of yards through the operation of National Shipbuilders' Security in the thirties, as well as by amalgamation.

The thirty leading shipbuilders in the industry today produce between them about 90 per cent of the tonnage of new ships launched in the United Kingdom, and six of these companies, with about 100 berths under their control, account for over half the tonnage of mercantile output. Thus the bulk of the output of new ships is concentrated in relatively few hands, and it is upon their affairs that much of the fortunes of the industry turn. The six largest companies comprise: Harland & Wolff (with yards at Belfast and Glasgow); the Lithgow group (Lithgows' yards, Fairfield and Hamilton —all on the Clyde); Vickers-Armstrongs (with yards on the Tyne and at Barrow); Swan, Hunter & Wigham Richardson (at their Tyneside yards and through their wholly owned subsidiary, Barclay Curle, on the Clyde); the Furness Co. (on the Tees); and the recently amalgamated companies of J. L. Thompson and Sir James Laing & Sons on the Wear.

The comparative importance of these companies has grown since 1920 and 1921; in those years they accounted for less than 40 per cent of output. In 1954 and 1955 their combined output was somewhat greater absolutely, while the output of the remainder of the industry had declined, largely as a result of the extinction of firms and capacity in the inter-war period.

There are two other companies whose output in the post-war period has not exceeded 100,000 tons in any year, but has been approaching this level, and, having regard to their production of passenger liners and warships

---

[1] Treating the armament and warship producers as independent producers, though in fact there was a good deal of collaboration between them.

25

(which are much more costly to construct than other vessels of comparable dimensions), they must be included amongst the largest producers in the industry. These two companies are John Brown's and Cammel Laird, each of which has produced 80,000 g.r.t. of merchant shipping in recent years within their own yards. The remaining score of shipyards not enumerated above each produce some 20,000 or more g.r.t. of merchant ships in a good year.

III

There are a number of ways in which shipbuilding and ship-repairing firms can be said to specialise. They may, for example, concentrate exclusively on construction or repair, or combine both in the same establishment; they may cater for naval requirements or large passenger vessels; they may produce tankers, or dry-cargo vessels, or some of each; and within any one of these broad divisions they may select some narrower field. But whatever form of specialisation is considered, it cannot generally be regarded as much more than a tendency for some types of activity to take a preponderant place.

It is usual for shipbuilding companies to undertake a measure of repair work, though not all do so. Bartram's, Connell's, Denny's, Doxford and Furness are the main exceptions, but, as we have already indicated, repair work is generally of less importance in the shipbuilding areas than new construction.

Warship building calls for high standards and often for special plant and equipment, but there are a number of shipyards catering for this kind of work. Eight of them, Vickers-Armstrongs, John Brown, Cammell Laird, Harland & Wolff, Scotts' Shipbuilding and Engineering, Fairfield, and Swan, Hunter & Wigham Richardson are equipped to build capital ships, while others, including Hawthorn Leslie, Alexander Stephen, Yarrow & Co., Samuel White, Thorneycroft and Denny Brothers, have in varying degrees the facilities and experience to construct smaller naval vessels.

The warship yards also cater for passenger vessels, as might be expected since elaborate facilities are required for both warship and passenger ship construction; and their output ranges from the 'Queens' constructed by John Brown's to the cross-channel vessels constructed by Denny's. This points the way to one generalisation that can be made with safety about specialisation in the United Kingdom shipbuilding industry: the larger the yard the more likely is it to cater for a wide range of different kinds of vessels. Of the eight largest companies ennumerated above, only Laing & Thompson and Furness tend to concentrate their output on tankers and dry-cargo vessels; the former, however, is also listed as a warship producer, and the latter has built a number of special-type ships as well as floating docks

26

and caissons. John Brown, Cammell Laird, Vickers-Armstrongs, Harland
& Wolff, Fairfield and Swan, Hunter & Wigham Richardson have at one
time or another built nearly every kind of vessel. Very few ships are too big
or too small, too simple or too complicated, too new or too conventional
for them to undertake if opportunity presents or necessity dictates.

In the main this diversity of output reflects the fact that the volume of
naval, or high-class passenger or merchant work, is entirely insufficient to do
more than provide partial, and often intermittent, employment for those
whose specialities they are. In the four years 1952–5, for example, when
warship building was on a moderate scale, only 22 passenger liners were
launched. Of these six were built by Harland & Wolff and five by John
Brown, the remaining eleven being spread amongst the other passenger-
liner builders. All these shipyards would have been unable to operate at
full capacity had they not been ready to construct dry-cargo and tanker
vessels. While orders have been plentiful they have experienced no difficulty
in supplementing the high-quality work they prefer with other types of
ships, but in the past they have generally considered themselves at a disadvantage in this kind of work and in danger of applying warship building
methods, or a liner finish, to dry-cargo ships or oil tankers. It is said, for
example, that the extreme accuracy insisted on for Admiralty work tends to
be applied also on other types of construction, since it is difficult to get
workmen to change from one way of working to another. Moreover, with
the present distribution of orders between main types of vessels, it is difficult
to obtain a proper balance between the facilities of these yards, the manpower needed in the finishing trades and the type of vessel on the stocks.

The position may be improved in some respects by the trend to tankers
of larger sizes and perhaps by the use of nuclear power. The facilities needed
for warships and passenger liners are admirably suited to the construction
of super-tankers, and it may be possible, as orders for these are received, to
spread the overheads of warship and passenger-liner construction over
super-tankers as well. Without this, it may be questioned whether, with
the present distribution of orders, there are not too many yards equipped
for the production of warships and passenger liners. The advantage to the
great liner companies in having a number of suppliers competing for their
orders, with all the kudos that these bring, and the advantage to the Admiralty
of having a reserve of warship-building capacity, is not necessarily reflected
in an economic use of resources within the industry itself—a subject to
which we will return in a later chapter. And it may be, therefore, that if
the facilities necessary for the production of the larger warship and, in-
cidentally, passenger liners, are to be preserved in less prosperous times,
the Admiralty, and not as happened in the 1930's[1] the Bank of England, will

[1] See p. 30.

have increasingly to accept the need to provide for warship-building capacity.

Below the large warship and passenger-liner producers, specialisation proceeds largely by exclusion. Thus no warship or passenger-liner work may be undertaken, or the size of berths available or their width may limit the length or capacity of ships which can be constructed. The smaller shipyards can, on this principle, be classed as specialist producers; for their work may be restricted to, say, the production of tugs, trawlers or coastal vessels; but it is not always easy to say whether a yard produces a certain type of vessel because it has acquired special skills in its construction, or merely because it has not extended its facilities to cater for more varied types. The dredger-building of Lobnitz is an example of specialist building in the true sense of the word, and, although Cammell Laird, for example, has produced dredgers from time to time, the four firms of Lobnitz,[1] Simons,[1] Fleming & Ferguson and Ferguson Bros. have provided an example of a concentration of firms in a small area specialising on dredger work. Even they, however, are by no means engaged exclusively on dredger construction.

For most of the thirty leading shipbuilders there is a considerable amount of common ground in the construction of some run-of-the-mill tankers or dry-cargo vessels. But within this broad band some preferences, if not specialities, are discernible. In the post-war period two firms, the Furness Co. and Blythswood, have concentrated on the production of tankers, but neither of these two companies should be regarded as tanker specialists irrespective of what is available in the market; as we have indicated, the Furness Co. has produced a variety of different types of vessels, even post-war, as well as other products. Similarly, Bartram and J. Readhead have tended to concentrate on dry-cargo vessels rather than tankers.

Outside the general run one can point to various specialities for which individual firms have got a name, such as the banana boats built by Stephen's for Fyffes, whalers built by Smith's Docks or combined ore-oil carriers by Fairfield's, but these are often few and far between, and it will be exceptional for any one shipyard to average one a year. The best examples of specialisation on a large scale date to the beginning of the century, when the long runs of Doxford's turret ships or the standard ships produced by the Northumberland Shipbuilding Co. ran into scores or even hundreds, and it is interesting that the north-east coast still tends to concentrate on the simpler type of cargo ship, or today tankers, to a greater extent than the Clyde or the more diversified output of Barrow, Belfast or Birkenhead.

---

[1] Lobnitz and Simons are controlled by G. & J. Weir; Simons also does non-shipbuilding work.

CHAPTER 3

Industrial Affiliations

I

In spite of a number of large units, the industry is very far from a condition of monopoly selling or of unified control. At times the tendency towards establishing larger units of control has been strong. The Swan, Hunter & Wigham Richardson group, the Lithgow group, Vickers-Armstrongs, Thompson & Laing, Harland & Wolff, the Burntisland group, Austin & Pickersgill, are all illustrations of the incorporation of various shipbuilding companies under one control. C. S. Swan & Hunter amalgamated with Wigham Richardson & Co. in 1903 in order to command the resources necessary to construct the *Mauretania*; the new company acquired a controlling interest (which in 1957 was extended to complete ownership by the purchase of outstanding shares) in the Wallsend Slipway and Engineering Co., a marine-engineering and ship-repairing firm and purchased the Tyne Pontoon & Dry Docks Co. which was connected with John Wigham Richardson through his directorship and the shareholding of his company. In 1912 a further amalgamation was completed between Swan, Hunter & Wigham Richardson and Barclay Curle, giving the combined companies interests on both the Tyne and the Clyde,[1] and in 1914 Swan, Hunter & Wigham Richardson absorbed, for a time, H. & C. Grayson, a Merseyside firm with repair facilities in Liverpool, Birkenhead and Garston.[2]

Although Fairfield's is the best-known company included in the Lithgow group, it was not in fact incorporated into the group until 1935. Lithgows owes its origin to the partnership between Joseph Russell, Anderson Rodger and William Lithgow; the three shipyards included in the partnership were divided when Joseph Russel retired in 1891, and it was not until 1918[3] that two of them were brought together again under the control of William Lithgow's two sons, James and Henry, and not until 1918 that the name

[1] For more details of these companies see *Launching Ways*, published by Swan, Hunter & Wigham Richardson in 1953.

[2] Pollard, *op. cit.* p. 456. At this time H. & C. Grayson were in close connection with the other ship-repairing firms of Clover, Clayton & Co. (Liverpool), R. & H. Green & Silley Weir (London), and Joseph T. Eltringham (Willington Quay). H. & C. Grayson was reorganised in 1928 when its business was consolidated with that of David Rollo & Sons Ltd. under the title of Grayson, Rollo & Clover Dry Docks Ltd. This concern acquired the undertaking of Clover, Clayton & Co. Ltd. in 1935 and is no longer connected with the Swan, Hunter & Wigham Richardson group.

[3] For a more detailed account see 'Shipbuilders of other days, xi, Joseph Russell', *Shipbuilding and Shipping Record*, 13 September 1945. p. 253.

was changed to Lithgows Ltd. The Lithgow group also incorporated the yards of Robert Duncan & Co. and Dunlop Bremner & Co., all in Port Glasgow (the latter yard was closed in 1928), and in 1919 the shipyard of William Hamilton & Co. was acquired. On the marine-engineering side the group controls the small company of Rankin & Blackmore, as well as David Rowan. A number of other companies on the periphery of ship-building and the Dornoch Shipping Co. are also included in the group.[1]

The amalgamation of the shipbuilding interests of Vickers and Armstrong Whitworth owes itself to the misfortunes of the latter company and the happy accident that it banked with the Newcastle branch of the Bank of England. The foundation of the success of Armstrong Whitworth had lain in the skill and the facilities it developed for manufacturing heavy guns and gun mountings, armour plate and warships, and the agreement to build no more capital ships at the Washington Conference created a serious problem for Armstrongs. An attempt was made to diversify the firm's activities through commercial shipbuilding, locomotive building and pulp and paper manu-facture, but these activities proved to be disastrous, and by June 1925 the overdraft at the Newcastle branch of the Bank of England had risen to £2,600,000. The solution to the difficulty was seen to lie in a merger of the interests of Armstrongs with those of Vickers, which, although it offered little prospect of the recoupment of the Bank's losses on the overdraft it had authorised, would at least stop the drain of further loss and avoid the increase of unemployment and disturbance of labour which would be involved in the closure of Armstrong Whitworth's works. In this way the idle and deserted Walker shipyard was kept in readiness until the *Monarch of Bermuda* was built in 1931.[2]

The extension of the direct interests of Harland & Wolff started in 1912, when they bought the shipyard of the London & Glasgow Engineering Co. and later in the year that of Mackie & Thompson. This was followed by the acquisition of control of A. McMillan & Son, of Dumbarton, through Lord Pirrie's interest in Lamport & Holt. In 1916 Cairds were acquired, and in subsequent years D. & W. Henderson and A. & J. Inglis.

The formal amalgamation of Laing & Thompson is recent (1954), but they have been closely associated since 1909 when Sir James Marr, a director of Thompson's, joined the Board of Laing's. The interests of the companies were widened to include John Lynn & Co., T. W. Greenwell and John Crown & Sons Ltd. (ship-repairers), the Walsingham Steel Co., and Sunder-land Forge, and these, together with the shipbuilding companies, are incorporated as Sunderland Shipbuilding Dry Docks & Engineering Co. Ltd.

[1] For details, see *The Shipbuilder*, 1952, p. 139.
[2] For more details of the merger of these interests see Sir Henry Clay's account in his book *Lord Norman*, pp. 318–23.

Other comparatively recent amalgamations include that of the medium-sized Burntisland Shipbuilding Co. with the smaller yards of Alexander Hall & Co. and Hall Russell & Co., all located in the east of Scotland. The Burntisland group was taken over by Scottish & Mercantile Investments in 1951. Another merger taking place recently was that of S. P. Austin & Son and Wm. Pickersgill, both Sunderland firms. The entire capital of Austin Pickersgill was bought by London and Overseas Freighters, Lambeth Bros. and Philip Hill Higginson & Co., who plan to reconstruct the shipyard facilities.[1]

The reasons prompting the amalgamation of shipbuilding companies have varied. There has often been an element of misfortune and frequently a need to strengthen the financial position of one or perhaps both parties; but at the same time larger units have been required to produce economically modern ships of increasing size and complexity; the amalgamation of Swan, Hunter and Wigham Richardson, for example, opened the way to the production of large passenger liners and warships at a time when there were profitable outlets for these products. On the other hand, the control of a number of companies of varied output may be undertaken not with the intention of increasing the range of a company's activities, but of promoting greater specialisation within a group. Lord Pirrie had something of this in his mind when he established the shipbuilding interests of Harland & Wolff on the Clyde, and similarly there are opportunities for specialisation in the operation of the Lithgow yards.

II

The major attempts at industrial combination in the shipbuilding industry were not undertaken with the intention of rationalising production through greater specialisation, or indeed mainly with the intention of obtaining economies through horizontal integration. The largest and most powerful combinations in shipbuilding were organised either with the intention of establishing a monopoly or quasi-monopoly selling position or of integrating shipbuilding with either steel production or shipowning.

There are some outstanding examples of such forces at work in the association of the armament producers in the late nineteenth and early twentieth centuries, in the integration of the shipping interests of Christopher Furness with shipbuilding and coal and iron, in the varied interests of Lord Pirrie in shipping and shipbuilding, and in the monopolistic tendencies of the Sperling combine.

The activities of the armament producers were founded on the control of armour plate. Compound armour plate was made at first only by Charles

[1] *Journal of Commerce, Shipbuilding and Engineering Edition*, 28 February 1957.

Cammell and John Brown, who divided the markets between them before tendering. The entry of Vickers and Beardmore and later Armstrong was no improvement.[1] The monopoly position of Armstrong in the manufacture of guns was assailed by the entry of Vickers and Beardmore at the instigation of the Government and later by the promotion of the Coventry Ordnance Works by John Brown, Cammell Laird and the Fairfield Co.[2] The latter company was only one of the common meeting-points of the armament and warship producers, who joined forces in innumerable ways whenever their interests were favoured by combination. These ranged on the one hand from the complete merger of Vickers and Armstrong (1902) with Robert Napier under their joint control, the merger of Cammell Laird and Fairfield (1907) and the merger of John Brown and Thomas Firth (1902), to the joint control of establishments overseas such as that of the Muroran Ordnance Works in Japan by Armstrong and Vickers and to the establishment of syndicates, for example, for the purposes of reconstructing the Portuguese Navy (John Brown, Cammell Laird, Fairfield, Palmer), reconstructing the Spanish Navy and the Ferrol Dockyard (Vickers, Armstrong, John Brown, Thorneycroft and Parsons Steam Marine Turbine Co.) or supervising the building of dreadnoughts in St Petersburg (John Brown and Armstrong).[3] In 1907 Harland & Wolff and John Brown exchanged shares and directorships and the arrangement was in being until the death of Lord Pirrie (Harland & Wolff) brought it to an end in 1924, and in the same year Lord Aberconway (John Brown) ceased to be a director of Harland & Wolff.[4]

The armaments ring was an example of horizontal control of shipbuilding based both on a common end-product—that of warships—and the use of a common raw material—steel and armour plate. These relationships were developed by vertical integration between the steel and armament producers and the warship yards prompted by the desire of the steel producers to tighten their hold on the warship-building market and the profitable opportunities afforded by it, and to find outlets for their steel products. Armstrong's purchased the Mitchell yard on the Tyne in 1882. In 1897 Vickers found a natural avenue of expansion from the production of guns and armour plate to the ship which carried them and they purchased the Barrow Shipbuilding Co. The Sheffield firm of John Brown are described as purchasing the shipbuilding company of J. & G. Thompson on the Clyde in 1899 (now, of course, John Brown's) in order to secure an outlet for their steel-forging plant, and as securing a controlling interest in Harland & Wolff for the same reason; and Beardmore's acquired a shipyard, that of Robert Napier on the Clyde, in 1900. The amalgamation of Charles Cammell and Laird Brothers

---

[1] Pollard, *op. cit.* p. 265.
[2] Pollard, *op. cit.* p. 451.
[3] See Pollard, *op. cit.* p. 245.
[4] See the Company file at Bush House.

in 1903 also united a producer of steel and armour plate with an important user of these products.

When, before the First World War, warship building accounted for some 20–25 per cent of the employment and output of the shipbuilding industry, the major warship building yards with their steel interests behind them were in a commanding position. It was, however, the peak of their achievement in their combined endeavours. Disarmament and depression reduced their numbers and prosperity, bringing Armstrong, who had once treated with the British Government on the basis of equality,[1] to the verge of bankruptcy, destroying the warship-building activities of Beardmore's and closing Palmer's shipyards as well as others outside the control of the leading firms.

The value of the armaments monopoly was thus largely destroyed, though it is doubtful if any comparable exploitation of a government market could have survived in the face of political changes and altered social pressures. As it was, the links between the companies were largely torn asunder and independent operation resumed. The activities of the surviving companies have broadened and their shipbuilding output has declined in relative importance, so that today, for Vickers or John Brown's, shipbuilding contributes only 10–20 per cent of profits.[2] Besides the shipbuilding and engineering works operated by Vickers-Armstrongs, the Vickers group includes, for example, such diverse interests as the manufacture of malt and grain machinery, scientific instruments, printing machines, brewery plant, power presses, accounting machines and aircraft. Vickers also own half of the Metropolitan-Cammell Carriage & Wagon Co., the remaining half being owned by Cammell Laird & Co. The latter company also has interests in steel production through its holdings in the English Steel Corporation. The activities of John Brown's are equally diverse, including the manufacture of aircraft, machine tools, land boilers, structural steelwork, and a number of other products.

This diversity of interests has only tenuous relations with shipbuilding today, and it is doubtful if it serves to strengthen shipbuilding activities to any appreciable extent. There is no need, for example, at the present time to secure supplies of steel, although the control of steel capacity may be advantageous to users in securing preferential treatment in delivery, or the production of the most needed or economical shapes and sizes of plates and sections. In the 1920's the position was different. One after another of the steel producers had fallen under the control of shipbuilders, and as

---

[1] Pollard, *op. cit.* p. 244.

[2] In the year ended March 1956 shipbuilding contributed 10 per cent of the profits of John Brown's, though the assets of the shipbuilding subsidiary company accounted for 27½ per cent of the total (see *The Financial Times*, 3 January 1957).

Stephen's and other Scottish producers felt themselves in danger of being cut off from their supplies, they combined to purchase the Steel Co. of Scotland.[1]

The production of land boilers and power equipment in addition to marine engines has obvious indirect advantages in the field of technical developments, but the production of land and marine boilers does not necessarily result in integration of production. John Brown's, for example, considered it best to establish a separate company for the production of land boilers distinct from their marine activities, though both are on the Clyde. The tendency to establish separate companies for the shipbuilding activities of these large producers may represent the acceptance of the fact that diverse activities do not lend themselves easily to integration, and that in changing circumstances new links may be necessary for efficient production and new departures. Thus the shipbuilding activities of John Brown's were transferred to a subsidiary company in 1953 and Cammell Laird took the same step in 1954[2], but it has also been necessary for a number of shipbuilding companies to form new liaisons in order to cater for atomic-powered ships. For this, the widely based diverse company engaged in shipbuilding is at an advantage in commanding the financial and technical resources necessary to undertake new departures.

III

There have been other industrial combinations affecting shipbuilding which were not based primarily on armament production. It was as a shipowner that Sir Christopher (later Lord) Furness first entered the field of shipbuilding. Out of his shipping profits he took the opportunity to develop interests in iron and steel, coal, engineering and shipbuilding—generally in conditions of depression when they could be purchased cheaply. By 1911 he controlled the Henry Withy Shipyard at Hartlepool, Irvine Shipbuilding & Dry Dock Co., also at Hartlepool, and the Northumberland Shipbuilding Co. at Howden, besides having a dominant interest in Palmer's at Jarrow. He also acquired marine-engineering facilities which he combined in Richardsons Westgarth & Co. Since he controlled about $1\frac{1}{2}$ million t. of shipping he was in a position to keep his shipyards plentifully supplied with orders as well as to give orders to other yards.[3]

One of the Furness interests, the Northumberland Shipbuilding Co., acquired Smith's Dock Co. Ltd., when the latter was formed by amalgamation

[1] Subsequently sold to Colvilles.
[2] Doxford also found it convenient to separate shipbuilding and engineering into two companies in 1956.
[3] See *The Statist*, 11 January 1908, for an account of a year in which 180,000 t. of shipping were launched for Furness, Withy & Co.

of the previous company of Smith's Docks with the family businesses of H. S. Edwards & Sons and Edward Bros., in 1899. The former company provided in later years the nucleus of a determined effort to secure control of a number of shipyards by the Sperling Combine, organised by a group of London financiers. Besides the Furness interest in the Irvine Shipbuilding & Dry Docks Co., the Sperling Combine owned by 1921 the whole of the share capital of Doxford's, 85 per cent of the capital of Fairfields', the whole of the share capital of the Monmouth Shipbuilding Co. and all the capital of Workman Clark in addition to a controlling interest in Blythswood.

For a time the Northumberland Shipbuilding Co. figured in the finance of the newly established Furness Shipbuilding Co., but this appears to have been a purely temporary arrangement, the shares being transferred to Furness Withy after a short interval, and later to Viscount Furness (the founder of the Furness Shipbuilding Co. and the son of Christopher Furness). Viscount Furness, who had been a director of a large number of the Furness interests, including the Irvine Shipbuilding and Dry Dock Co., severed all his other interests shortly after establishing the Furness Shipbuilding Co., concentrating on shipbuilding.[1]

The Furness Shipbuilding Co. was thus immune from the difficulties of those companies who fell under the control of the Sperling group. In the depressed years of the inter-war period the financial links holding together the Sperling group were overstrained. The Northumberland Shipbuilding Co. collapsed and with it Workman Clark, in spite of attempts to keep it in existence by a financial reorganisation. The Clyde firms were more fortunate; Fairfield's and Blythswood were bought back by private shareholders and their independence preserved.[2]

Lord Pirrie, Chairman of Harland & Wolff and wartime Controller General of Merchant Shipping in the First World War, was another figure linking shipping and shipbuilding. We have already referred to his activities in extending Harland & Wolff's interests on the Clyde, and of the connection between Harland & Wolff and John Brown's. His shipping connections were far flung. In 1891 he had put the Union Castle on its feet by arranging for Harland & Wolff to provide it with ships more suitable for its trade. He was an important figure in the Pierpont Morgan Combine of six British and American Shipping Companies in International Mercantile Marine and the recipient of their shipbuilding orders, and in 1910, acting in conjunction with Sir Owen Philipps, later Lord Kylsant, he purchased Elder Dempster & Co. At his death he was a director of twenty companies and interested in a good many more. In 1932, when the financial interests of

---

[1] See the Company files.

[2] Fairfields is, of course, now a member of Lithgows' yards, Blythswood is connected with Furness Withy.

the Royal Mail Steam Packet Co. fell to be reconstructed, the Elder Dempster group of companies, the Royal Mail Steam Packet Co., and a host of other companies had large financial interests in Harland & Wolff and through them in the Clyde Companies of the latter.

The spread of the interests of the Northumberland Shipbuilding Co. from the east and the Harland & Wolff interests from the west, in addition to the already close connection built up by the warship builders, could have resulted in a gigantic combine of shipbuilders closely associated with shipping interests. It is by no means certain that such an association would have been undesirable if it could have been properly organised and if efficiency could have been put before the chance of monopoly gains. But it failed to come into being. The profits out of which it could have been fed did not materialise, the Northumberland Shipbuilding Co. collapsed and Lord Pirrie did not succeed in consolidating his ventures so that the incursion of Harland & Wolff into Clyde shipbuilding was not on the scale originally intended.

IV

The value to shipbuilders of an association between shipbuilding and shipping interests lies in the possibility of securing orders and achieving a steadier flow of production in slump as well as boom. Complete integration, however, requires that the scale of organisation should be large. A shipyard producing, say, 100,000 g.r.t. of shipping per annum would be able to maintain a fleet of some 2–3 million t. There is only one shipyard in the world at the moment with an output approaching this figure which sells exclusively to one owner. This is the Kure shipyard in Japan, owned by Daniel K. Ludwig, which by the terms of its lease is required to build exclusively for the owner's companies—National Bulk Carriers, Universe Tank Ships and Sea Trawlers Incorporated, all 100 per cent personally owned, and American Hawaiian Steamship Co., in which Mr Ludwig has a 59 per cent interest.[1] The decision of Mr Ludwig to place orders for five oil tankers in 1957, when tanker freights were at an unrewarding figure for many operators, strongly recalls the similar policies adopted by Christopher Furness half a century earlier.

In this country the major oil operators have tended to avoid associating themselves with shipyard operation, although the size of their fleets and the rate at which they have been expanding would have made vertical integration of shipbuilding and tanker-owning a possibility. It is likely that the advantages of this course will commend themselves most strongly to Mr Leonard Clore, who controls the Furness Shipbuilding Co. In recent years, this shipyard has concentrated on the production of tankers, and is in a position to meet

[1] See *The Financial Times*, 3 October 1957.

the needs of British Oil Ships, of which Mr Clore is chairman. Like Mr Ludwig, Mr Clore does not hesitate to extend his shipping activities even when the general outlook appears far from favourable, and this is likely to increase the value of integration.

The reluctance of the major United Kingdom oil companies to enter the shipbuilding field may be soundly based. Their capital requirements are so large as to make them reluctant to add to them by an avoidable departure into new ventures, and although oil extraction has led them into tanker operation they have found it advisable to leave a large share of this to specialist tanker operators; all the more reason therefore for not branching further outside their major field. Nevertheless, as we shall see later, the failure of the oil companies to enter the shipbuilding field has probably prevented the full benefit of standardisation from being reaped. It has not, however, impaired the bargaining position of the oil companies *vis-à-vis* the tanker builders, as the orders placed by these companies are too valuable a prize to be considered lightly by any shipbuilding company.

It might be possible for the larger groups of liner operators, also, to link their fleets exclusively with the output of one shipyard, but it would not be so easy for them as for tanker operators. The composition of their fleets is generally varied, and if passenger liners and cargo liners are mixed, there may be much greater advantage to the liner operators in buying from specialist producers of these vessels than in attempting to integrate the operation of their fleets with the output of a single shipyard under their control. In short, there must be some compromise between drawing on the advantages of having a number of competing specialised producers and the close liaison of policy and interest which is possible when shipping and shipbuilding are closely integrated.

In the United Kingdom, as the industries are organised at present, the balance appears to lie in the separate control of shipping and shipbuilding; it is unusual to find shipbuilding and shipping companies under common control; and when this does occur it does not necessarily reflect much integration in their operation. An example of a shipyard controlled by a shipping company is the Greenock Dockyard, previously owned by the Clan Line, and now owned by the British & Commonwealth Shipping Co. Ltd., after the amalgamation of the Clan Line with the Union Castle Mail Steamship Co. Ltd. It is clear from a scrutiny of the ships in the Clan Line fleet, half of which have been built by the Greenock Dockyard, that a policy of integrating the output of the shipyard with the requirements of the Clan Line has been followed. It is difficult to say whether there will be any change in the policy of the Union Castle Mail Steamship Co. in the direction of purchasing from the Greenock Dockyard, though there are signs that the long connection between the former company and Harland & Wolff mentioned above has been broken, as recent orders have been placed elsewhere.

Complete ownership of a shipbuilding company by a shipowning company does not necessarily imply that one serves the other. The United Molasses Co. owns the small shipbuilding company of W. J. Yarwood & Sons Ltd., but since the vessels built by the latter company are much smaller than the bulk of those operated by the United Molasses, only one vessel built by Yarwood was included in 1957, in the Athel Line, and Anchor Line fleets, owned by United Molasses. Similarly, the connection between Blythswood and Furness Withy has not meant that any large number of the latter company's ships, or the ships of the associated companies, have been built in the Blythswood shipyard. The large shipowning company of Alfred Holt holds 49 per cent of the shares of the Caledon shipyard, but this has not given Caledon any larger stake in the Holt fleet than Harland & Wolff. The connection between the Southampton & Isle of Wight & South of England Royal Mail Steam Packet Co., and the shipbuilding and engineering firm of Thorneycroft is reflected in the number of ships which have been constructed for the latter by Thorneycroft, but this is not necessarily more than would have resulted from the geographical nearness of the two companies, and, of course, this constituted only a small part of Thorneycroft's output.

The two ships of the Hopemount Shipping Co. have been built by their owners Swan, Hunter & Wigham Richardson, and the two ships of the Dornoch Shipping Co. by Lithgows and engined at their associated company Rankin & Blackmore. A more recent development has been the association of the British Steel Corporation with a number of companies in order to provide for the movement of iron ore. These include financial association with the Denholm-Lithgow group through Scottish Ore-Carriers Ltd., and with Smith's Dock Co., in the North Yorkshire Shipping Co.[1]

A complete unravelling of shipping and shipbuilding interrelations would, no doubt, reveal connections between the two industries of greater extent and significance than those quoted above; but vertical integration between shipowners and shipbuilders is not likely to characterise the shipbuilding industry so long as the scales of operation of shipbuilders and shipowners do not coincide. The variety of ships required by shipping companies makes it difficult for them to deal with one shipyard; and informal connections between shipowners and shipbuilders make it possible to combine flexibility in the ordering of ships with something approaching the closer relations between companies operating in a common group.

Informal connections exist in abundance. A shipowner satisfied with the delivery of a ship from one shipbuilder is likely to place subsequent orders in the same yard. The Cunard Line in recent years has ordered a succession

[1] *Journal of Commerce, Shipbuilding and Engineering Edition*, 2 May 1957, p. 2.

of passenger liners from John Brown's, though both it and its subsidiary companies own many more ships produced at other yards than John Brown's. The New Zealand Shipbuilding Co. has built mainly, though not exclusively, with Alexander Stephen's and John Brown's; Elders & Fyffes' have placed a large number of orders with Alexander Stephen's; most of the ships of the Asiatic Steam Navigation Co. were built by Lithgows'; most of those of the Bibby Line by Fairfields'; nearly half the ships of the British India Steam Navigation Co. have been built by Barclay Curle or Swan, Hunter & Wigham Richardson; over half the ships of Salvesen & Co. have been built by Smith's Docks; and many other examples of shipowners purchasing a high proportion of their ships from particular shipbuilders could be given. In foreign countries much the same kind of connections may be built up; for example, the Svenska Ostasiatiska Komp A.B., or the Forenede Damp-skibs-Selskab A/S. have bought the bulk of their ships from two shipyards.

A succession of orders from one shipowner to a shipbuilder may be due solely to personal connections. It is often said of shipyards that the sales department is the managing director, and while this is not invariably true and is unlikely to apply to companies urgently seeking export business, the personal contacts of the owners of privately controlled, as well as other companies, are often an important source of orders. The relationship between the owners and builders concerned in such cases is likely to be one of mutual confidence so strongly felt that the precise terms of an agreement to buy and build a vessel may never be set down in detail or completed only after much of the construction of the vessel is in hand.

Such personal relationships may be formed or broken during the life of the companies, but close cooperation is likely to develop between companies as the shipbuilding company acquires special knowledge of the requirements of its customer, and, perhaps, begins to specialise on the type of ship required. It is partly because of this that many of the relationships established have stood the test of time, but an assured connection is an important asset to a shipbuilder and he is likely to make every effort to preserve it by giving value for money.

CHAPTER 4

Marine Engineering

Marine engineering is a different business from the building of ships, and although many important shipbuilders in the United Kingdom, and for that matter abroad, construct both hulls and engines in close proximity, the two industries need separate consideration. The association of marine-engineering establishments with shipyards rather than with companies producing land engines of comparable powers is, in fact, an historical accident. It was a natural development in the second half of the nineteenth century for ship-builders to attempt to establish themselves in marine engineering, on which so much of the performance of their vessels depended; and in an expanding market in which few engine-producing firms were established, they saw new opportunities for profits.

Of the larger shipbuilding firms with marine-engineering facilities, the oldest foundations are probably those of Scotts', 1825, and Hawthorn Leslie, 1820. Denny's shops date to 1850[1], those of Smith's Docks probably to about the same date,[2] Cammell Laird's to 1857, Stephen's to 1872, Doxford's to 1878, John Readhead's probably to 1881, John Brown's facilities to 1883 when they were established by their predecessors, and Wm. Gray's facilities, in the control of Central Marine Engineering, to 1884. The marine-engineering companies still extant either independently or in combination with other marine-engineering companies or shipbuilding companies were also started for the most part in the second half of the last century. On the Clyde, Rowan's were established in 1866, and Kincaid in 1868; in the north-east, George Clark commenced marine-engine building in 1854 and the North-eastern Marine Engineering Co. in 1865; Richardsons Westgarth and Parsons Marine Turbine Co. were founded at a later date than these other companies, and British Polar Engines in 1927 when they commenced business as Fiat British Auxiliaries Co. The move to establish marine-engineering facilities was not, however, universal. Connell's founded in 1861, Hamilton's in 1865, Laing's in 1793, Thompson's in 1846 and Bartram's in 1837, for example, did not add marine-engineering facilities

---

[1] As Tulloch and Denny, a partnership between Peter Denny and John Tulloch. In 1862, when John Tulloch retired and John McAusland joined Peter Denny as partner, the name was changed to Denny & Co. This company was formally incorporated in William Denny & Brothers Ltd. in 1917.

[2] No date is given in *Ships and Men*, 1899–1949, an account of the Smith's Dock Co. Ltd., but the first steamship was built in 1852 and a plan of the time shows a building marked machinery.

to their shipbuilding activities, and it is not without relevance to this that Laing & Thompson have grown to be amongst the largest hull constructors in the country, and that Connell's and Bartram's have established a reputation for high efficiency.

Those companies which were founded at the end of the First World War also did not embark on marine engineering. Neither Furness, Blythswood nor Burntisland constructed their own engine works. At first it was the intention of the Furness company to take this step, but in the post-war slump the idea was shelved, and it cannot be said in the event that it has proved disadvantageous.

The control of a marine-engineering establishment must not, therefore, be considered as a necessary adjunct to shipbuilding. Nor, as we shall argue, is it certain that the two go well together. On the one hand, marine engineering may be as profitable a venture as shipbuilding, and the production of ships and engines in the same establishment may be a convenience in the planning and building of a vessel, even though in practice the marine-engineering shops and the shipbuilding sheds may be far removed and largely under independent administration. On the other hand, bending the output of a marine-engineering shop to the particular requirements of an individual shipyard presents some difficult problems, and may inhibit specialisation on the production of particular types of engines in a number of ways which cannot be got over entirely by buying one or two engines in and selling others out.

In the main, the marine-engineering establishments of shipbuilders tend to engine most of the ships produced in their own shipyards; perhaps 10–15 per cent of the ships will be engined by other firms. This is quite a small percentage when it is remembered that it is exceedingly difficult for a small engineering works to cater adequately for all types of engines and that it will not always be possible to match the ships constructed to a programme suitable for the engine works. Indeed, the need to keep both a shipyard and engine works operating at full capacity while synchronising the delivery of engines with the launching of ships is likely to exercise some considerable influence on the type of ships which are laid down when orders are easy to get.

It might have been expected that by producing a large number of engines each year and specialising on certain types the 'independent' marine-engineering works would have succeeded in cutting costs to a point at which it was not worth while for marine-engine works attached to shipyards to continue. In fact this is not what has happened. There appears to have been little, if any, tendency for the outside works to grow at the expense of the combined shipbuilding and marine-engineering firm, and the largest marine-engineering establishments are to be found in these latter firms. The output of Harland

& Wolff, or of Vickers-Armstrongs for example, may exceed that of the separate establishments of companies specialising in marine engineering exclusively by a substantial margin, and in 1955 Hawthorn Leslie, a combined shipbuilding and marine-engineering firm, both met its own requirements and produced for sale to other shipbuilders a greater horsepower than a number of other marine-engineering establishments produced in total.

Recently, however, there has been a move to incorporate the independent marine engineers of the north-east coast under unified control. In 1938 the firm of George Clark amalgamated with the North-eastern Marine Co. and Richardsons Westgarth, and in 1957 Richardsons Westgarth acquired the Parsons Marine Turbine Co.[1] by an exchange of shares. The Richardsons Westgarth group also includes Richardsons Westgarth Atomic Ltd., and participates in Atomic Power Construction Ltd. The total horsepower produced by this group exceeds considerably that of any other specialised marine-engine builders.

There are three engine builders on the Clyde who have no shipyard attached. The first of these—David Rowan & Co.—is a subsidiary of Lithgows and largely supplies the shipbuilding companies in the Lithgow group; Kincaid & Co., another large engine works, supplies a variety of customers as does British Polar Engines.

There is thus no clear-cut pattern in the relationship between shipbuilding and marine engineering. A large combine exists side by side with other independent producers and with many integrated shipbuilding and marine-engineering establishments; and on occasion output is supplemented from the resources of companies concentrating on the production of machinery for non-marine purposes; British Thomson-Houston, English Electric, General Electric, or Metropolitan Vickers, may all supply marine installations often of a specialist character; B.T.H., for example, has supplied a gas-turbine engine in recent years, while all the companies cater for diesel-electric and turbo-electric installations.

The structure of the marine-engineering industry cannot be considered independently of the practice of producing engines under licence. There are, in fact, only five makes of diesel engine in widespread use, but in the United Kingdom alone there are almost a score of establishments manufacturing one or more of the various alternatives. In terms of the horsepower installed annually, the leading makes are those of Burmeister & Wain (Denmark), M.A.N. (Germany), Doxford (United Kingdom), Sulzer (Switzerland) and Gotaverken (Sweden), the countries of the parent firms being indicated in brackets. The Doxford engine has been installed in about three-quarters of the ocean-going motorships built in Britain since the war,

---

[1] In addition to the Humber Graving Dock & Engineering Co. Ltd.

as well as in ships built in Continental countries, but in 1956, for example, only about one-fifth of the horsepower installed was built in the Doxford works. The rest was constructed either on the Continent, a comparatively small amount, or, mainly, by other marine-engineering establishments in the United Kingdom.

The Doxford engine is produced under licence in the United Kingdom by nine marine-engineering establishments, including John Brown, Fairfield, Scotts', Alexander Stephen, Swan, Hunter & Wigham Richardson (and its associated companies), Vickers-Armstrongs, and the North-eastern Marine Engineering. Most of these companies produce diesel engines of other makes, and the tendency to add to their range of output has become more pronounced, as the Doxford engine, unlike other designs, does not yet offer the possibility of supercharging up to outputs of at least 24,000 h.p.,[1] and cannot, therefore, be used as an alternative to steam turbines for large vessels. Burmeister & Wain were early in this field, but production is limited to Harland & Wolff and their sub-licensee, Kincaid, on the Clyde; and in consequence a number of shipbuilders who might have preferred to build Doxford engines of large horsepower, had suitable designs been available, or Burmeister & Wain engines, are likely to rely increasingly on Sulzer engines.

The production of turbine machinery is less widespread than the production of diesel engines, but here again it is the usual practice to produce under licence. A number of designs are prepared by the Parson and Marine Engineering Turbine Research and Development Association, a research establishment set up by the industry, and licences for foreign designs including gas turbines are also available.

The fact that marine engineers have been able to secure the right to build engines of various designs under licence has made it possible to operate marine-engineering establishments without incurring the expense of development work and research, and indirectly it has tended to maintain a large number of establishments in being. It does not, however, follow that the whole of the research necessary to improve existing types of engines is carried out in the parent establishment. It frequently happens that developments and improvements of existing types of engines are made by licensees, and an engine designated jointly by the name of the licenser and licensee may be the result. What is gained, however, by this diversity of effort may be lost if development programmes are not co-ordinated.

In Chapter 11 it is argued that the marine-engineering industry would benefit if it were possible to arrange for greater specialisation and the production of longer runs of engines from fewer establishments, and it is of

---

[1] See *The Times*, 6 June 1958.

interest to consider here whether the introduction of new types of engines or ships is likely to affect the organisation of marine engineering in this way.

Three new types of engine may come into service in appreciable numbers in the foreseeable future. Two of these, the gas-turbine and the free-piston gas-turbine engine appear unlikely to alter the structure of the industry; both require turbine machinery and to this extent favour turbine producers rather than specialists on diesel engines, but on present showing it appears doubtful if the gas turbine will gain ready acceptance as a marine engine and the future of the free-piston engine is by no means assured. The third possibility is, of course, the use of atomic energy, and this could have considerable repercussions on the organisation of marine engineering.

As a first step towards the production of atomic-powered ships some shipbuilding companies have joined forces with other firms interested in atomic power. John Brown joined with Hawker Siddeley to form John Brown Nuclear Construction Ltd. in 1957, and Cammell Laird with Babcock & Wilcox, while Vickers Nuclear Engineering, Rolls-Royce and Foster Wheeler have been collaborating in the atomic field. In April, 1959, Fairfield Shipbuilding and Engineering signed an agreement with Mitchell Engineering for the same purpose. It may seem a natural development to these shipbuilding companies, accustomed to carrying out a large proportion of all the details of ship construction themselves, to embark on the application of atomic energy to marine propulsion. So far as can be seen at the present time, heat generated in atomic reactors will be converted into productive energy by conventional means, of which steam and gas turbines are possibilities. Presumably the designs of these turbines and their associated equipment will not differ greatly from that now in vogue, and the existing productive equipment and experience of marine-engineering works will largely suffice for their construction. If this is so, engine work may be relatively little affected, and it will be possible for shipbuilding firms to rely on specialists for the development and production of atomic reactors while retaining the production of more conventional items of engine-room equipment themselves. This may be what they intend. On the other hand, it seems unlikely that many atomic-powered ships will be ordered for some time and the few that will be put in hand are likely to be built with special purposes in view. It is difficult to see, therefore, what prospects there are of an adequate volume of work in shipbuilding being secured by even three companies. The addition of the Richardsons Westgarth group to the list gives a total of five marine engineering companies who are potential suppliers of atomic equipment, and there are also a number of other engineering companies which have designed reactors suitable for ship propulsion. It may be, however, that shipbuilding companies, particularly those with interests in outside fields, see in the new associations they have formed the opportunity to develop their activities in a new direction and that they have other applications of atomic energy in mind as well as its use for marine purposes.

The most suitable ships for atomic propulsion are large in size (perhaps 100,000 d.w.t.), and for such ships comparatively small ratios of horsepower per deadweight ton emerge for optimum speeds. Although at the present time one horsepower for every 1½ d.w.t. is an average requirement for the size of ship produced in the United Kingdom, for the largest tankers 1 horsepower for every 5 d.w.t. is all that may be needed. Thus, for a 100,000 d.w.t. tanker an engine of no more than 20,000 h.p. may suffice, although up to 30,000 h.p. might not be excessive. But, whatever choice within this range is made, it is clear that in relation to tonnage, the industry, and more particularly shipbuilders concentrating on large vessels, will need less engine-producing capacity in relation to the tonnage of ships produced, and this points to fewer establishments producing smaller numbers of larger engines.

There may, however, be two offsetting tendencies at work which will make it possible both for larger and more specialised marine-engineering establishments to develop and for smaller establishments to maintain their output. The first of these is the possibility that in the long term the output of ships will increase and that in consequence the demand for engines of medium power and conventional design will continue about the present level, the whole of any increase going into larger units. It is quite impossible to say how this will work out. Ships of all kinds have tended to increase in average size over the years, but as might be expected there has been a considerable dispersion about average or modal sizes; and it is to be expected on the whole that conventional engines will continue to be used side by side with atomic reactors for a considerable time, particularly now that diesel engines of large powers are available. It seldom happens that new inventions either gain instantaneous acceptance, or are, in fact, as suitable for all applications as existing devices. It is possible, for example, that fears of nuclear contamination or arrangements for the refuelling of nuclear-powered ships will limit the types and kind of traffic for which nuclear propulsion can be applied or restrict ships powered by these means to prescribed routes; and it cannot be considered very probable that the use of submarine tankers for the transport of oil, which depends on the use of atomic energy for its feasibility, is likely greatly to accelerate the change-over from engines of conventional type.

The second factor tending to maintain the work of marine-engineering establishments is the tendency for shipowners to demand higher powers in ships of all sizes. This has gone a good way already, and since the horsepower needed to increase the speed of a ship of any given size rises progressively, further gains from this source are likely to be limited.

The most that can be concluded from the various opposing movements at work is that while it is highly probable that the demand for marine engines of greater powers will increase, and it is reasonable to suppose that this will be to the advantage of the larger producers, an increase in the output of new ships and the tendency to increase engine powers in ships of all sizes could still mean that sufficient horsepower of engines of conventional design and smaller size would be required to maintain the output of smaller marine-engineering establishments at its present level.

III

THE DEMAND FOR SHIPS

CHAPTER 5

The Future Course of Demand

I

The four main elements of shipbuilding output—building of new tankers and dry-cargo vessels, naval work, and repairs—must be distinguished in discussing the course of demand, for they are affected by different considerations and have changed markedly in relation to one another over the course of time. Table 2 shows the proportion of the gross value of the output of the shipbuilding industry represented by certain main items in the Census years from 1907 to 1954. The percentages are not all compiled on the same basis; post-war figures include government establishments (in this case the naval dockyards), whereas figures for earlier years, with the exception of 1935 for which two sets of figures are available, relate to private industry; figures for 1948 also refer to Great Britain, whereas other figures refer to the United Kingdom.

Table 2

United Kingdom shipbuilding output analysed according to type of work*
(percentages)

	1907†	1912†	1924	1930	1935	1935‡	1948‡§	1954‡
New merchant ships	60	62	65	63	47	37	42	52
New warships	11	14	1	6	18	20	3	11
Repair work	25	20	32	26	33	37	47	34
Other work	4	4	2	5	2	6	8	3
Total	100	100	100	100	100	100	100	100
Index of the value of output at constant prices	—	—	100	95	58	—	—	—

* Except for 1954, the figures have been abstracted from an unpublished analysis of the shipbuilding trade in the Census of Production prepared by Dr C. E. V. Leser.
† Eire is included in the figures for 1907 and 1912.
‡ Including government establishments.
§ Great Britain.

It is evident from Table 2 that there were considerable differences in the importance of the three main categories of work in Census years; and it is reasonable to suppose that if figures for all years could be shown, even greater differences would emerge. As it is, for Census years, the construction of merchant ships varied, in the inter-war period, from 47 per cent of output in 1935 (exclusive of the naval dockyards) to about 65 per cent in 1924, and that of warships from only 1 per cent in 1924 to 14 per cent in 1912, 18 per cent in 1935 and, it may be estimated, about 40 per cent in the very unusual conditions of 1939.[1] Repair work tended to grow in relative importance during the inter-war period partly because new work fell off, and whereas it accounted for about one-fifth of output in 1912 when output was high, it accounted for about one-third of output in 1935 when new construction was at a low ebb.

The post-war year for which the analysis can be made, that of 1948, shows a small amount of warship work, a moderate proportion of new merchant building and a heavy load of repair and conversion work. The latter figure is inflated in relation to the earlier pre-war years by the inclusion of the naval dockyards which concentrate on repairs, but there is no doubt that the proportion of repair work was greatly swollen by the need to make good wartime damage and neglect, and the conversion of ships from naval to merchant purposes which was still incomplete at that juncture. By 1954, the distribution of output had settled down to a more normal pattern with, however, somewhat greater emphasis on repair work than pre-war. The distribution of employment roughly corresponds to that of output with new merchant building accounting for about 50 per cent of employment, new naval work for about 10 per cent, and repairs for about 40 per cent.[2]

It is clear from the Census figures that the fortunes of companies engaged mainly on merchant building, naval work or repairs will vary greatly as one or another of these classes of work comes to the fore or declines in relative importance. Thus, in 1939, there was abundant work for warship yards though merchant output had fallen to small proportions, and in 1935, repair work suffered less than new construction. Of the various classes of work warship construction is probably the most sporadic and repair work the least subject to variation, but there were violent ups and downs for all of them in the inter-war period.

The future output of the shipbuilding industry will depend on how the demand for tanker vessels, dry-cargo vessels and warships develops as well as on the amount of repair work that is required. In the following pages we examine some of the factors which have a bearing on the matter.

---

[1] Sir Amos Ayre, *op. cit.* p. 11, gives a diagram showing the equivalent output of naval output and merchant output in 1939 as 700,000 g.t. (merchant equivalent) and 600,000 g.t. respectively.

[2] See, for example, Cmd. 9085, *Report of a Court of Inquiry into a Dispute between the Shipbuilding Employers' Federation and . . . the Confederation of Shipbuilding and Engineering Unions,* February 1954, p.5.

II

The gradual reduction of ocean transport costs with the use of large steam-driven vessels and the development of special ships such as refrigerated cargo vessels, luxury passenger liners and oil-tankers, acted as an encouragement to trade. But today, when transport costs have become exceedingly low for most commodities, any further reduction in costs is unlikely to have any marked effect in promoting trade, and it is reasonable to regard the demand for ships as being in the main determined by the demand for ocean transport, and this in turn by the expansion of world trade. Whichever is cause or effect, however, in the relations between trade and transport, the

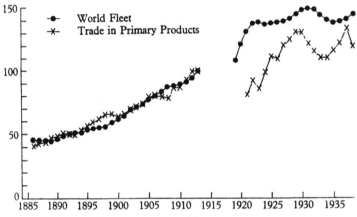

Fig. 2.—World Trade in Primary Products and the Tonnage of World Ships, 1886–1938
(1913 = 100)

tonnage of ships in the world's fleet must keep roughly in step with movements in world trade. If the pattern of trade alters, or if sea transport is more efficiently operated, some divergence between the two may occur, but in general, if the supply of ships fails to keep pace with world trade, freight rates will be increased to abnormally high levels and new building will be stimulated; while, contrarily, if trade falls away, or fails to expand as quickly as the world merchant fleets, freights will fall and new building will be retarded.

Fig. 2 shows the rate of growth of world trade in primary products as measured by a volume index and the tonnage of ships in the world fleet, also in index form, from 1886 to 1938. In the main, both curves can be considered to be dominated by the movement of non-tanker cargoes, although no attempt has been made to separate the shipment of oil products in either series. Tankers, however, accounted for a negligible proportion of the tonnage of the world fleet at the beginning of the century and even by 1938 accounted for no more than 15 per cent of the total.

It is evident from Fig. 2 that both trade in primary products and the tonnage of ships in the world had a marked upward trend before the First World War. Whether they increased together so closely as the figure suggests is much more doubtful. The movement of indices of world trade in primary products is not necessarily a good indicator of the amount of ocean transport

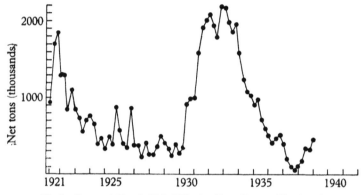

Fig. 3.—Tonnage laid up in United Kingdom Ports (Source: Chamber of Shipping of the United Kingdom)

involved; and the development of the fleet recorded in the figure probably understates the growth of its carrying capacity, for, throughout this period, steamships were replacing sailing vessels and ton for ton the former may have carried four times as much cargo as the latter.[1]

Once the immediate dislocation of post-war shipping had been overcome and trade returned to its normal routes, it became evident that post-war building had increased the size of the fleet much beyond the growth of trade, and it was not until 1929 at the earliest, and more probably 1937, that trade and a stagnant merchant fleet came roughly into balance. This

[1] Maier, for example, quoted in *Palgrave's Dictionary of Statistics*, assessed the carrying capacity of one net ton of a sailing vessel at only one-quarter of that of a steamship. It is arguable that between 1886 and 1913 the carrying capacity of the world fleet increased much more rapidly than the world trade in primary products. This view is supported by a comparison of the movements of freight rates over the period in relation to wholesale prices with the movement of trade in primary products in relation to the tonnage of the world fleet. Over the period as a whole freight rates fell in terms of wholesale prices and carrying capacity appears to have increased in relation to trade. But the precise relationship between the series is uncertain and of little moment in the development of the argument.

is evident both from the movements of the two series in Fig. 2 and from the tonnage of ships shown as laid up in Fig. 3.

From 1929 onwards it is possible to follow the comparative evolution of the demand for non-tanker ocean transport and the world non-tanker fleet from the figures compiled by the United Nations staff with a greater pretension to accuracy than can be attained with the figures readily available for a long-term historical analysis. It appears from these figures that there was little increase in the weight of dry cargo to be moved by sea between 1929 and 1954. In 1955, there was a sharp increase to 450 million tons and expansion continued in 1956 and 1957 (490 and 510 million tons respectively). In 1958, however, according to the Institute of Shipping Research at Bremen, there was a sharp decline, leaving the total at little more than the 1955 level.

Table 3.—*Dry-cargo movements and the world dry-cargo fleet*

	1929	1937	1950	1954
Tonnage of cargo to be moved (million metric tons)	390	375	300	390
Average length of haul (nautical miles)	3090	3230	3310	3330
Ton-nautical-miles	1200	1210	990	1330
Tonnage of dry-cargo vessels actively engaged in external trade (million d.w.t.)	50·2	46·7	44·6	49·9
Average rated speed (knots)	11·3	11·6	12·8	13·2
Index of utilisation	95	100	78	85

Source: *United Nations Bulletin of Statistics*, March 1956, pp. viii and ix, and January 1959

Between 1937 and 1950, the size of the fleet engaged in external trade fell by less than the amount of transport required (measured in ton-miles). This was not due to a tendency for world shipbuilding to outpace the growth of world trade, or for more ships to be kept in operation than were justified by prospective employment, but to a fall in the efficiency of utilisation of the world fleet. The higher average speeds available to non-tanker vessels were more than offset by port delays and other factors. In 1950 the world dry-cargo fleet carried 20 per cent less goods than would have been possible if it could have been utilised as effectively as in 1937 and, although in 1954 the position had improved, roughly 15 per cent more ships were required than would have been necessary with the degree of utilisation attained in 1937.

Apart from this factor it is broadly correct that the demand for ocean transport of dry cargoes was roughly in balance with the available tonnage of ships until 1958. This is not to say that there were not quite large swings in both directions from time to time. The Korean War in 1951, and the Suez crisis in 1956, strained world-shipping resources for the transport of dry cargoes, as did periodic demands for the transport of coal across the Atlantic from the United States to Europe; and at times, particularly in the aftermath of scarcity, a surplus of vessels emerged which could not find employment. But the surplus of tonnage that emerged in 1958, when a high rate of new building coincided with a sharp contraction of trade, was much more serious, and by 1959 it had all the signs of heralding a prolonged depression.[1]

Leaving out of account the market situation as it appeared in 1959, it is possible to examine in general terms the outlook for the construction of non-tanker vessels in future years. In the first place, an examination of past trends provides no reason for thinking that the demand for dry-cargo transportation will rise any more quickly than world trade. This is not a case of some new product with unbounded prospects in front of it, or of the sale of some commodity or service that has been observed to increase more rapidly than the growth of industrial production and national income over the years, but of a demand widely related to materials needed in many spheres of production, or to the growth of population in so far as it is reflected in a movement of foodstuffs in world trade. At the best, the demand for dry-cargo vessels is unlikely to increase more than industrial production, and on the basis of some past experience it is likely to increase more slowly. Between 1937 and 1950 there was, as we have seen, a fall in dry-cargo transportation (largely reflecting the substitution of oil for coal in movements in international trade), though world industrial production was 45 per cent greater in the latter year. Between 1950 and 1955, on the other hand, the trend was more favourable and trade grew more rapidly than industrial production.

In assessing future demand for dry-cargo vessels, it is difficult to go beyond certain simple propositions without running the risk of seriously misreading the course of events. On the whole it seems likely that the growth in demand for ocean dry-cargo transport will not be very rapid. On the basis of the expansion of trade before the First World War an annual increase of 3 per cent per annum might appear to be reasonable, though a smaller increase could not be ruled out if autarky regained a foothold or if production became less dependent on trade in other ways; but equally a higher figure, perhaps 5 per cent per annum or even more, might be recorded in favourable circum-

[1] See J. R. Parkinson, 'The demand for ships', April 1959, *Scottish Journal of Political Economy*, June 1959.

stances, judging by the expansion that took place between 1950 and 1955. An increase of 3–5 per cent per annum would mean that $1\frac{1}{2}$–$2\frac{1}{2}$ million d.w.t. of new shipping (say 1–$1\frac{3}{4}$ million g.r.t.) of the same kind as that in use would be needed for ocean transport work. If other services such as passenger transport and coastal trade increased in the same proportion the figure might be as much as $1\frac{3}{4}$–3 million g.r.t. per year. In fact, it might be possible to provide for a given increase in the amount of ocean transport work required, with a rather smaller increase in the world fleet as some improvement in the efficiency of new tonnage is likely, either because its rated speed will be greater than the average of existing ships or because improved facilities are provided in other ways. If past trends are any guide average rated speeds might increase by $\frac{3}{4}$ per cent per annum, and allowing for time spent in port the carrying capacity of the world fleet might increase on this account by $\frac{1}{2}$ per cent per annum; at the same time improved designs and special ships, such as those used for the transport of iron ore, will help to increase the effective carrying capacity of a given tonnage. Both these effects will reduce the need to supply new tonnage in the future as they have in the past. It can be inferred from the United Nations figures, for example, that the carrying capacity per deadweight ton of the world dry-cargo fleet increased by $4\frac{1}{4}$ per cent between 1929 and 1937 and by $3\frac{1}{2}$ per cent between 1950 and 1954, increases of $\frac{1}{2}$ and 1 per cent per annum respectively.

In addition to the demand for non-tanker vessels in order to increase the size of the world fleet in line with trade and production, there will also be some demand for replacement purposes. The effect of this in augmenting the demand for new ships is likely to be very variable in the short run but reasonably predictable over long periods of time. When trade is slack and freights at rock-bottom levels, scrapping of older vessels may proceed apace without any substantial quantity of replacement orders being placed; and contrariwise replacement orders may be given when at the height of the boom vessels are kept in service. In 1925–30, for example, few vessels were scrapped though new orders were given fairly readily, whereas in 1932–4 scrapping was at a high level without replacement orders being placed. Over a long period, however, replacement demand for non-tankers may average about 3 per cent per annum for a fleet of 'normal' age composition (e.g. one that has been built up over a long period by an invariable amount of new building exactly making good wastage). This corresponds to the average experience in the inter-war period, though in fact wastage rates varied considerably at different periods. For a fleet which has been increasing in size over a period of time, the amount of tonnage coming due for replacement will be less than that for a normal age distribution. In a fleet growing at the rate of 3 per cent per annum, for example, the tonnage of ships scrapped each year will not be 3 per cent but nearer 2 per cent of the strength of the fleet at any given time.[1] This is due to the fact that, with an increasing fleet, an abnormally small percentage of vessels is in the upper age-groups where the incidence of marine casualty and scrapping is greatest.[2] On the average in the inter-war period, of each 100 g.r.t. of new shipping about 90 g.r.t. remained at $12\frac{1}{2}$ years, about 88 g.r.t. at $17\frac{1}{2}$ years and about 78 g.r.t. at age $22\frac{1}{2}$. Of the tonnage over 20 years of age, about 5.7 per cent left the register each year.[3]

It may be that wastage rates experienced in the inter-war period will not be characteristic of future years. There is no reason to suppose that ships have any predetermined span of life irrespective of type, construction, technical developments, the requirements of Governments and classification societies or economic factors; but an average length of life of 30 years or thereabouts appears to have been characteristic of ships built in iron and steel, irrespective of when they were constructed, and there is some reason for supposing that it will not alter radically in the next few years. We may not, therefore, go far wrong in assuming that it will be necessary to replace something of the order of 2 per cent of the world fleet of dry-cargo vessels if it expands at the rate of 3 per cent per annum.

The orders of magnitude set out above do not, of course, form a basis for prediction of the course of events. Doubts will be felt by many informed observers as to whether an increase in world trade of even 3 per cent per annum is a justifiable assumption in an uncertain world subject to slumps and other interruptions to the course of economic expansion; the increase in the weight of dry cargo to be carried by sea may well depart from the rate at which trade measured in economic terms may develop; and again, in the short run, much depends on the ability of ports to handle cargo expeditiously. If the weight of dry cargo to be carried by sea increased by 3 per cent per annum and replacement demand for ships averaged 2 per cent per annum, the total demand for new ships might be of the order of 5 per cent per annum

---

[1] If l is invariably the length of life of a ship, r the arithmetic rate of increase of the fleet per annum and a the tonnage of ships built l years ago, the size of the fleet may be taken to be

$$\frac{a + (a + lar)}{2} \cdot l = \frac{al(2 + lr)}{2}$$

and the proportionate wastage rate will be

$$\frac{a}{al\left(\dfrac{2 + lr}{2}\right)} = \frac{2}{l(2 + lr)}$$

for $r = 0 \cdot 03$ and $l = 33$

this gives a wastage rate of approximately $0 \cdot 02$; while for $r = 0 \cdot 05$ and $l = 33$ the wastage rate is reduced to about $0 \cdot 017$ of the strength of the fleet.

[2] This was not, however, so true of the period before 1914 when marine casualty was an important source of wastage and seemed to affect all groups almost indiscriminately.

[3] See J. R. Parkinson, 'Ship wastage rates', *Journal of the Royal Statistical Society*, 1957, p.75.

of the existing fleet, but such a figure would appear to some to represent a highly optimistic view. The upper limit to optimism could be placed with some degree of confidence at 7½ per cent, composed of an increase in trade of 5 per cent per annum and a replacement rate of some 2½ per cent per annum. Thus a demand of 3–4½ million t. of new dry-cargo shipping per annum corresponding to 5–7½ per cent of a fleet of about 60 million g.r.t. is more likely to err on the side of optimism than pessimism.

In fact the world output of dry-cargo vessels fell somewhat below this range until 1956, when it increased rather suddenly, although, as we have seen, the growth of ocean transport of goods was rather more rapid on the average than the figure of 5 per cent suggested as the upper limit to the likely increase in future years. What appears to have happened is not that the dry-cargo fleet has been under-maintained but that an increase in the efficiency of the fleet has made it possible to carry some part of the increase in cargo without an increase in the tonnage available.

Table 4

World fleet of dry-cargo vessels and new construction

	World fleet excluding the U.S. reserve fleet (million g.r.t.) (100 g.r.t. and above)	New construction (million g.r.t.) (100 g.r.t. and above)	New construction as a percentage of the world fleet
1950	53	1·9	3·6
1951	57	2·1	3·6
1952	58	2·4	4·1
1953	58	2·2	3·8
1954	57	2·4	4·2
1955	60	2·9	4·8
1956	63	4·0	6·3
1957	68	4·7	6·9
1958	70	4·5	6·4

Source: *Lloyd's Register of Shipping: Statistical Tables*

III

Our broad survey of the possible evolution of the world demand for dry-cargo vessels provides a general background to the prospects of the United Kingdom shipbuilding industry, but although shipping and shipbuilding remain international industries in spite of nationalistic tendencies in some directions, there is no reason to expect that any country will follow the general pattern at all closely. In the long run, the United Kingdom shipping industry will be more closely bound up with the evolution of United Kingdom trade than with what happens in the world at large, even though United Kingdom shipowners may be active in carrying goods between third countries, and other countries continue to share in both inward and outward trade of the United Kingdom. And much the same is likely to be true of the United Kingdom shipbuilding industry, for the bulk of the orders are for the home market and it is the general practice of United Kingdom shipowners to place orders with United Kingdom shipbuilders rather than abroad.

Both United Kingdom trade and even more the United Kingdom fleet are expanding rather more slowly than is the case in the rest of the world. Table 5 is of interest in this connection. It can be argued that irrespective of the predominance of coal in 1913 as the export or import *par excellence* requiring shipping space, it has been the weight of imports (and the distance over which they have had to be carried) that has determined the needs of the United Kingdom in the present century. Coal was shipped mainly to Europe and mostly in Continental ships; when this was not the case and it was sent farther afield it travelled mainly as an alternative to ballast for ships which had entered fully loaded but otherwise would have returned empty to the more distant centres of world supplies. The fact that the weight of dry-cargo imports into the United Kingdom has shown no increase since 1913 is revealing and explains in large measure why there has been no increase in the United Kingdom dry-cargo fleet over this period of time. Indeed, the United Kingdom fleet of dry-cargo vessels is no larger than it was in 1939 or 1913, and it has shrunk from about 40 per cent of the world total in 1913 to 17 per cent in 1956. Thus the United Kingdom, far from keeping pace with the expansion of world trade in the present century, has fallen well behind, and the trend has continued in recent years. Between 1950 and 1956 the weight of United Kingdom imports increased by 30 per cent, but even then the expansion was less than that of world non-tanker trade and the weight of imports in 1956 was still less than it had been in 1937. Over the same period, the tonnage of the United Kingdom non-tanker fleet showed virtually no change. This suggests that the United Kingdom is likely to continue to lose part of her share of world trade unless the dry-cargo fleet increases in future. It can be argued that in the inter-war period not only was the United Kingdom losing ground in world shipping, but also that at times of high activity she was becoming more dependent on foreign shipping to carry her own imports.

These divergent trends make it even more difficult to judge what changes are likely in the size of the United Kingdom non-tanker fleet over the years than to appraise the probable evolution of the world fleet. It may be that United Kingdom trade will increase in the next decade at much the same rate as world trade and that the non-tanker fleet will follow suit, but there are good reasons for caution in appraising the outlook in view of past experience, and it might be more realistic to assume that the increase will be rather smaller.

Table 5.—United Kingdom imports and exports by weight (million tons)

	1913	1920	1929	1937	1938	1946	1947	1948	1949	1950	1951	1952	1953	1954	1955	1956	1957	1958
Imports																		
Food, tobacco, wines, etc.	18·7	15·6	19·0	22·0	22·0	10·6	14·0	16·0	15·4	14·5	17·0	16·3	18·3	16·7	18·9	19·0	18·9	21·3
Raw materials (excl. crude petroleum)	27·0 {	22·6	27·0	35·6	26·3 {	21·0	23·7	24·0	27·4	25·5	28·3	28·1	28·0	30·1	33·0	32·9	35·1	29·3
Crude petroleum	1·9				2·3 {		2·5	4·7	6·2	9·5 {	34·3 {	30·5	33·8	39·3	50·3	—	43·9	47·3
Refined petroleum	1·8	3·1	6·1	9·1	9·4	11·7	10·2	12·5	11·5	9·4 {								
Manufactures (excl. refined petroleum)	6·6	4·2	8·4	8·6	7·2	3·7	4·5	4·7	4·8	4·3	5·8	6·2	6·2	5·3	7·7	7·1	6·4	6·3
Total	56·0	45·5	60·5	75·3	67·3	47·0	54·9	61·9	65·3	63·2	79·6	81·1	86·3	91·4	109·9	104·5	104·3	104·2
Exports																		
Other than coal	16·9	12·3	17·0	13·5	11·5	10·9	10·1	11·6	16·0	15·5	19·1	19·7	21·7	23·0	22·7	24·7	23·1	24·3
Coal	76·7	28·9	64·4	43·5	38·2	5·0	1·1	11·6	16·0	16·2	9·1	13·7	15·7	15·6	14·3	11·2	10·0	5·8
Total	93·6	41·2	81·4	57·0	49·7	15·9	11·1	23·2	32·0	31·7	28·2	33·4	37·4	38·6	37·0	35·9	33·1	30·1

Source: *Liverpool Steam Ship Owners' Association's Annual Reports*

On the basis of past experience it might be expected that the United Kingdom would have a rather higher tonnage replacement rate than the world as a whole. United Kingdom shipowners have tended to sell much of their tonnage overseas before it reached the end of its useful life and to replace it with new modern tonnage. In the period 1885–1914 about 2½ per cent of the total strength of the British fleet was sold abroad each year, compared with 1¾ per cent lost or broken up. In the inter-war period the United Kingdom fleet was turned over consistently more rapidly than ships owned by the rest of the world. For ships over 20 years old, twice as much tonnage was disposed of by the United Kingdom as by other countries, and in the lower age-groups the difference was, if anything, even more marked.

Table 6.—*Percentage of tonnage surviving 5 years on the average during the period* 1922–29

(Steamships and motorships 100 *g.r.t. and over)**

	Initially in age group			
	5–10	10–15	15–20	Over 20
United Kingdom fleet	90·9	83·6	69·2	44·7
World fleet	94·0	93·6	88·7	71·6

* Tankers as well as non-tankers are included in the figures.

It can be concluded from Table 6 that a wastage rate of 4 per cent rather than 3 per cent is likely to be typical of the United Kingdom fleet in stationary conditions, though this would be the equivalent of about 3 per cent of the strength of a fleet increasing by 3 per cent each year. This means that, allowing for an improvement in efficiency, rather less than ½ million g.r.t. of shipping might be needed each year to provide for the replacement of the United Kingdom fleet, and in addition to this there might be sufficient demand to increase the non-tanker fleet by, say, 3 per cent per annum, giving, say, a total demand for replacement and expansion of ¾ million g.r.t. per annum.

IV

The orders of magnitude discussed in connection with the size of the market which may develop for dry-cargo ships are, of course, of a very general nature. Within whatever total of non-tanker vessels is required there will be shifts in the relative importance of different types of vessels, and some of these will be of consequence to the shipbuilding industry. Since 1939 a number of trends have become evident: there has been, for example, a growth of liner tonnage and a decline in the importance of tramps and coasters; certain types of specialised vessel have come to the fore while competition from the airlines has imposed a check to the expansion of passenger-liner tonnage. The tonnage of tramps has fallen from about 30 per cent of the total dry-cargo tonnage in 1936 to about one-quarter in 1956; more recently, however, there have been some signs of a reversal in the trend with tramp launchings rising to one-third of the total.[1] The essential distinction between tramps and liners lies in the type of trade on which they are engaged rather than in the vessels themselves—tramps carry cargo in bulk wherever it can be found, whereas liners sail at predetermined times on regular routes and cater for a variety of cargo—but the cargo liner is likely to be bigger, faster and better equipped and consequently more expensive to construct than the handy tramp, and since it is often constructed with a specific route in mind it is likely to be designed to meet special requirements. In recent years there has been an increasing demand for vessels which, because of the bulk nature of the cargo they carry, should properly be classed as tramps but which, in the regularity of their employment on certain routes and the specific nature of the cargoes for which they are designed, have some resemblance to liner tonnage in their operation; such vessels include bulk-sugar carriers, ore-carriers and combined oil/ore-carriers. It has sometimes been found that vessels of this kind are sufficiently versatile in operation to be used for a variety of purposes, and in some respects they may be regarded as a rather larger version of the pre-war tramp. This tendency is also notice-able in the design of larger tramping vessels specifically for the transport of coal on the Atlantic run.

The substitution of liner for tramp tonnage, as well as an increase in the size of tramps, has meant that fewer ships of larger average size have been constructed. This tendency has been reinforced by the decline in the number of vessels used in the coastal trade from 1000 in 1939 to under 500 in 1956.[2] Only in passenger liners does the trend seem to have been against an increase in the average size of ships. The expansion of passenger traffic on the most important Atlantic route has been slow compared with the growth of air travel. The numbers crossing the Atlantic by sea increased by over 20 per cent between 1952 and 1956 and exceeded 1 million in the latter year; but in 1958 they fell by 7 per cent. Over the same period, however, the number of passengers by air roughly trebled to reach 1,200,000.[3] Sea travel is still cheaper than air transport, but in order to maintain their advantage the liner com-

---

[1] See L. Isserlis, *Journal of the Royal Statistical Society*, 1938, pt. I, p. 102, and the *Annual Report of the Chamber of Shipping of the United Kingdom*, 1956–7, pp. 168–9.

[2] See the report of a speech made at the Eightieth Annual Meeting of the Chamber of Shipping by Mr W. F. Robertson (*Annual Report of the Chamber of Shipping of the United Kingdom*, 1956–7, p. 265).

[3] *Maritime Transport*, a study by the Maritime Transport Committee of the O.E.E.C., May 1957, p. 37.

panies are finding it necessary to cut costs by providing less space per passenger. Thus a new P. & O. liner with a gross tonnage of 45,000 will carry the same number of passengers as the *Queen Elizabeth* with a tonnage of 84,000 and require a crew of 960 against 1260. But the general trend to larger ships is not likely to be much affected by this move, and the larger and better-equipped shipyards will tend to profit from the changes that are taking place.

v

In contrast to the moderate change that took place in world trade in dry-cargo products between 1929 and 1958 shipments of oil have increased at a phenomenal rate. Not only has increasing production required a steady increase in fuel supplies but, within a rising total, an increasing proportion of consumption has been met by the use of petroleum products, which could be more readily provided than coal or hydro-electricity. Between 1929 and 1937 the *weight* of oil carried by sea increased by over a half and between 1937 and 1958 it increased 4 times. The number of ton-miles involved appears to have increased rather more quickly than the quantity of oil; there was an increase in the average haul from 2700 nautical miles in 1929 to 3050 nautical miles in 1954—largely the result of a shift to Middle East sources of supply. The world tanker fleet, on the other hand, increased rather more slowly than either—by roughly 4½ times between 1929 and 1958 compared with an increase of roughly 7 times in the number of ton-miles performed. This was possible because the new tankers added to the world fleets in increasing quantities were capable of higher average speeds than those built in previous years. There may also have been some contribution from a reduction in loading and unloading times, but tanker turn-round is accomplished in a matter of hours, and even a marked improvement in the time taken makes only a small difference to effective carrying capacity.

The increase in the rated speeds of newly built tankers is a continuing feature of the tanker market. Owners have moved decisively in the direction of having speedier vessels at their disposal, either to maintain higher average speeds or to provide a working margin against bad weather or unforeseen contingencies, or to take advantage of favourable market conditions. In this they have been helped by the movement towards the use of larger vessels which has been an outstanding feature of the post-war period. The larger a vessel the greater can be its speed without raising fuel costs exorbitantly. But, irrespective of size, there comes a point at which higher speeds can be attained only at the expense of a steep and progressive increase in fuel consumption. Thus there are limits beyond which it does not pay to increase speed in order to make fuller use of tanker capacity but is cheaper to increase the tonnage of tankers employed in order to save fuel costs. The upper limit to economical speeds in present circumstances is likely to be about 17 knots, though atom tankers may reach higher speeds, but it is possible that operating speeds of conventional tankers will tend to be appreciably lower, and for the largest tankers speeds of only 14 or 15 knots may be adopted.[1] Since every knot increase in average speed has the effect of increasing effective tanker capacity by 7 per cent (the average rated speed of the world fleet of tankers was about $13\frac{1}{2}$ knots in 1954), the rated speeds of tankers to be built in future years and the speeds at which they are intended to be operated will have a considerable bearing on the amount of new tonnage that will be required. It is clear, however, that in the next few years tanker tonnage will not need to increase quite so rapidly as the anticipated increase in the transport of oil by sea measured in ton-miles.

The outlook for oil consumption over the next 10 or 20 years is almost certainly one of rapid growth. How rapid the expansion is likely to be is difficult to say, and the various estimates attempted from time to time of the likely trend of consumption are inevitably influenced by the date at which they are made; there would be little point, therefore, in attempting any detailed estimate here. The most that can be done is to describe some of the factors influencing the likely evolution and to give some very rough indication of the magnitude of the expansion in order to provide a background to the future of tanker construction.

It appears that growth of consumption of oil in Europe is likely to be the major factor affecting oil transport by sea. It is possible that the United States will draw large quantities of oil from overseas, and particularly from the Middle East, in order to provide for higher consumption, while safeguarding her own sources of supplies against over-consumption and the encroachments that this would make on strategic reserves, but it is possible that much of her needs will be met out of Canadian production or from the South American producers, such as Venezuela, closer at hand.[2] In Europe some increase in indigenous production of oil is likely, but the major source of Europe's oil requirements will continue to be Middle East supplies so long as political conditions permit. Thus in an O.E.E.C. study[3] of member countries' oil requirements indigenous production was expected to increase from (in round numbers) 9 million t. in 1955 to about 36 million t. in 1975, while imports were expected to increase from roughly 84 million t. in 1955 to about 334 million t. in 1975.

[1] See *The Financial Times*, 8 September 1956.

[2] Between 1952 and 1956 United States imports from this source were increasing at $16\frac{1}{2}$ per cent per annum. See *The Financial Times*, 16 May 1957, reporting a speech by Mr A. S. C. Hulton to the Institute of Tankers. Since import restrictions were imposed in 1958 in the interests of home producers, it is possible that imports will increase less spectacularly in future.

[3] *Oil. The Outlook for Europe*, O.E.E.C., 1956, p. 32, Table 7.

The increase in the requirements of oil by Europe from the Middle East will be the most important factor governing the demand for tankers, but the figures cannot be more than an indication of the orders of magnitude involved and any number of events could alter them markedly. They serve only to illustrate how quickly oil consumption is increasing and what dimension it could reach if it expanded in an uninterrupted manner. Between 1950 and 1955 oil consumption in the O.E.E.C. countries increased by no less than 13 per cent per annum and, although this rate of increase was expected to drop by the late sixties and seventies, it was expected to fall only slightly in the first decade after 1960. World figures of the weight of oil transported given in Table 7 also show smiliar magnitudes of increase in some recent years. The increase in 1955 was 9 per cent, and in 1956, 11 per cent. In 1957, when the transport of oil was interrupted by the closure of the Suez Canal, this was reduced to 8 per cent; and in 1958 it appears that there was a further decline in the rate of increase to 6 per cent. Nevertheless, in four years the weight of oil moved by sea had increased by 125 million tons to reach 445 million tons in 1958.

Table 7.—*Movements of oil and the world fleet of tankers*

	1929	1937	1950	1954	1955	1956
Tonnage of cargo to be moved (million metric tons)	65	105	230	320	360	400
Average length of haul (nautical miles)	2700	2680	2960	3050	—	—
Ton-nautical-miles	180	280	680	960	—	—
Tonnage of tanker vessels engaged in external trade (million d.w.t.)	5·8	9·0	17·7	24·4	—	—
Average rated speed (knots)	10·0	10·4	12·9	13·6	—	—
Index of utilisation	102	100	99	96	—	—

Source: *United Nations Bulletin of Statistics*, March 1956, pp. viii and ix, and January 1959

It is difficult to say whether the slower increase in oil consumption registered in 1957 and 1958 is good ground for modifying previous estimates of the rate of increase that is likely to be sustained over a long period. One effect has been to make both oil companies and independent tanker operators scrutinise their requirements more closely and cancel orders placed when the outlook appeared more favourable. In 1957 some orders were on the books of shipbuilders for the delivery of tankers as far ahead as 1965, and this indicates the strength of the boom that swept the tanker market at the time. There was, of course, no co-ordination in the placing of orders; some were given by the international oil companies operating mainly under United Kingdom direction, others by American-controlled companies and a great many by independent 'tramp' tanker operators, some of whom, like Onassis or Niarchos, are almost household names and control fleets of tankers running into millions of deadweight tons. Orders for tankers were placed all over the world, and it was no mean problem in the circumstances to determine what tonnage had been ordered in total. The Suez crisis prompted the American government to ask for a special study of the tonnage of tankers on order in an attempt to pin down widely differing estimates. This study, as well as others conducted at the time, pointed to an unprecedented rate of deliveries in future years, and also provided an illustration of how rapidly the situation can change within a matter of months. On 14 December 1956, for example, the total tonnage of ocean-going tankers on order according to the United States Survey amounted to about 29 million d.w.t.—sufficient to increase the effective carrying capacity of the fleet of some 41 million d.w.t. of ocean-going tankers by 82 per cent.[1] Yet by March 1957 the figures of tankers on order had jumped from 29 million to 38 million d.w.t. Had the United States matched estimates of new tankers on order against consumption trends it would no doubt have concluded, as did John I. Jacobs & Co. or the Westinform Service in conducting a similar review of order books, that the tonnage of tankers due for delivery in future years would very likely outrun requirements. The former study foresaw an average annual delivery of tankers with a capacity equal to 16–17 per cent of the existing world fleet against a rise in consumption of only 10 per cent,[2] while the latter concluded that on the basis of a rather higher increase in oil consumption than many would consider reasonable over the period 1957–61 there could well be a surplus of super-tankers ranging from as little as ½ million to 5½ million d.w.t.; and yet another estimate given by Mr A. S. C. Hulton[3] put the likely surplus at 7½–15 million d.w.t. by 1961. These estimates were prepared before a slackening in the growth of industrial output in a number of countries became clearly apparent later in the year.

On the basis of these conclusions it would be easy to accuse the various oil interests of over-ordering and in so doing risking the precipitation of a slump in tanker construction. It is, however, difficult to make any such accusations when the circumstances in which many of the orders were placed is considered: with the Suez Canal closed the sea route to the Middle East was doubled in length, and something like an additional 5 million d.w.t.

---

[1] Tankers owned by Russia and satellite countries as well as United States and government and military tankers were excluded from the figures.

[2] See *The Journal of Commerce, Shipbuilding and Engineering Edition*, 28 February 1957.

[3] In a speech to the Institute of Tankers. See *The Financial Times*, 16 May 1957.

of tankers would have been needed to carry the same volume of oil round the Cape as passed through the Suez Canal. As oil consumption continues to increase a correspondingly higher tonnage of tankers would be needed to by-pass the Suez Canal in future years. It may be, therefore, that the oil companies would not see it amiss to have a reserve of tankers available to ensure a passage round the Cape if the need arose. Thus the Westinform Survey concluded that the tanker building programme in 1957 could be justified only by the need to provide sufficient capacity to by-pass the Suez Canal.

Underlying all discussion as to the balance between tanker construction and the movement of oil lie certain assumptions as to the wastage rates appropriate to tankers in future circumstances. Generally, with a fleet increasing as rapidly as the present oil-tanker tonnage, wastage is likely to be of rather small moment in the total picture. The calculation of wastage rates for the inter-war period referred to earlier made no distinction between tanker and non-tanker vessels, though in fact there are good reasons for believing that the longevity of tankers is less than that of non-tankers. In the main this is due to corrosion caused by the combined action of sea water and petroleum on the plates and structure of the tanker. It has happened with some tankers that corrosion has been so far advanced in even the first 15 years of operation that economic repair was impossible, but generally there can be no doubt that the serviceable life of a tanker is much greater than 15 years, and it is almost certainly in excess of 25 years, which was the average age of tankers broken up or lost in the period.[1] Even on a 25-year span of life the tonnage of tankers likely to be broken up each year is a rather small percentage of a fleet growing at the rate of 10 per cent per annum and, on the formulae adopted for similar calculations for dry-cargo vessels, would amount to less than 2 per cent of the fleet. The past few years have, however, been ones of great technical change, and many of the smaller tankers which have seen some years of service are getting outdated and, while not worn out, are approaching obsolescence as repair costs rise and super-tankers drive down the cost of oil transport to lower levels. Thus it is possible that an excess of new tanker production over a few years could be offset in part by an increased rate of scrapping due to obsolescence; there was however, no more than $6\frac{1}{2}$ million g.r.t. of tankers more than 15 years old out of a total of 34 million g.r.t. in the world fleet in 1958, and this sets a limit to what could be done by this means to keep supply and demand in balance.

Large tankers are far more economical to operate than smaller sizes. Cost estimates given in a 'Survey of the future of the Suez Canal' prepared

[1] The average life calculated in this way is almost certainly weighted too highly with vessels lost or broken up prematurely which are over-represented in a growing population.

by Ebasco Services Inc. for the Suez Canal Co. suggested that the cost of a 16,000 d.w.t. tanker built in European yards in 1957 would be about $265 per ton, compared with $175 per ton for a tanker of 90,000[1] d.w.t. Running costs per ton also fall steeply with an increase in the size of tankers. The *World Glory*, a 45,000 d.w.t. super-tanker, costs twice as much to run as a T 2 tanker of 16,600 d.w.t. and a speed of 14.6 knots, but its carrying capacity is three times as much. The reason for this is partly that it is not necessary to increase the size of the crew in proportion to the size of the vessel and partly that fuel consumption also does not rise in proportion. A 30,000 d.w.t. tanker requires 12,000 shaft-h.p. but a 50 per cent increase in power

Table 8.—*Age distribution of world fleet of tankers* (100 *g.r.t. and over*), 1958

	Million gross tons
Under 5 years	12·6
5 and under 10 years	8·7
10 and under 15 years	5·8
15 and under 20 years	3·5
20 and under 25 years	1·2
25 years and over	1·8
Total	33·6

Source: *Lloyd's Register of Shipping, Statistical Tables*, 1958

suffices to drive a tanker of 90,000 d.w.t., and, since fuel consumption is roughly proportionate to shaft-horsepower, there is a considerable saving in running costs. Similarly, 55 men are needed to run the *World Glory* but only 70 men would be needed for 100,000 d.w.t. tanker.

It is not surprising that with such decisive cost advantages progressively larger tankers are being ordered each year. At present the use of large tankers on the trunk routes appears to be limited only by berthing facilities, or in the case of the Middle East run to Europe the draught that the Suez Canal can accommodate.[2] A super-tanker carrying oil round the Cape would be less costly to operate than a 16,000 t. tanker carrying oil through the Suez Canal, though a 37,500 t. vessel (the maximum size that can pass

---

[1] It appears however, that the most economical size to build (though not to operate) is in the 45–65,000 d.w.t. range, largely because steel requirements per ton increase thereafter (see *The Times*, 11 June 1959).

[2] The lack of adequate berthing facilities and dry docks and the fact that much of the United Kingdom oil comes through the Suez Canal is a partial explanation of why somewhat smaller sizes of tankers are building in United Kingdom shipyards than in the rest of the world. Suitable terminals for the largest tankers are scarce in the United Kingdom and Milford Haven is one of the few examples of a suitable site with sufficient depths of water to accommodate the largest tankers without extensive works being required.

through the Canal fully loaded in normal circumstances) would transport oil at slightly less cost than either. This by no means exhausts the possibilities; a tanker of 90,000 d.w.t. can utilise the Suez Canal in ballast and intermediate sizes can carry part cargoes; and there may also be other ways of loading super-tankers at the northern end of the Canal; but it is rapidly becoming a matter of indifference as to whether oil should be transported round the Cape in the largest super-tankers available or carried through the Canal in smaller vessels.[1]

The realisation that this is the case has played a part in stimulating the ordering of larger tankers. Until recently the characteristic size of tankers

Table 9.—*Size distribution (thousand d.w.t.) of tankers: end* 1956

	In service	On order
24–30	188	93
30–35	103	191
35–40	20	119
40–45	3	69
45–50	7	116
50–60	—	9
60–75	—	17
75 and over	1	8
Total	322	622

Source: John I. Jacobs & Co., as given in the *Shipping World Year Book*

was in the 10,000–15,000 g.r.t. group and the 12,500 g.r.t. tanker with a deadweight tonnage of a little short of 20,000 was typical. Table 9 illustrates how the size distribution of tankers is changing in the larger size groups. The average size of tankers in the world fleet of ocean-going vessels was 16,900 d.w.t. at the end of 1956 compared with 26,400 d.w.t. for new tankers constructed in the second half of 1956 and 31,000 d.w.t. for those on order. Even more instructive, however, was the large number of 45,000–50,000 d.w.t. on order at the end of 1956 and the number of orders for tankers over 60,000 d.w.t. which had been placed. The 65,000 d.w.t. tanker is now thought of as a handy size, thus usurping the place of the 32,000 d.w.t. tanker a year or two previously or the 18,000 d.w.t. tanker before that. In face of the rapid rise in the average size of tankers that has taken place in recent years it is difficult to be sure that the present size distribution will not in turn be greatly modified in the future. But the continued increase in tanker sizes brings difficulties in its train with the need to provide port

[1] See *The Financial Times*, 12 March 1957, using data compiled by Harley Mullion & Co.

facilities to accommodate giant vessels and, no less expensive, the need to construct docks able to accommodate tankers of 100,000 d.w.t. for repair and overhaul.

The increase in the average size of tankers that has already taken place means that perhaps only half the number of tankers will be required in future as would have been necessary with the modal sizes in use in 1956. This is to the advantage of firms that are accustomed to building large ships and have the facilities for the job. But many firms, large, medium and small, are enlarging the size of their berths in order to be able to move up the size scale; and by this means they hope to maintain their place in the tanker market.

The tonnage of orders placed at the end of 1956 included almost 10 million d.w.t. on order for the oil companies and about 20 million d.w.t. for 'tramp' operators, compared with 17 million d.w.t. owned at the end of 1956 by the oil companies and 23 million d.w.t. by tramp operators.[1] At this juncture tramp operators were hoping to undertake a rising proportion of oil shipments. At mid-December 1956, nine companies, including their affiliated interests, had placed about one-third of the orders in hand. These included Standard Oil, N.J., Royal Dutch Shell and British Petroleum, each with orders placed of about $1\frac{1}{2}$ million d.w.t., A .S. Onassis, S.S. Niarchos and Gulf Oil with orders of about $\frac{3}{4}$ million d.w.t. and D. K. Ludwig, P. & O., and Caltex with $\frac{1}{2}$ million d.w.t. on order. There were also a number of other companies with orders of a little less than $\frac{1}{2}$ million d.w.t.; and a number of contracts were in the course of negotiation by the larger companies.[2]

VII

It is very difficult, if not impossible, to analyse the deman for United Kingdom controlled tankers irrespective of the world operations of the oil companies and the 'tramp' tanker operators. The total of imports of crude and refined petroleum into the United Kingdom has been rising more steeply than that of the world as a whole, and imports in 1955 were $2\frac{1}{2}$ times as great as 1950 compared with $1\frac{1}{2}$ times for the world. There was a check to the rate of increase in 1956 when United Kingdom imports fell, and the extent to which imports will recover and continue their expansion in future years is uncertain, but the United Kingdom need for imported fuels may continue to be greater than that of other countries for some time. The United Kingdom ocean-going tanker fleet, on the other hand, has been

[1] John I. Jacobs, & Co., *loc. cit.*

[2] *The Financial Times*, 8 March 1957. These figures were compiled at a slightly different time from those of John I. Jacobs & Co., a material point affecting comparability since orders were rising very steeply at the time.

increasing rather more slowly than the world fleet. The size of the fleet registered in the United Kingdom is not necessarily a good indication of the tonnage of ships under the control of United Kingdom companies. Although the bulk of tonnage operating under the flags of convenience is Greek-owned it is becoming increasingly common for United Kingdom controlled tanker operating companies to be registered in other countries. But this movement does not appear to have been of sufficient magnitude to disturb the general conclusions that the United Kingdom controlled fleet has been increasing less rapidly than both United Kingdom oil imports and the fleets controlled by other countries. Finance has been one difficulty in the way of a more rapid expansion, and it has not been confined to the taxation of company profits but has extended to the raising of the new money that would have been needed if the United Kingdom fleet had kept pace with the growth of

Table 10.—*World tanker capacity* (2,000 d.w.t.)

	1939		1946		1950		1956		1958	
	%of total	Tonnage (mill.)	%of total	Tonnage (mill.)	%of total	Tonnage (mill.)	%of total	Tonnage (mill.)	%of total	Tonnage (mill.)
United Kingdom	27	4·5	18	4·4	20	6·0	18	7·8	17	8·4
United States	27	4·5	57	13·5	29	8·6	18	7·9	16	7·9
Norway	17	2·9	10	2·3	14	4·3	15	6·7	15	7·3
Panama and Liberia	4	·7	4	·9	12	3·6	20	9·0	24	11·8
Other	25	4·1	11	2·6	25	7·3	29	13·0	28	14·2
Total	100	16·7	100	23·7	100	29·8	100	44·4	100	49·6

Source: John I. Jacobs & Co. as given in the *Shipping World Year Book*, 1958–9

oil imports and the fleets of other countries. It is only recently that efforts have been made to find new sources of finance for tanker purchases. There was, for example, the formation in 1957 of a new company, Tanker Charter Co., owned jointly by Robert Fleming & Co. and the Ship Mortgage Finance Corporation, which intended to raise £40 million by way of loans on the security of charters to the B.P. Tanker Co. Tanker Finance Ltd. was set up to finance Shell Petroleum's purchase of tankers by raising £30 million in 3 years from Lloyds Bank and certain insurance companies and institutions, and London and Overseas Freighters was able to finance tanker construction by issuing £7½ million of debentures.[1] In 1958, another new company, Tankship Finance (United Kingdom), was being formed to finance the building of four tankers for use of the Caltex group, from the proceeds of an

[1] See *The Financial Times*, 24 January 1957 and 28 February 1957.

issue of £10 million of loan stock.[1] The system of raising loans to pay for tankers on the strength of charter agreements is widely used in the United States and has been used in Sweden in post-war years, and it is capable of being operated in such a way as to make bank participation easy.

The United Kingdom fleet expanded by 5 per cent per annum between 1950 and 1958, and it would be disheartening if it expanded more slowly than this in future years. A 5 per cent increase in the United Kingdom fleet is, however, likely to be at least adequate to cater for any foreseeable increase in the consumption of oil in the United Kingdom, and although, in favourable circumstances of finance and opportunity, it might increase more rapidly than this, perhaps by as much as the anticipated rate of increase of oil transportation by sea, it will do so only if it shares in the increased shipment of oil to other countries.

The importance of the size of the United Kingdom fleet to the United Kingdom shipbuilding industry is the usual one: the larger the United Kingdom fleet and the faster its rate of growth the more work is likely to be placed in United Kingdom shipyards. United Kingdom oil companies, no less than liner companies or tramp operators, have a certain preference for buying British, and since oil tankers are likely to continue to be an important source of shipyard employment, the United Kingdom shipbuilding industry has an important interest in the progress of United Kingdom controlled tanker fleets.

VIII

We have seen that over the years there is likely to be a substantial demand for dry-cargo and tanker vessels. For the world, demand for non-tanker vessels may be between 3 and $4\frac{1}{2}$ million g.r.t. of new shipping each year on optimistic assumptions, and for tankers 3 million g.r.t. may well be required. These figures correspond reasonably well to the average yearly output of 6 million g.r.t. of ships launched in 1955–6; but they are rather lower than the average of 9 million tons launched in 1957–8 and they give no grounds for thinking that the 1958 level of output could be sustained year in and year out. For the United Kingdom shipping industry, it is even more difficult to judge what level of new orders may be forthcoming. We have suggested that a figure of $\frac{3}{4}$ million g.r.t. may be the right order of magnitude for dry-cargo vessels, while for tankers, taking account of replacement needs, demand might be of the order of 5–10 per cent per annum of the existing fleet, say $\frac{1}{4}$–$\frac{1}{2}$ million g.r.t. per annum. So long as the United Kingdom industry remains reasonably competitive with its neighbours it is likely that the bulk

---

[1] *The Times*, 19 June 1958.

of these orders will be placed in United Kingdom shipyards, which in this case would receive 1 to 1¼ million g.r.t. of orders each year from British sources. Since the industry is certainly capable of producing 1½ million g.r.t. annually and perhaps as much as 1¾ million g.r.t.—its target figure—if plentiful supplies of steel, improved organisation and a better use of existing production facilities can be realised, it is clear that full employment is likely to depend on securing a substantial share of new orders for dry-cargo vessels and, more particularly, tankers placed by foreign shipowners. There could be no confidence in 1959 that the United Kingdom industry was sufficiently competitive to be able to attract as much as ½ million g.r.t. of foreign orders on the average each year, even in favourable conditions of demand. Most foreign orders given at that time were being placed overseas, particularly in Japanese shipyards, and the output target of 1¾ million g.r.t., though well within the potential capacity of the industry and its existing manpower, looked remote from reality.

So far as naval work is concerned, it is exceedingly difficult to form any opinion as to the course of development, since political factors are likely to be of overwhelming importance whether Admiralty orders or orders for export are concerned. A gradual increase in merchant repair work, however, would be in line with the expansion of the United Kingdom fleet that seems likely over the years. A growth in the combined fleet of tankers and non-tankers of, say, 3 per cent per annum, which is not an unreasonable expectation, would ultimately increase the amount of repair and maintenance required at the same rate. After a period of stagnation in the size of the merchant fleet the increase in repair work would not, of course, occur simultaneously with the increase in the size of the fleet, for major repairs and overhauls arising out of wear and tear would not be required immediately; some maintenance, however, is required from the start and this would increase progressively as time went on. An increase in the amount of repair work at even 3 per cent per annum would mount up with surprising rapidity. Without an appreciable increase in productivity approximately 10 per cent more men would be required every third year. Since some 60,000 men are employed on repair[1] at the present time, the additional labour required is likely to be quite considerable, particularly in localities used by tankers. There will also be a need to expand ship-repairing facilities in a number of ways, notably in the provision of an increased number of dry docks of adequate capacity. If this is not done, or if the necessary labour cannot be found to repair the ships, an increasing number of vessels in the United Kingdom trade will be driven to seek repair in Continental centres. Already a high proportion of ships are repaired on the Continent which, if competitive

---

[1] A figure of 61,000 men employed by members of the Shipbuilding Employers' Federation is given in Cmd. 160, p. 5.

facilities were available, would be repaired in this country. And it is important that the increasing demand for repair work that is likely in the future should not be turned away, since it is one of the main avenues along which the shipbuilding industry should be able to expand its output with confidence and with the prospect that it will enjoy a measure of assurance against setbacks of a cyclical nature in world trade.[1]

The general prospect for the United Kingdom over the coming years depends, therefore, largely on its competitive ability. If the industry can increase its efficiency, if the slump in output threatened in 1959 is averted and if demand again increases, there may yet be opportunity to expand production. But since an increase in output per man is indispensable for this, there can be little prospect of expanding employment on merchant shipbuilding. No conclusions can be reached about the prospects for warship work, but the amount of repair work required may increase rapidly. Repair work is likely to provide at least as good an opportunity for profitable employment as new building, and if a greater proportion of the industry's activities is directed towards it the balance of work will be tilted in an anti-cyclical direction.

[1] Note, however, that in January 1958 nearly 1,000 shipyard workers were unemployed in the Tyne because of a dearth of repair work during the shipping recession, while new building continued without interruption. (See *The Daily Telegraph*, 13 February 1958.)

CHAPTER 6

Fluctuations in Demand and their Consequences

I

The world output of merchant ships fluctuated markedly from year to year in the period 1886–1939. Fig. 4 shows that before the First World War output might fluctuate in an extreme case from 50 per cent below its trend to 50 per cent above its trend in 2 years, while swings of 50 per cent from slump to boom and back again were usual. In the inter-war period, output fell from the post-war peak of 150 per cent above the average to 80 per cent below in 1933, and there were considerable variations in other years. From

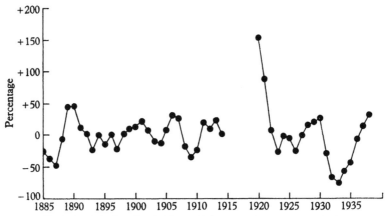

Fig. 4.—Deviation from Trend of the World Output of Merchant Ships, 1885–1938. (For the interim period no clear trend for output is discernible and fluctuations have been measured against average output.)

1946 to 1957 there were no obvious signs, in the world output of ships, of the extreme instabilities of demand characteristic of the shipbuilding industry; in each year the tonnage launched increased by comparison with the previous year, sometimes by quite small amounts but between some years substantially. Up to 1957, therefore, it was true to say that there had been no recession in the world output of ships during the post-war period. Nevertheless, it would be quite wrong to infer from the figures for total output that shipbuilding in all countries was unaffected by fluctuations in orders for new ships, or that during the period the underlying causes which led to fluctuations in output in the nineteenth century and in earlier years in the present century had subsided or even lost much of their force. Although total output has increased without pause, a number of countries suffered a check to their output even in the post-war period. Output of ships in Italy, for example, declined between 1953 and 1954, output by Japan between 1952 and 1954 and output by the United States between 1950 and 1951. The falling-off of output on all these occasions was not due to temporary difficulties on the side of production but to the fact that at the time output declined all these countries were marginal producers. Their yards were kept employed so long as a large reservoir of orders had been built up in other countries, but were the first to suffer as soon as orders became more difficult to get and the overflow from other more competitive producers dried up.

There can be little doubt that the effect would have been much more widely felt if long order books had not cushioned output against fluctuations in demand during the post-war period in other countries. The tonnage of vessels in hand or on order in the world remained comparatively high until mid-1948, when it amounted to roughly 9 million g.r.t.;[1] in the second half of the year it fell steadily and continued to fall throughout 1949 until it reached a level of 6¾ million g.r.t. before the outbreak of the Korean War. Orders then rose rapidly and reached a peak of roughly 15¾ million g.r.t. in mid-1952. Thereafter a falling trend set in again and continued until the fall was checked towards the end of 1954 and reversed in 1955 before the Suez crisis developed and orders on hand doubled between January 1956 and August 1957. This in turn was succeeded by falling order books continuing into 1959.

It is possible that suitable analysis of the changes during the post-war period in the order books either of individual countries or of all countries combined, would show a number of identifiable cyclical patterns, but the predominant causes of the timing and the extent of the most striking monthly or yearly variations in the inflow of new orders were political in nature, and, in consequence, the extent to which fluctuations in order books can be explained by economic analysis alone is limited. In earlier periods, however, it is possible to regard fluctuations in the output of ships as being more purely economic in character and to attempt to explain them along economic lines, and it is useful, therefore, to see what can be learned from an examination of the relevant figures.

In the first place it appears that fluctuations in output can take place in vastly different sets of economic circumstances. Before 1914 both shipping and shipbuilding were expanding in contrast to the virtual stagnation of

---

[1] The figures of the tonnage of ships under construction or on order are compiled by the Shipbuilders' Council of America and published in the *Bulletin of the American Bureau of Shipping*. They relate to vessels of 1,000 g.r.t. and over.

the merchant fleet and of the output of new ships during much of the inter-war period, but we have seen that fluctuations characterised both periods. The post-war period has been different again, for the world fleet (tankers and non-tankers combined) and the tonnage of ships launched have not failed to expand from one year to the next. But if fluctuations in order books when output proves to be inelastic can be considered as equivalent to fluctuations in output when capacity is more than adequate, it can be said that the same tendency for orders for new ships to be given in fits and starts is discernible in all three periods, and it is possible that a generalised explanation can be developed which would be valid in spite of differing economic circumstances.

A number of economists have attempted to probe into the reasons for fluctuations in new orders for ships, and various theories have been developed which purport to 'explain' the fluctuations in terms of other economic or technical factors. One explanation of fluctuations, resting heavily on technical factors, is that advanced by Einarsen following in some respects the lead given by Professor D. H. Robertson in 1914,[1] that reinvestment cycles once generated would be maintained if there were a marked tendency to replace ships, when they reached a certain age, with new tonnage. This would give rise to an echo effect. Einarsen showed that for the Norwegian fleet it was more usual to replace vessels about the modal ages of 8, 15 and particularly 20 years than at other ages, and that the tendency appeared to hold in the various phases of the trade cycle. He argued from this that shipbuilding for replacement was determined mainly by the typical age of replacement of the ships and by the age distribution of the fleet.[2] Shipbuilding for new investment, on the other hand, was held to be determined primarily by the prospects of the freight market.

Einarsen's replacement theory is not, however, easy to sustain. His data was confined to the Norwegian fleet, and although it could be claimed that this was the fourth fleet in the world at the time Einarsen made his study it represented only 7 per cent of the world total, and the practice of its ship-owners in disposing of the older tonnage of certain ages to other countries makes it impossible to apply his conclusions to the world fleet. The definition of replacement as opposed to new investment demand used by Einarsen also raises several difficulties, particularly in regard to the relation between the timing of replacement and the timing of new investment during the trade cycle. More important, however, is the fact that although the modes are clearly discernible in the data a substantial amount of tonnage is, never-

---

[1] 'Some material for the study of trade fluctuations', *Journal of the Royal Statistical Society*, 1914, pp. 159–73.

[2] Einarsen, 'Replacement in the shipping industry', *Review of Economic Statistics*, vol. XXVIII, 1946, p. 226.

theless, replaced at non-modal years. It follows from this that any incipient reinvestment cycles are likely to be quite strongly damped.

A more extensive investigation of wastage, as opposed to reinvestment, rates for the world fleet in the latter part of the nineteenth century and the inter-war period has shown that although wastage rates do tend to cluster around certain age-groups there are, in fact, wide variations in wastage rates and in their incidence in different groups from year to year, depending on economic conditions as well as other matters. This is brought out in Table 11, showing the percentage of ships in various age-groups surviving a further 5 years during certain periods of time. The first line shows the average percentage of tonnage initially in the various age-groups in the years 1922–5 which was still in the world register 5 years later, and subsequent lines treat later periods.

Table 11.—*Percentage of tonnage surviving 5 years* (*world fleet of steam and motorships* 100 g.r.t. *and over*)

	Initially in age group			
	5–10*	10–15	15–20	Over 20
1922–25	90·6	96·4	92·1	74·1
1926–28	93·2	94·2	90·8	74·6
1929–31	96·3	90·0	83·2	64·6
1932–34	97·3	92·7	87·4	71·6

* The high rate of wastage in the 5-10 age group is due to the disposal of war-built ships.

It is apparent from the table that a much higher proportion than is usual of the tonnage of ships on the world register in the years 1929–31 was scrapped in the following 5 years during the depression of the thirties, and it is also clear that considerable proportions of tonnage were scrapped on occasions in all the three age-groups 10–15, 15–20 and over 20 years. In other words scrapping covers a wide band of ages and is not really very highly concentrated about characteristic ages.[1] A numerical exercise carried out for the United Kingdom fleet to show what would happen to the tonnage of shipping ordered on the assumptions that wastage was made good ton for ton, and that wastage rates characteristic of 'normal' years in the inter-war period applied, did not suggest that replacement cycles were likely to be important in the next decade or so and that without a marked change in the practice of United Kingdom shipowners of selling aged tonnage abroad

[1] It is interesting in this connection that in the subdivisions of the Einarsen data the tonnage of vessels scrapped and replaced in non-modal age groups during revival and prosperity are often as great as and sometimes greater than the tonnage of ships replaced in modal groups in depression and recession.

or some other drastic change in habit, replacement cycles were likely to be damped down considerably.[1]

It is difficult, therefore, to assign any great importance to the simple-echo effect as an explanation of the trade cycle in shipbuilding. This does not, however, mean that a number of special variations of the echo theory may not be applicable. It is possible, for example, to develop a replacement cycle theory in terms of the rate of scrapping of ships in a band of age-groups, or even within the whole fleet, provided certain other assumptions are made, such as that replacement proceeds only after a fleet has contracted to some stated level. Cycle-generating models of this kind were sketched by Mr Kaldor and elaborated by Mr Black.[2]

Cyclical models of this type have something in common with an 'explanation' of the shipbuilding cycle developed by Professor Tinbergen.[3] This explanation rests on the observed relationship between the tonnage of merchant ships launched in various years with the size of the fleet 2 years earlier. Professor Tinbergen showed that for the priod 1880–1911 fluctuations in the rate of increase of the fleet (corresponding approximately to the tonnage of ships launched) had an amplitude 50–100 per cent of the amplitude of the tonnage of ships on the register about its trend 2 years earlier, the two series moving inversely. In other words, the relation of the figures was such that if the tonnage of ships was below its trend at some time this would be followed by a rise in output 2 years later. In due course this process would bring the strength of the fleet above its trend and the cycle would reverse, the whole process taking some 8 years in the material used by Professor Tinbergen. It could be argued from an econometric model of this kind that once the pattern of new building had been established it would be automatically self-repeating. Presumably the underlying economic assumptions would be that whenever the level of the fleet fell below its trend, freight rates would tend to rise and this would stimulate shipowners to place new orders until the fleet increased to the point at which it was excessive in relation to requirements and freight rates consequently tended to decline. There would, therefore, be something akin to a pig cycle in the shipbuilding output.

The explanation of the working of the cyclical causes is interesting as an econometric exercise, but it has the disadvantage of masking some of the economic causes of fluctuation. It ignores the fact, for example, that trade in primary products fluctuated during the period studied by Professor Tinbergen inversely with the size of the fleet. Thus when the world fleet

[1] For the illustration and more details of the figures quoted above see my 'Ship Wastage Rates', *Journal of the Royal Statistical Society*, vol. 120, 1957, p. 71.

[2] N. Kaldor, 'The relation of economic growth and cyclical fluctuations', *Economic Journal*, March 1954, pp. 53–71. J. Black, 'A note on Mr Kaldor's trade cycle model', *Oxford Economic Papers*, June 1956, p. 151.

[3] J. Tinbergen, 'Ein Schiffbauzyklus', *Weltwirtschaftliches Archiv*, 34 Band, 1932, II, p. 152.

deviated from trend in one direction the volume of trade in primary products deviated in the opposite direction, tending to increase the disparity between changes in the size of the world fleet and changes in the amount of ocean transport required. It might, therefore, be more satisfactory to link the production of ships to world trade than to the size of the fleet at some previous date or perhaps, more realistically, to the ratio between the size of the fleet and the growth of trade.

This returns us to the central core of trade-cycle theory as applied to shipbuilding. The stimulus to increased investment in ships, if not to building for replacement, appears to be the rate of profit. Thus Einarsen explained new building with reference to freight rates some 12–18 months earlier and Koopmans showed that a rise in freight rates tends to encourage the building of tankers.[1] It is not clear how far a statement of this kind can be regarded as justifying the description of a theory or for that matter how far its mechanism differs from that described by Tinbergen, yet the approach is a useful one in giving an understanding of the economic and arithmetical considerations that would need to be examined before a shipowner decided to place or to withold a new order.

The fact that shipowners appear to be influenced in the placing of orders by temporary variations in freight levels may give the impression that they are always either over-optimistic or over-pessimistic, and that they tend to assume that the present can be indefinitely projected into the future. It is true that improvements in freights lead to a tendency to over-order and depressions to a tendency to postpone even replacements—unwisely as events usually show—but it would be wrong to conclude that optimism and pessimism are so strongly felt that shipowners assume that present conditions will inevitably set the tune for the whole future operation of a new ship. Ships last for 30 years, and the decision to order a new ship must largely be taken on the view that is formed of prospects over 30 years coloured, perhaps, by present happenings, but not to the exclusion of all other possibilities.

A sudden rise in freight rates is not likely to be evenly spread in its incidence. Even in the worst of depressions there will be some trades which are operating at a profit because the specialised nature of their services provides some protection against competition in the short run. Any general increase in freights is likely to increase the profitability of already profitable undertakings quite considerably, and in some cases the opportunity to earn large profits with a ready ship may make it possible to write-off a good proportion of the value of a ship in the true economic meaning of the term. If, for example, it can be assumed that depreciation accounts for no more than

---

[1] T. Koopmans, *Tanker Freight Rates and Tankship Building*, an analysis of cyclical fluctuations, Netherlands Economic Institute, study no. 27, pp. 140–56.

one-fifth of total costs, doubling freight rates for a year above some level which was already yielding normal returns, while other costs remain unaffected, would make it possible to write-off 5 years' life of a vessel in 1 year's operation even without the improvement in loading factors which would be likely to result under the pressure of intense demand.

Before 1914 it was unusual for freights to fluctuate from year to year by more than $\pm$ 15 per cent about their trend (see Fig. 5), and this variation can have given no great opportunity to accelerate the writing down of new tonnage. Fluctuations in the inter-war period, apart from the early 1920's and late 1930's, also were not very large. The fluctuations of freights since the Second World War as a result of tonnage shortages in 1951 and 1956, on the other hand, were violent. In 1951 and 1956, for example, the charter rates for Liberty vessels averaged about 40–45s. a ton for 4- to 7-monthly periods against about 15s. a ton in 1953 and 1954 and about the same level in 1950. It is interesting that these fluctuations were closely reflected in the price of Liberty ships. A Liberty vessel worth about £200,000 during much of 1953 and 1954 was worth about £400,000 in 1951 and 1956.[1] At first sight it might be supposed that shipowners would be taking an unjustifiably optimistic view if they were prepared to double the price they were ready to pay for a ship in response to a temporary upward movement in freight rates of the same order of magnitude. But the fact that in the face of a stickiness of costs it is possible to earn very high profits and write down the value of a vessel very rapidly throws a cloak of rationality over the whole operation. Generally speaking, construction costs increase by a smaller amount than freight rates during a boom, and fall by a smaller amount in the depression, although this is not always the case. In the boom of 1907, for example, the rise in construction costs was much the same as that in freight rates. The rise in costs which can be justified by an increase in freights is, however, limited; a 100 per cent increase in freights expected to last for a year, which would make it possible to write 5 years off the value of the vessel in a year's trading, would justify paying only some 25 per cent more for a vessel expected to last 25 years. It would, however, make it worth while to pay double the previous price of a vessel with only a few more years' life in front of it.

These arguments lead to the conclusion that when freight rates are unusually high a case can be made for bringing forward orders, and conversely. It is reasonable in some circumstances to hasten the purchase of a new vessel because it is of very much greater value when freights are high than when they are low, and also because costs may be rising and there is a danger that they will rise further; and equally it is reasonable to keep vessels in

---

[1] The figures are based on data compiled by Messrs Harley, Mullion & Co. Ltd.

service which otherwise would have been unprofitable and broken up. It must also be remembered that it is difficult to justify new capital commitments, unless freights are high, so that it is only in the boom that money is forthcoming. In practice, however, only ordering or abstaining from ordering new ships in anticipation of events and not in response to present events is

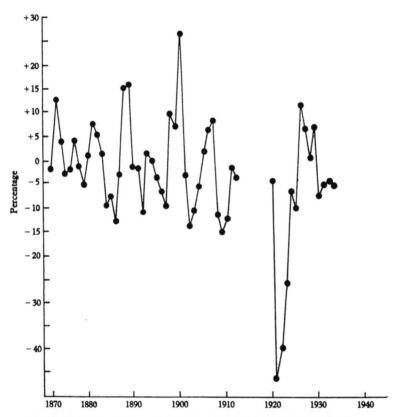

Fig. 5.—Fluctuations of Tramp Freights about their Trend (Source: L. Isserlis, 'Tramp Shipping Cargoes and Freights,' *Journal of the Royal Statistical Society*, vol. CI, 1938, p. 77)

likely to bring about the desired result for, as we have seen in the analysis of Tinbergen, some time is likely to elapse before scarcity and high freight rates are translated first into decisions to order new ships, and secondly into vessels ready to put to sea. Thus it often happens that a tonnage scarcity has to be met by a policy of making do, by delaying the scrapping of new vessels and by increasing average speeds and loading factors, and that before the new tonnage is available the worst of the immediate shortage is over. It requires both a bold and an exceptionally shrewd shipowner to place orders in contrary motion to cyclical trends—a process which, as we have seen, is facilitated when shipowners and shipbuilders are linked.

Up to the Second World War it could be said that shipowners acted with moderation in the placing of orders. If the usual relation between the world fleet and the amount of trading to be done became out of balance for a time, there was no attempt to restore it completely by new building. Thus new orders placed in the boom were less than sufficient to carry the increase in traffic at the previous rate of loading, and likewise orders in slump conditions did not fall off to zero while the fleets lived off their fat, but continued at a lower level.

It would have been possible before the First World War to have met the growth in ocean transport requirements by a steady rate of new building, and since in practice the launching of new ships ordered during the boom often coincides with the downturn or slump, it can be argued that this would have been a preferable procedure for all concerned. But individual owners in advancing or postponing new orders by months or even years were not in fact making very large alterations in the rate of growth of the world fleet. Giving or withholding even $\frac{1}{2}$ million g.r.t. of new orders for ships meant only a 1 per cent change in the rate of growth of the world fleet before 1914. Nevertheless, such a fluctuation in orders made all the difference to shipbuilders who, in any case, were catering for new requirements of, perhaps, 4 or 5 per cent per annum and consequently withstanding fluctuations in either direction of 25 per cent or even more.

It is, of course, the long life of ships which underlies the large effect on shipbuilders of even small increases or decreases in the total stock of ships. Wastage rates, as we have seen, are likely to be only $2\frac{1}{2}$ or 3 per cent of the size of the fleets depending on their rate of expansion, while the demand for new tonnage to increase capacity is often no more than 5 per cent. With these orders of magnitude normal replacement demand constitutes only a small part of total output—perhaps one-third—and since replacement demand may be postponed or advanced considerably, and very likely will be in response to the self-same factors that affect the need to increase (or decrease) the size of the world fleet, there is scope for very wide fluctuations in orders. Demand in consequence is not greatly stabilised by the need for substantial and regular replacements which is the case for things that wear out quickly. It follows from these considerations that the greater the rate of expansion of a fleet the more likely is the shipbuilding industry to suffer from intense fluctuations in orders, for new orders will be unusually large in relation to orders for replacement. This is one reason for thinking that fluctuations in orders are likely to be quite wide in the coming years, for, as we have seen, the indications are that there will be a rapid expansion in the fleet of tanker vessels and probably also an appreciable expansion in the fleet of dry-cargo vessels.

There may also be other reasons for anticipating quite marked fluctuations in orders. As we have seen, shipowners have frequently ordered ships when delivery delays mounted into years, sometimes 4 or 5 years ahead, and they have been prepared to do this apparently in response to stimuli that are unlikely to last more than a few years. It is possible that this practice reflects the confidence of shipowners in the future of their industry, and that they are prepared, in consequence, to commit themselves for several years ahead. But, in the main, extended ordering must be regarded as something in the nature of an insurance policy which, for the price of a cancellation, offers the certainty that a new ship can be secured. It is not possible to move up a queue for the delivery of new vessels, but, once established in the queue, it is generally possible to leave it either by paying a comparatively small sum, or if the order is for delivery some time ahead or the reservation has been largely tentative, without cost to the shipowner. Long-order books enable shipbuilders to plan some way ahead and in this way they are of assistance to the industry. But they are not without their dangers. Cancellations may rapidly reduce a shipyard's orders to nought, and if large-order books encourage too great a commitment of the world's economic resources to shipbuilding, as appeared likely in 1957, the backlog of orders, which has so far acted as a buffer for the United Kingdom shipbuilding industry, will disappear and once again leave the industry at the mercy of the strong forces which made shipowners order their ships in fits and starts prompted by cyclical disturbances. It is at this juncture that a scramble for world markets may be expected to arise, and it is with this in mind that the possibilities of combating future cyclical disturbances or the flow of orders to the shipbuilding industry has to be considered.

No estimate can be made of the likely severity of fluctuations in demand in future years. It is possible that, with a rising demand for ships over the years, and with a much closer control of world demand than could be attempted in the first part of the century, fluctuations in demand and trade may be subdued; it is possible also that the avoidance of severe fluctuations in the output of the United Kingdom shipbuilding industry will become an accepted part of the responsibilities of the large shipping companies that place the bulk of orders. But in an international industry subject to competition from all comers, in spite of the device of shipping conferences, the prospects for voluntarily smoothing the flow of orders to shipbuilders cannot be viewed with equanimity and, as we have seen, there is always the danger that uncoordinated ordering of ships will exaggerate requirements at times and, in boosting the output of the shipbuilding industry, denude it of orders in subsequent years. The possibility that orders will be sufficiently irregular to cause the output of ships to expand or contract by as much as 50 per cent cannot be excluded.

Fluctuations in output of this order could not readily be absorbed by the shipbuilding industry. There are about 65,000 men engaged in the construction of new ships at present levels of output. If output were to fall by 50 per cent about 30,000 men would become unemployed. In itself this is not a big number, but there would be some associated unemployment in industries supplying shipbuilding with materials and components. Much of this also would be concentrated in the shipbuilding areas and sometimes in a few streets clustered round the berths, so that in selected areas the dislocation of the labour market would be considerable and it would not be easy for the men concerned to find alternative employment quickly. Provided demand outside the industry remained at a high level skilled men would, in time, find plenty of opportunity in other industries; the same also might be true for the comparatively unskilled helpers or labourers. However, the loss to the shipbuilding industry of its labour force would be likely to become permanent if this occurred; once shipyard men found other occupations it would not be easy to attract them back into the industry when orders again flowed into the yards, and there would be a danger that gradually the centre of gravity of shipbuilding in the world would move to those countries where unemployment can be countenanced and every advantage taken of fleeting increases in demand to find employment for a surplus labour force. Apart from the effects of fluctuation in demand on the labour force of the industry which are by far the most serious effects, fluctuations are expensive because surplus capital equipment is needed to deal with what are frequently ill-timed and capricious peaks of demand.

The measures likely to be needed to deal with fluctuations in orders for new ships will depend on the severity of the fluctuations which are encountered. If the fluctuations in demand are not very marked—say within the range of 10 per cent on either side of average output—and are short-lived, no special measures are likely to be needed. Industries producing capital goods must expect to see some variations in their output and rate of growth and be prepared at times to work below capacity or to seek other outlets for their plant. It might be possible for many firms in the industry to find some alternative employment for men on the prefabrication of structural steelwork which is carried on by a number of shipbuilding undertakings either within their shipyards or in separate undertakings. For a moderate recession in demand it might be possible also to increase the flow of orders for ships by reducing prices. We have seen how a rise or fall in freight rates can be considered as equivalent to an increase or decrease in the market value of a new ship, and there is some possibility that shipbuilders by reducing prices in years of depression and increasing them in years when demand is high, might be able to smooth the flow of orders somewhat by price adjustment. The price of raw materials and bought-in components is not likely to be very responsive to the fortunes of shipbuilding and when wages are sticky costs cannot readily be reduced. The brunt of any contribution to a reduction in prices would tend to fall on overheads, and since these may account for only 20 per cent of the cost of a ship it is not generally possible to cut prices very considerably. There are few examples in the period 1850–1938 of prices being reduced from one year to the next by as much as even 10 per cent, and there were a number of instances of prices actually increasing as output fell off.[1] No great reliance can therefore be placed on the hope that a fall in prices will serve to stimulate demand in a depression as severe as that occurring in the years 1908–10 when the tonnage launched was little more than one-half that launched in 1906.

A slump in orders and output of this severity would require much more drastic measures if unemployment were to be avoided. The possibilities would range from attempting to stimulate shipbuilding indirectly by assisting the shipping industry, to taking direct measures to increase shipbuilding output by placing government orders, offering subsidies or by other means. Nearly all maritime and shipbuilding countries have had occasion at one time or another to take government action to protect or develop their interests. Direct assistance given to the shipbuilding industry in this country has been slight, hardly extending beyond guarantees given under the Trade Facilities Acts; indirectly, however, the industry has benefited to some extent by the succession of measures taken in the thirties to restore prosperity to shipping and encourage the ordering of new tonnage.

The main weight of government assistance in the thirties was put into subsidising tramp shipping. Tramp owners were also encouraged to protect their interests by observing minimum freight rates and combining amongst themselves where possible to force up freights to a level at which more provision could be made for tonnage replacement and some return on capital invested. The extent of the financial assistance given was too slight, however, to give much encouragement towards the placing of new orders. Payment was made on the basis of a sliding scale varying with the level of freights, subject to a maximum expenditure of £2 million. In 1935 and 1936 virtually the full amount of the subsidy was paid out, but in 1937 no payment was made as the level of freights exceeded the maximum for which any payment was provided under the Acts. Although freights in 1937 were 30–40 per cent greater than in 1929 and roughly double what they had been when the subsidy was instituted, so that it was possible to provide for depreciation and a modest dividend, it was not possible to make any significant contribution

---

[1] For figures of construction costs see K. Maiwald, 'The construction costs and the value of the British merchant fleet 1850–1938', *Scottish Journal of Political Economy*, February 1956, p. 50.

to arrears of depreciation, which between 1930 and 1935 had amounted to roughly £10 million in spite of transfers from reserve, assistance from interest on investments and very restricted dividend payments.

It is not surprising in the circumstances that the subsidy did little more than stave off a catastrophic decline in United Kingdom tramp shipping and failed to reactivate new building on a substantial scale. The scrap and build scheme introduced with the intention of promoting new construction while at the same time removing older ships from the market was no more successful. The scheme provided for loans for new building or modernisation at 3 per cent per annum repayable over 12 years, on condition that 2 tons of shipping were scrapped for every ton built with assistance and 1 ton scrapped for every ton modernised in the same way. The terms proved to be so unattractive that at the termination of the scheme in 1937 only £3½ million had been sanctioned for the purpose, and the tonnage of vessels constructed under the scheme (much of which no doubt would have been built without it) amounted to only 186,000 g.r.t.[1] Even in 1939, when renewed depression in shipping and the imminence of war necessitated fresh assistance to shipping and grants for new building were instituted without any scrapping provisions, the scale of assistance was too small, the grant for new construction serving only to reduce the cost of building by some 2 per cent.

The measures taken in the thirties illustrate the difficulties that can be encountered in dealing with fluctuations in international industries. In acute depression assistance has to be given on a generous scale if it is to be effective. It was not until the tonnage laid up fell to small proportions and freights rose in 1937 to 30–40 per cent above the level of 1929 that orders were given for launching 1 million tons of shipping from United Kingdom shipyards in 1938. Subsidies, which were given at a diminishing rate when freights reached 93 per cent of the 1929 level and ceased entirely when parity was reached, could not be expected to restore prosperity to the British shipbuilding industry without a growth in shipping activity.

If the main object of government policy had been the stimulation of shipbuilding output rather than the maintenance of the merchant marine it would probably have been better to have subsidised shipbuilding directly. Yet any attempt to stimulate shipbuilding without an attempt to improve the profitability of shipping operation would have been doomed to failure and the payment of steadily increasing subsidies, unless the new tonnage had proved so much more effective than the old that the wholesale scrapping

---

[1] Under the scheme, vessels to be scrapped had to be disposed of in the United Kingdom, where the price was less than that paid abroad for obsolete tonnage; another difficulty was that the intense rate of scrapping in the early thirties had left few vessels on the United Kingdom register eligible for scrapping, for it was one of the conditions of the scheme that the tonnage offered for scrapping must not be non-competitive tonnage and in consequence suitable tonnage had to be sought from foreign owners at enhanced prices.

of existing tonnage (which in the thirties was so vastly in excess of requirements) had resulted.

A period of depression as prolonged as that of the 30's requires international action to deal with it effectively. This might involve attempts to maintain freight rates either by government-sponsored restrictions or by industrial action through Shipping Conferences[1] which might be of the same pattern as the International Tanker Owners' Association's scheme put into operation in May 1934 for the laying up of tankers.[2] This would mean in effect that a surplus of shipping would be treated along much the same lines as those so frequently advocated for commodities; a buffer stock would be created by agreement with the intention of absorbing variations in the balance between the supply and demand of shipping and smoothing out variations in freight rates. A precedent for such arrangements has already been set by the establishment of the American reserve fleet, and the release of ships from it has been made to meet conditions of unusual scarcity of shipping space. The reserve fleet includes only a few tankers, and there would be scope therefore for the creation of a tanker reserve if over-production threatened the stability of tanker operation and shipbuilding. International action is not, however, to be expected in view of the difficulties likely to arise in the operation of measures designed to safeguard shipping and shipbuilding interests, unless a prolonged and exceptionally severe depression is encountered.

[1] A Committee was set up in 1958 by the International Chamber of Shipping to discuss possible stabilisation schemes.

[2] Under this scheme a levy was made on tankers in operation to finance the withdrawal of tankers from operation. The contribution to the pool varied from 15 per cent for voyage charters and 18 per cent for time charters, shortly after the scheme was set up, to very small contributions from June 1937 to May 1938. The laid up allowance was 24s. per g.r.t. per half-year, falling to 15s. after five half-year periods. Most European owners joined the Association but the United States did not, and there were different forms of membership for owners who chartered on the market and oil companies.

CHAPTER 7

Home and Export Markets and Competition for Orders

I

All shipbuilding countries enjoy a measure of protection in producing ships for their own nationals, and it is rare for other shipbuilding companies to break into their rivals' home market on a substantial scale.

Table 12.—*Percentage of ships registered in various countries supplied by home producers*

	United Kingdom	Japan	Germany	Sweden	Netherlands	France	United States
1949	90	100	100	86	74	71	100
1950	100	100	100	83	58	72	100
1951	100	100	100	71	84	67	100
1952	98	100	100	73	89	77	100
1953	95	100	100	100	96	71	100
1954	94	100	100	94	81	77	100
1955	96	100	100	85	94	91	63
1956	89	100	100	68	78	95	100
1957	88	100	100	74	75	80	92
1958	79	100	99	80	61	85	100

Both Japan and Germany have supplied their own requirements of ships, and apart from 1955, when tonnage was imported from Japan, and to a lesser extent 1957, the same is true of the United States. Sweden, the Netherlands and France, on the other hand, have remained importers of tonnage throughout the post-war period. Sweden imported ships both to meet some of her own needs for tonnage while she was simultaneously exporting to other countries on a substantial scale, and to provide herself with the types of ships, mainly passenger liners, which she is not accustomed to produce. The sharp rise in imports in 1956 included a passenger liner built in Italy as well as tonnage from Belgium and Germany. The Netherlands also is a net exporter of ships but imported an exceptionally large tonnage of dry-cargo vessels from Germany in 1957 and 1958. France, on the other hand, has had difficulty in competing with other producers and until recently has imported substantial amounts of tonnage from the Netherlands in most years. The United Kingdom is not normally an importer of tonnage on any considerable scale, but in recent years appreciable tonnages of ships have been imported from the Continent, mainly from Germany and the Netherlands, though some ships have been built elsewhere.

United Kingdom shipowners are reluctant to build their ships outside the United Kingdom. They appreciate the convenience of having ships built close at hand, but more important, they believe in buying British and have great confidence in the quality of ships produced in British shipyards and in the men who build them. There is no doubt that they are prepared to pay more for a British-built ship than one of comparable design built elsewhere, and it is extremely doubtful if a price differential of 5 per cent or even more would drive United Kingdom shipowners to build elsewhere. There are, however, occasions when, because of excessive price differentials, delivery delays, or for other reasons, ships are ordered from foreign yards. We have already referred to the purchase of five motorships ordered from the German yard of Deutsche Werft in 1924. Again in 1936 and 1938, when Germany was using foreign exchange restrictions to force foreign orders into German yards, about 100,000 g.t. of shipping was launched for the United Kingdom alone. This was, however, quite exceptional. Some sales were made in other years but they were not large and purchases from other countries, including Dutch coasters readily bought by United Kingdom owners in 1937 and 1938 and larger vessels purchased from Denmark in 1938, were small in relation to home output. In recent years United Kingdom orders from the Continent have been prompted mainly by the need to secure earlier delivery than United Kingdom shipbuilders have been able to offer rather than by price considerations, or they have been placed by shipping companies with international affiliations—tankers ordered by the Shell interests in Holland are a case in point.

The comparative self-sufficiency of the merchant fleets of the most important producing countries has a number of consequences. It is likely, for instance, to inhibit international specialisation in different classes of ships, although as we have seen it has not had this effect in the case of Swedish producers, and by providing an assured market at home it weakens the forces of competition. It also means that the output of a major shipbuilding country is likely to be rather closely linked to the fortunes of its own shipowners. This was an important factor affecting the position of United Kingdom shipbuilding in the inter-war period when the comparative stagnation of the United Kingdom's fleet made itself felt. One of the advantages of the expanding Continental shipbuilding centres and Japan in the thirties was that their merchant fleets either increased or contracted only slightly. Between 1929 and 1938 the German and Swedish fleets each increased by 10 per cent and the Japanese fleet by 20 per cent while the Dutch fleet declined by only 4 per cent. The United Kingdom, the United States and the French fleets, on the other hand, declined respectively by 12, 17 and 14 per cent.

At the same time, in countries where the shipbuilding industry is highly developed, the fortunes of the shipping industry are dependent (so long as shipowners tend to buy exclusively at home) upon the progress made by the national shipbuilding companies. One of the reasons why the United Kingdom fleet expanded comparatively slowly was that both United Kingdom ship-builders and shipowners were slow to adopt the diesel engine, though it is probably an exaggeration to say that 'the slowness of British shipping and shipyards to adopt the important innovation in this field seems to be the main explanation of the relative decline in British shipbuilding'.[1] Sufficient motor-ships were being produced by British shipbuilders, even in the 1920's, to provide for the needs of foreign owners had the United Kingdom shipbuilding industry been competitive in other ways; and in 1930 over ¾ million g.r.t. of motorships was launched from United Kingdom yards, an output greater than the whole of that produced by any of her competitors in an inter-war year. Although, in the 1930's, it is true that the United Kingdom produced ton for ton of steamships with her rivals overseas, the latter drew ahead in motorships, and before the Second World War were producing three times the tonnage of the United Kingdom; but they were also drawing ahead in the production of tankers, which in the United Kingdom, as in other countries, were predominantly motorships. It would seem, therefore, more reasonable to look to the greater cost of diesel-engined ships in the United Kingdom than abroad as the main explanation of the relative decline in British shipbuilding and perhaps as a factor contributing to the difficulties of the shipping industry.

II

Outside the markets of the main producing countries there is much greater scope for competitive selling in export markets by the United Kingdom or other producers. The opportunities range from the sale of warships to foreign navies to the large-scale export of cargo vessels and tankers to Norway and companies operating under flags of convenience, and they include the variety of repair and conversion work that is on offer within range of the northern European ports. Production of warships is a much less important source of export business than it was at the beginning of the century. The world export market for merchant ships, on the other hand, has expanded greatly from perhaps ½ a million g.r.t. in a good year[2] to over 3 million g.r.t. in 1956, and repair work has grown in line with the expansion of world fleets.

There has, however, been a considerable change in the composition of export markets. In the twenties the United Kingdom exported mainly to

[1] Ingvar Svennilson, *Growth and Stagnation in the European Economy*, 1954, p. 155.
[2] The tonnage exported from the United Kingdom alone in the three years 1904–7 was 1·5 million g.r.t. (see Sir Amos Ayre, *op. cit.* p. 14.) At this time the United Kingdom was the main exporting country.

the Commonwealth and to Norway (which rather exceptionally in 1930 bought no less than 300,000 g.r.t. of shipping from United Kingdom ship-yards), but appreciable amounts were sold to other European countries, including France and Holland, while smaller tonnages were constructed for Greece, Argentine and a number of other countries. Norway has continued to import tonnage on a considerable scale in the post-war period (between 1949 and 1958 it purchased some 6 million g.r.t. of shipping from outside suppliers), and Commonwealth countries and Greece have continued to import ships in varying quantities, in addition to imports by the major European producers discussed above. The outstanding feature of the post-war market, however, has been the tonnage of ships registered under the Liberian flag and to a lesser extent the Panamanian flag. These markets have taken roughly 7 million g.r.t. and $2\frac{1}{2}$ million g.r.t. respectively since 1949, and between them they accounted for 2 million g.r.t. out of a total of $9\frac{1}{4}$ million g.r.t. launched in 1958.

The flag of convenience is a well-known device for escaping either safety or labour regulations or taxation. In the post-war period new ships have been registered under flags of convenience in order to avoid taxation, and they are every bit as lavishly equipped and well found as ships registered under other flags. Much of the tonnage registered is owned by international shipping operators to whom it is a matter of indifference where ships are purchased provided that they represent good value for money, and in consequence the markets of Liberia and Panama provide a better opportunity of assessing the competitive position of the main shipbuilding countries than their performance in home markets.

The figures of sales to Norway, Liberia and Panama given in Table 13 must, however, be interpreted with some care if they are not to be misleading. Not all sales to these flags represent genuine export sales, since nationals of a shipbuilding country may also register their ships under flags of convenience while continuing to purchase ships in their own countries, and some sales to these markets have been subsidised; French and United States output for registration under the flags of Panama and Liberia, for instance, cannot be taken as indicating that these countries are competitive in the ordinary way in world markets, since it is generally acknowledged that their prices have been well above those of other countries. It should not be forgotten also that, when order books are long, what proportion of export orders should be catered for is sometimes a matter of policy rather than of purely commercial considerations; in the early post-war years United Kingdom shipbuilders were urged to export a substantial proportion of their output, sometimes as part of an agreement to help make good war losses of an ally, whereas in later years there may have been a change of heart in the direction of giving preference to the home market.

Nevertheless, with all these reservations in mind there can be little doubt that the United Kingdom has steadily been losing ground in export markets. For all practical purposes the United Kingdom supplied the whole of the export market in ships at the beginning of the century; in 1913 she still provided 80 per cent of the ships exported; and in 1927–30 her share was still 40–50 per cent. By 1936–8, however, her share was little more than 20 per cent, and after the assumption of a more dominant position in the early post-war years it had again fallen to 20 per cent in the 4 years 1953–6 and in 1957, probably exceptionally, it was down to 7 per cent.[1]

Table 13

Tonnage (1000 g.r.t.) *built for the Norwegian, Liberian and Panamanian flags*
(100 g.r.t. *and over*)

Importer	Exporter	1949–51 (average)	1952–54 (average)	1955	1956	1957	1958
Norway	Sweden	214	199	267	288	327	325
	Germany	1	78	94	175	162	403
	United Kingdom	235	175	234	144	19	113
	All exporters	524	493	631	711	584	1074
Liberia and Panama	Japan	3	151	444	1124	1324	1098
	United Kingdom	73	146	146	155	128	70
	Germany	0	179	94	82	195	134
	Sweden	0	32	69	11	71	107
	United States	220	142	0	0	64	308
	All exporters	307	702	899	1499	2110	1977

There is a warning in the steady encroachments of other countries in the export market previously dominated by the United Kingdom which cannot be ignored. It would not be wise to assume that the United Kingdom was becoming steadily more and more uncompetitive solely on the basis of figures relating to the share she secured of the export market, or that she was able to hold her own only in protected home markets. The United Kingdom was able to add to her order books when considerably shorter delivery times were quoted by foreign countries, and this applied to export as well as home orders. The fact is that the United Kingdom industry failed to expand output in line with the world demand for ships; this was itself sufficient to prevent her keeping the same share of both home and export markets.

[1] The figure for 1913 follows from a study in *The Glasgow Herald*, 5 February 1926; the range for 1927–30 is based on an analysis of figures given in *The Glasgow Herald's Review of Shipbuilding, Engineering and Commerce*; figures for subsequent years are based on *Lloyd's Register's Annual Summary of Ships Launched*.

Home markets were largely held, export markets suffered and a unique opportunity was given to other countries to cut into the United Kingdom's share by expanding their production and filling the void created by stagnation of United Kingdom output. In so doing they greatly improved their efficiency and competitive position, making it difficult for the United Kingdom subsequently to maintain her share of a diminishing market.

The challenge to the United Kingdom has come from Germany, Sweden and Holland over a long period, and more decisively and on an unprecedented scale from Japan since 1955, and it may yet be taken up by other countries on the fringe of shipbuilding. The United Kingdom, which supplied a high proportion of the needs of Norway in the immediate post-war years, is gradually being ousted from that position by Continental shipbuilders. The

Table 14.—*Tonnage of ships exported as a percentage of tonnage launched* *

	United Kingdom	Germany	Holland	Sweden	Japan
1925–30	24	37	36	60	—
1931–38	18	53	22	63	—
1950–55	35	45	53	64	41
1956	31	62	27	68	71
1957	19	63	33	66	62
1958	23	60	57	62	61

* Figures for the Continental producers during the inter-war period are based on an analysis of *The Glasgow Herald's Review of Shipbuilding, Engineering and Commerce*, published annually; they are approximate only, other figures are based on *Lloyd's Register's Shipbuilding Statistics*. The percentage of Japanese output for foreign registration was small in the inter-war period.

close ties of Norway and Sweden have been maintained, but in default of an adequate volume of deliveries from Sweden or the United Kingdom Norwegian owners have had recourse to the German market, and the Norwegian shipbuilding industry has been encouraged to expand its output. Similarly, Panamanian and Liberian owners have had little hope of meeting their requirements in the United Kingdom, and have ordered liberally in Germany and Japan. As a result in 1954 Germany exported a greater tonnage of ships than the United Kingdom; in 1955 United Kingdom sales in foreign markets exceeded those of Germany, but Japan launched a greater tonnage for export than either, and in 1956, when Germany once again overtook the United Kingdom, Japan launched nearly as great a tonnage for export as the United Kingdom launched in total. One consequence of the expansion of German and Japanese output in this way is that they are now much more dependent on foreign orders than the United Kingdom. This is brought out in Table 14.

With the fortunes of Japanese, Swedish, German and Dutch shipbuilders closely tied up with the export market, intense competition is to be anticipated from these countries whenever there is any general decline in export sales. United Kingdom shipbuilders may be relieved therefore that their fortunes are more closely dependent on the home market than those of their competitors. But it should not be forgotten that this independence has not been so much a matter of deliberate choice as a reflection of the inability of the United Kingdom to expand her output at a time when world markets were opening up, and of a gradual decline of the comparative advantages of the United Kingdom as a shipbuilding centre over the years, and it is to these problems that we turn in the next sections.

IV

THE SUPPLY OF SHIPS

CHAPTER 8

The Course of United Kingdom Output

One consequence of the slow expansion of the United Kingdom's output of ships is that it has continued to decline in importance as a shipbuilding country in the post-war period. This is evident from Fig. 6, which shows the changing proportion of United Kingdom output in the world markets for ships. Three-quarters of the world's ships were produced in the United Kingdom in the 1890's and the proportion was still 60 per cent in the years 1910–14. After a temporary eclipse in the shadow of the United States'

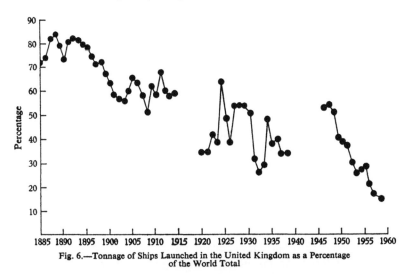

Fig. 6.—Tonnage of Ships Launched in the United Kingdom as a Percentage
of the World Total

post-war output, the United Kingdom's share of the world market again rose to over 60 per cent in 1924, only to fall again under the pressure of foreign competition in 1925 and the General Strike in 1926. The comparatively stable years, 1927–30, heralded a violent decline when, in conditions of deep slump, the United Kingdom output fell to little more than one-quarter of world output. Recovery in 1934 was not maintained; and the temporary ascendancy of the United Kingdom in 1947 and 1948 was lost when Continental shipbuilders and Japan re-established their shipbuilding output.

The decline in the relative position of the United Kingdom has been caused more by an increase in the output of the other countries—particularly Germany, Japan, Sweden and the Netherlands—than by a reduction in the output of the United Kingdom. It is true that in recent years United Kingdom output has not approached the peak levels attained in the early part of the century—before the First World War output exceeded 1·8 million g.r.t. on three occasions, and in 1920 it exceeded 2 million g.r.t.—but the average of the best five consecutive years, 1910–14, was 1·66 million g.r.t. compared with 1·38 million g.r.t. in 1952–6 and 1·47 million g.r.t. in 1955 (the best post-war year). Against this moderate reduction in average output must be set a growth in the output of all other countries from some 1·08 million g.r.t. in 1910–14 to 3·97 million g.r.t. in 1952–6 and 7·87 million g.r.t. in 1958. The tonnage of ships produced by Japan has exceeded that produced by the United Kingdom by a considerable margin, and although the United Kingdom produces on the average ships of a higher value per gross ton than Japan, this can hardly have changed their relative positions as ship-building countries in 1957.

The reasons for the decline of the United Kingdom's relative position in the post-war period have been rather different from those operating in the inter-war years, although there is a certain common thread running through-out the whole period. In the inter-war period the United Kingdom was unable to attract orders to her shipyards in the face of foreign competition for two main reasons: the first of these was the growing tendency of ship-building countries to subsidise both their shipping and their shipbuilding industries, and the second the growing efficiency of her competitors. Nearly all maritime countries subsidised their shipping in one way or another, and the efforts to promote shipbuilding, and so to weaken the position of the United Kingdom industry, were not always confined to the countries in-stigating them. Germany, Italy and Japan built more ships than they needed and made a determined effort to cut British ships out of established trades. Germany not only encouraged her own shipyards by a variety of devices, but also supplied Italy and Japan, Scandinavia and Holland with uneconomi-cally cheap material and machinery, enabling them to produce cheap ships.[1] Much of the progress of the leading Continental shipbuilders at this time has been attributed to the effect of their shipping and shipbuilding subsidies, and to the pursuit of autarkic economic policies, but it was by no means the whole story. Subsidies failed to stimulate output to any marked extent in Italy, France or the United States. The effectiveness of subsidies depends on producers being, at least, in measurable distance of being competitive; otherwise they are either ineffectual or prohibitively expensive, and there can be little doubt that the expanding centres of Continental shipbuilding were capable of meeting the United Kingdom on her own ground.

This is the continuing thread in the relation of the United Kingdom output

---

[1] See 'Full employment in British shipyards': a Presidential Address by Sir A. Murray Stephen to the Institute of Engineers and Shipbuilders in Scotland, 1944.

of ships to the output of her competitors; the leading Continental and Japanese shipbuilders are as efficient as the best in the United Kingdom and able to compete effectively in the world markets. But it was not foreign competition or a dearth of orders that limited the achievements of the United Kingdom in the post-war period up to 1958, so much as a physical inability to expand output. The pessimistic view taken of the prospects of the industry at the end of the war and on later occasions was in some measure responsible for failure in this respect. Anxiety about the future, resting largely on previous setbacks, robbed the industry both of the will and the means to increase its output rapidly in an economy in which so many other industries seemed to hold out the promise of almost unlimited expansion. In the event pessimism was shown to be ill-founded; 10 years of output at full capacity followed the Second World War and culminated with the placing of a record volume of new orders in world shipyards. Whatever the future may hold, the economic signs in the early post-war years were misread both by the industry and by those responsible for guiding the economy in an era of direct controls.

Table 15.—*Tonnage* (1000 g.r.t.) *launched of ships* 100 g.r.t. *and over*

	Tankers	Non-Tankers	Total
1946	—	—	1121
1947	—	—	1193
1948	—	—	1176
1949	434	833	1267
1950	614	711	1325
1951	834	507	1341
1952	643	660	1303
1953	762*	555*	1317
1954	714	694	1408
1955	648	826	1474
1956	518	865	1383
1957	535	879	1414
1958	577	825	1402

Source: *Lloyd's Register: Annual Survey of Merchant Ships Launched*

* Before 1952 the figures of tankers launched are for vessels of 1000 g.r.t. and over. Tankers under 1000 g.r.t., of which there are very few, are included in the values for non-tankers in these years.

The stagnation of output has given a unique opportunity for the United Kingdom's competitors to increase their share of what has proved to be a growing market for ships. First Germany, then Japan, recommenced shipbuilding on an extensive scale, drawing on state aid in both cases to re-establish and expand industries put out of action by the war, while the Netherlands and Scandinavian countries have been expanding the output of their yards. In the United Kingdom, output has increased very slowly. Between 1946 and 1951 it increased by 13 per cent, but output fell off in 1952, and it was not until 1955 that previous levels were exceeded; in 1956 again, however, the growth of output was interrupted and there was no significant recovery in 1957 and a further fall in 1958.

It is to be expected that the growth of output should not be entirely regular; a few launches advanced in one year and retarded in another can alter the figures quite considerably, as can variations in the proportions of tanker and non-tanker tonnage launched, the number of passenger liners

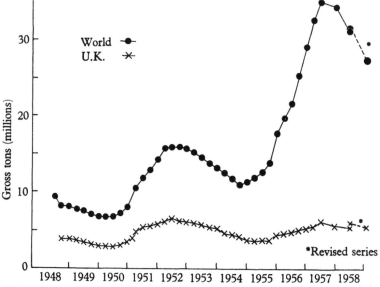

Fig. 7.—Orders on Hand in the United Kingdom and the World for Ships of 1000 g.r.t. and over
(Source: *Bulletin of the American Bureau of Shipping*)

included or the number of men diverted to warship work. But whatever the precise interpretation to be placed on the trend of output up to 1959, it bore little relation to the volume of orders on hand. These fluctuated widely but, even at their lowest ebb, could scarcely be described as small. Order books fell to under 3 million g.r.t. (about 2 years' output in hand) in 1950, only to rise to over 6 million g.r.t. (about 4½ years' output in hand) in 1952. Both in 1950 and again in 1954 fears were expressed about the future level of activity, but the influx of orders in 1956 and 1957 again carried order books to record levels. There was, therefore, over these years the strongest pressure to increase output in order to meet delivery requirements. (Fig. 7.)

There have been three difficulties in the way of a rapid increase in the output of the industry in the United Kingdom. They can be summarised as difficulties in maintaining an adequate labour force, difficulties in getting adequate supplies of steel, and difficulties in reorganising and re-equipping the shipyards in line with modern shipyard practice.

The early post-war years were occupied with the repair and reconstruction of vessels used in the war, and it was not until 1949 that the way was cleared to transfer men to new construction. In the immediate post-war years the labour force employed declined year after year. In mid-1945 there were 230,000 men engaged in the industry; in 1947, 206,000; and in 1948 on the old basis of statistics about the same. The number continued to decline, on the new basis of statistics, from 219,000 in 1948 to about 190,000 in June 1951. It then rose to 206,000 in June 1956 only to fall at an accelerating rate to 186,000 in February 1959. Over the whole period female labour force fell, as might be expected, from 20,000 in 1945 to a more normal figure of 10,000, mainly composed of clerical workers.

A decline in the number of workers employed in the industry immediately after the war was to be expected in view of the wartime direction of labour and intense mobilisation of the labour force. But at the same time there was not the steel needed to sustain a switch in output from repair to new building. Had adequate steel supplies been available, there would have been a better opportunity of retaining wartime workers and using them to increase the output of new ships. The steel shortage was, however, a continuing obstacle to an increase in output. The position had improved somewhat by 1950, but rearmament brought with it heavy demands for steel, and the reintroduction of steel rationing, which set back the hopes of the shipbuilding industry of increased output and resulted in a check instead. By 1954 steel supplies were flowing more freely and output again rose, but with the easing of the steel shortage the obstacle in the way of increasing production became more one of increasing the available labour force or using it more efficiently than one of inadequate raw material supplies or even supplies of components. The supply of steel, however, was adequate only for the type of ships under construction and forward planning was impeded by the difficulty of getting steel of special types, shapes and sizes. With the shift of programmes to larger and larger tankers accelerated by the Suez crisis, it was clear that much greater supplies of steel would be needed, since with larger ships and heavier plates there is some increase in the weight of steel processed per man. Moreover, the large influx of orders, the second within a limited number of years, served to convince the industry that it must at all costs rise to its opportunities and press on with preparations to launch the largest tankers, while continuing to reorganise production facilities so as to increase output per head and expand the tonnage launched nearer to the 1¾ million g.r.t. per year considered to approximate to the potential output of the industry under prevailing conditions.

With these resolves came a recognition on a wider front both that the shipbuilding industry could make good use of larger supplies of steel and that it had been starved of supplies, while other industries, particularly the motor-car industry, had been favoured. When the United Kingdom shipbuilding industry was a major customer of the steel industry and took almost a quarter of the total output of ingot steel, it was much more the steel industry that looked to the shipbuilding industry for its markets than the latter which sought the steel for its needs. In the early years of shipbuilding the steel industry found outlets by securing control of shipbuilding undertakings, and apart from the boom of the twenties, when, as we have seen, some shipbuilders had to band together to safeguard their steel supplies from the encroachments of their competitors, by the purchase of steel works, any failure of the steel industry to meet the full requirements of shipbuilding companies could always be countered by imports of steel plates and sections or castings as occurred, for example, before the First World War when the foreign product was often cheaper by a quarter or more.[1]

In the post-war world the importance of the shipbuilding market for steel has declined, and the industry now takes only about 5 per cent of the output of ingot steel, and it is possible that on this account shipbuilding got less consideration than it deserved. But also it is clear that there was a marked miscalculation of probable requirements, not only of the shipbuilding industry, but also of other industries requiring similar types of steel. 'Even though the general trend of industrial demand may be correctly foreseen, it is possible for demand in particular industries to develop unexpectedly, and for the higher level of demand to continue over a long period; and it may be that fortuitously these sectors of industry are heavy users of the same form of finished steel. On the formation of the (Iron and Steel) Board there had just become available the result of an officially sponsored inquiry into the demand for plate. It contained estimates on the best advice then obtainable to the following effect: that by 1959–60 the demand for ships would be insufficient to keep shipyards working at more than 90 per cent of the rate achieved in 1953. In 1955 shortly after the issue of the first development report it had appeared that the shipbuilders would be working at full capacity for many years.'[2]

At the same time there appears to have been little attempt to right matters by importing steel. In part this has been a government responsibility. In the extreme shortage of 1951–2, for example, it required the efforts of no less a person than the Prime Minister to secure additional supplies of steel

---

[1] See the *Second Report of the Booth Committee*, Cd. 9092, p. 25, Appendix A. It appeared that in 1912–13 less than 10 per cent of the total requirements of steel for shipbuilding was imported; for forgings and castings the proportions were roughly 35 and 45 per cent respectively.

[2] Development of Iron and Steel Industry: Report by the Iron & Steel Board (see *Shipbuilding and Shipping Record*, 1 August 1957).

from the United States. Thereafter it became less difficult to secure supplies abroad, but until 1958 the demand for shipbuilding steel was increasing, and the price, particularly for marginal supplies for immediate delivery during the Korean War or at the time of the Suez crisis, was often very high in relation to United Kingdom prices. For all that, more plentiful supplies of steel would have greatly outweighed any increase in the price that had to be paid, for if sufficient steel had been available a considerable increase in output would have been possible if the frequent complaints by the industry about the shortage of supplies in relation to requirements are to be believed, and since this could have been accomplished without any expansion of shipbuilding capacity and up to a point without a corresponding increase in manpower, it would have paid handsome dividends. It may be questioned whether the industry did all in its power to remedy the situation; it appears to have been exceptional for shipbuilders to seek supplies of steel abroad, and all too common for thousands of tons to be locked away in the slow construction of hulls, which in times of shortage should have taken the water in a much shorter time than the year or more they lay on the berth. But shortage breeds shortage, and the completion of a massive piece of construction may be delayed until some scarce plate is delivered to the yard or alternatives can be devised to make do with available supplies. It is perhaps a sign of the times that a shortage of steel was accepted without greater protest; in the heyday of expansion a similar obstacle to production would not have been brooked for long, and the price necessary to eliminate a bottleneck would willingly have been paid. Cheap steel at the expense of steel in adequate quantities is not cheap, but dear, if it inhibits advance, however it may seem to Britain's competitors. And it is ironic in the circumstances that the shortage of steel for shipbuilding was due in part to the export of steel to the United Kingdom's shipbuilding competitors, particularly to Sweden, in return for materials for smelting steel, 95 per cent of which went to other industries.[1]

It is difficult to judge what tonnage of ships has been lost to United Kingdom shipyards by the steel shortage. But in the final count it will not be the ships that could not be produced that will loom on the debit side so much as the damage done to the workers and the management of an industry by real or imaginary obstacles to the expansion of output from causes outside the industry's control. By 1957, however, the steel situation showed signs of being resolved, partly as a result of a change in government outlook and determined negotiations by the Shipbuilding Conference to secure greater supplies, and deliveries of steel to the shipbuilding and repairing industry reached 822,000 tons compared with 783,000 tons in 1956 and

[1] In 1951 and 1952 about one-quarter of the shipbuilding industry's requirements of plates was exported.

689,000 tons in 1955. In 1958 steel supplies were no longer a difficulty; glut had succeeded scarcity and steel was obtainable on the Continent and Japan below United Kingdom prices. It is ironic that at this juncture cancellations and requests by shipowners to postpone delivery began to upset production programmes and reduce the need for steel; while the prospects of securing sufficient orders to keep the industry going, even at the rate of output recorded in 1958, appeared remote. In 1957, it had looked as if manpower shortage would succeed steel shortage as a factor limiting the rate at which ships could be produced. In Denmark, Italy, Japan and presumably Northern Ireland, it was still possible to recruit additional shipyard workers even in 1957; but shipyards in the Netherlands, Germany, Sweden and Norway, no less than those in Great Britain, were experiencing the utmost difficulty in training and recruiting labour. At this time increased output depended mainly on increasing labour productivity. In 1959, however, there was some redundancy of labour in nearly all shipbuilding centres.

It is still true that the prospects of the United Kingdom industry depend on increasing productivity. But this is important not so much because it is a way to increase output as because it is a way to reduce costs and improve competitive power. In the next chapters we proceed to consider a number of matters that have a bearing on this.

CHAPTER 9

Technical Change in Ships

I

Technical progress in the design of ships is a factor of the first importance in its effect on the competitive position of shipbuilders. We have already seen how the change from wood and sail to steel and steam destroyed the lead built up by the American industry in the nineteenth century, and how the slow introduction of the diesel engine impaired the competitive position of the United Kingdom shipping and shipbuilding industries in the inter-war period. No country that fails to keep pace with technical progress can hope, in the long run, to make good this deficiency by producing ships more cheaply than countries in the van of progress.

In the operation of ships running costs tend to be of the same order as capital costs and, broadly speaking, a given reduction in running costs resulting from technical innovation is of the same importance as a comparable reduction in construction costs. Historically the most important reductions in the real cost of moving a ship through the water have come about by the adoption of more efficient prime movers rather than by modification to the shape of the hull of a ship, or changes in the design of propellers or transmission systems. The simple and compound steam-reciprocating engines in vogue between 1854 and 1862 required about 4 lb coal to produce 1 shaft-h.p.; geared turbines employing superheated steam developed by 1934 required the equivalent of only 1 lb coal per shaft horsepower—a most remarkable improvement in efficiency. Over the same period improvement in transmission reduced the power required for a given propulsive force by about one-third. In total, 1 lb coal sufficed in 1934 to do the work for which 6 lb. would have been needed in 1854. As a record of progress over 80 years these figures are striking; they are even more significant when it is realised that the bulk of the economy effected took place between 1914 and 1934.[1]

The significance of new designs of engines is not confined to the direct saving of fuel involved. A reduction in the weight and size of engines as well as in the bunker coal or oil required makes it possible to increase the amount of cargo that can be carried.[2] Between 1924 and 1934, for example,

---

[1] The above figures are taken from an article in the *Shipbuilding and Shipping Record*, 22 March 1934, p. 295.
[2] The higher calorific value per ton of oil in comparison with coal has a similar effect.

105

improvements in steam plants were calculated to increase the net revenue of a dry-cargo ship of 9000 g.r.t. by about £4800 per year. The cost of such a ship in 1934 was about £75,000; if interest charges, depreciation and upkeep are reckoned on the average at about 20 per cent per annum of the capital cost, or £15,000 per annum, it can be calculated that the increase in revenue from installing the new type of engine would justify an increased capital expenditure of about one-third.

The introduction of the diesel engine with an efficiency of 35–40 per cent against the 20–25 per cent more normal for steam engines also had a very marked effect on running costs in certain conditions of operation. It was calculated in 1934, for example, that with the then ruling prices for oil and coal an 8000 d.w.t. vessel with a speed of 10½ knots would cost about one-third less in running costs than one fitted with coal-fired turbine or reciprocating engines, roughly one-fifth of the saving resulting from reduced labour costs. The cost of diesel engines, however, was greater than the cost of the equivalent steam machinery. Nevertheless, in suitable conditions a motorship may have earned 5 per cent more on the capital invested than one driven by steam.[1] The advantage was not, however, always so clear-cut;[2] it depended on the relative costs and availabilities of coal and oil fuel, on the use to which the vessel was put, and on its size. Even after diesel engines were used extensively they were fitted less frequently than steam engines to vessels of 1000–4000 g.t., and although above this range diesel engines predominated, oil-fired steam-turbine engines offered greater economy in operation for some purposes. In 1950, for example, geared turbines were still more economical in running costs than diesel engines in a number of uses requiring 7000 or more shaft-h.p.[3] The trend, however, has been against the steam turbine in recent years, since, as we have seen, developments of the diesel engine have made it possible to obtain very large horsepowers from a single shaft. A power of 20,000 h.p can now be obtained from a diesel engine, whereas previously vessels requiring 15,000 h.p. generally have been powered by steam turbines. These developments make it possible for even the largest super-tankers to be powered by diesel engines.

The advantages of the diesel engine have been enhanced by the use of heavy oils which was pioneered in the United Kingdom by Anglo-Saxon

---

[1] See J. Ramsay Gebbie, 'The evolution of the cargo ship during the last 35 years', Appendix A; a paper presented at a meeting of the Institution of Naval Architects on 9 January 1958.

[2] For a curious example of a calculation showing that diesel operation cost more than steam propulsion see the *Shipbuilding and Shipping Record*, 17 January 1924. In this case the additional weight of fuel oil needed to be carried in order to provide for the return voyage prevented a vessel from arriving fully loaded at a port with only a limited depth of water available. It appeared to be cheaper to use a coal-fired steamship which with exhausted bunkers could clear the bottom when entering fully loaded.

[3] See 'Trends in the choice of machinery for ocean-going merchant vessels', A. W. Davis, *Transactions of Institution of Engineers and Shipbuilders in Scotland*, March 1950.

Petroleum Co. This company converted the *Auricula* to the use of heavy fuel oils, which are appreciably cheaper than the special products normally required for diesel operation but require only comparatively simple treatment to make them suitable for diesel use.

It is doubtful whether these innovations represent the limit to which conventional diesel engines can be developed, but in the post-war period no fewer than three other types of propulsion, which ultimately may prove to have advantages over diesel engines, have been brought at least to the trial stage. These three are the free-piston gas engine, the gas turbine and, of course, atomic power. The free-piston engine, like all prime movers, had a long history before it became a factor in practical affairs. It was first developed in practicable form by R. Pescara in Italy although it was built and used in Germany by Junkers; in 1937, Pescara were taken over by the French interests, Société d'Étude et de Participation with its associated companies of Société Industrielle Générale de Mécanique Appliqué (Sigma) and Société d'Études Mécaniques et Énergétiques (Seme). In 1953 General Motors took an interest, and under an agreement with Sigma built the first engine of this type, the G.S. 34. Further developments followed and a new model was introduced in 1954. The main advantage of the engine is that it uses a wide range of fuel and is efficient and flexible in its space requirements. It has shown sufficient promise to range in the alternatives offered by a number of British shipbuilding companies and marine engineers, but although foreign-built ships have been engined by this means and some orders have been placed in this country,[1] optimum operating conditions appear to be rather critical and this might prove to be an obstacle to widespread use.

The gas turbine has yet to become well established as a marine prime mover although it offers many attractions to other users. This country was, of course, one of the pioneers of the gas turbine for use in aircraft, but although it was considered as a possible prime mover for ships at least as early as the 1920's much of the early development work for marine purposes was done abroad, for example by the firms of Escher Wyss and Sulzer.

The first gas turbine to be used for marine propoulsion, however, was manufactured by British Thompson Houston, and installed in the *Auris* by the Anglo-Saxon Co. alongside three engines of conventional diesel operation. The gas turbine proved to be able to power the *Auris* across the Atlantic without the aid of the diesel engines, and it was decided on the strength of these trials to convert the *Auris* to full gas-turbine operation. The United States maritime administration has also converted experimentally the *John Sergeant*, a Liberty vessel. So far, however, the gas turbine has found little favour in shipping circles. A main difficulty is that of securing

---

[1] The *Morar*, launched in January 1959 by Lithgows, was fitted with a free-piston gas engine.

high enough efficiency to compete with alternative engines, particularly the diesel, and this is likely to involve the use of higher temperatures and the development of suitable material to withstand the associated stresses and strains. The position of the gas turbine in relation to other forms of prime mover will not, however, turn on efficiency alone. It was claimed, for example, for one gas turbine, the *Saturn*, announced by the Solar Aircraft Co. in the U.S.A., that a 1000 h.p. engine weighed only 5000 lb., compared with the 10,000–20,000 lb. for a diesel engine of comparable power, and that at high speeds the gas turbine would be more efficient than a diesel engine. It may be, however, that oil-burning gas turbines of conventional design will fail to gain acceptance before atomic energy is in use for merchant-ship propulsion. At the same time it is possible that the gas turbine will be brought into its own by the use of atomic reactors, and some schemes at present under consideration envisage the latter being used as a source of heat to drive a gas turbine.

The economic advantages and disadvantages of atomic reactors as a means of powering merchant ships at present lie in the balance. There is a fair measure of confidence that atomic reactors will ultimately prove to be economic for merchant ships, and where the weight of fuel to be carried is important this may outweigh other considerations. Russia, for example, has constructed an ice-breaker powered with atomic energy, and since for this class of vessel fuel consumption amounts to 100 tons of oil a day atomic power makes for considerable economy in storage requirements.[1] More generally atomic energy is likely to be at an advantage over other types of power when the vessel concerned is large, the power required high and when a great deal of time is spent at sea. The super-tanker voyaging round the Cape fits these requirements well, and the first merchant vessel to be powered by atomic energy in the United Kingdom is likely to be a super-tanker.

Competition in the technical sphere of engine development is likely to be severe in the next decade. Pride of place may be given to atomic power, and most shipbuilding countries have set up research establishments either on a company or industrial basis, generally with government assistance, to develop designs of reactors and machinery suitable for ship propulsion. In the United States, A.M.F. Atomics, Atomics International, Ford Instrument Co. and General Motors are all in the field, and some of their designs are likely to be taken up by the United States Maritime Commission. The Swedish Foundation for Shipbuilding Research at Gothenburg, the Norwegian Shipbuilding Institute and the Norwegian Institute of Atomic Energy and Osaka Shosen in Japan are amongst the organisations studying atomic

---

[1] *Journal of Commerce and Shipbuilding*, 11 July 1957, quoting an article by Dr J. V. Dunsworth. The ship was launched in 1957 (*Sunday Times*, 8 December 1957).

propulsion and plans are also being prepared in Holland.[1] In this country, as we have seen, there are a number of organisations interested in the development of atomic power for marine propulsion and John Brown's and Vickers-Armstrongs have both announced their technical readiness to start construction. The latter company is already engaged on the construction of an atomic-powered submarine.

Many problems, including potential dangers from contamination, remain to be solved before atomic energy can be widely used with safety and economy. Both first cost and running costs have to be considered. Running costs depend both on the system used and the price that has to be paid for nuclear fuels. If the price of these falls as their supply is increased, which appears to be a reasonable expectation, running costs may well fall below the cost of using conventional fuels. It is possible that there will not be a great deal in the space requirements and weight of nuclear-powered propulsion units, with their associated screening, and engines of other kinds, including bunker requirements. If this is the case, the economic advantages of nuclear ships will depend on minimising the cost of constructing nuclear reactors.

Even if fuel costs could be reduced almost to zero by using nuclear power, this would not justify more than an increase of 50 per cent in the cost of a ship, since fuel costs generally may amount to about half annual capital charges. The reactor for the *Savannah*, built in the United States, cost the equivalent of £5 million; the reactor that the Japanese Atomic Industrial Forum plans to install in their 3,000 ton experimental vessel is expected to cost £2 million; but ultimately it is to be expected that costs will be lower. The various designs of nuclear units submitted by several companies to an Admiralty Committee in this country are being appraised by a sub-committee appointed for the purpose. It cannot be judged, in advance of this, whether they offer the reduction in capital costs below previous estimates that is needed if nuclear propulsion is to become competitive with other means of propulsion; or even whether costs will be brought sufficiently near this to justify the construction of an experimental merchant vessel. But when the designs were submitted there did appear to be some prospect that this might be so. The design submitted by de Havilland, for example, was estimated to cost £$\frac{3}{4}$ million for the reactor furnace, roughly £$\frac{1}{2}$ million more than a conventional boiler.

The possibility that nuclear power will make it feasible to use submarines for the transport of cargo under the polar ice or by more conventional routes relying on speed for economy appears to be remote. For the most part nuclear propulsion, if it is to be adopted on a wide scale, will have to compete with the use of conventional prime movers in conventional ships.

[1] See *The Financial Times*, 25 September 1956.

Technical development will not be confined to atomic energy. If past experience of engine development is any guide, conventional engines will continue to vie with atomic reactors for many years to come. Thus diesel-engine manufacturers expect that the market for their products will continue to be strong for many years, and they will continue to develop the engine and improve its manufacture in order to resist the encroachment of atomic reactors into any but the largest vessels, or those particularly suited to the use of atomic energy.

Although engines must be placed first in the field of technical development, there are a number of other ways in which the design of ships affects their performance and their value to shipowners. These include appearance (the lines which contribute so much to naval architectural art), general arrangements (the position of cabins in passenger liners or the position of the engine room in cargo ships), loading and unloading facilities (palletisation, roll-on-roll-off ships for lorry transportation of cargos, electric or other types of cranes, hatchways and their covers), navigational aids, new surfaces for easy maintenance and many more besides. All these things will be a matter for discussion between shipowners and shipbuilders, and there will be opportunity, therefore, for a shipbuilder to improve on the proposals of potential competitors.

Possibly the most significant development in the post-war period outside marine engineering has been the use of progressively larger and larger tankers. In this case the initiative has lain mainly with shipowners, for the technical difficulties of constructing very large warships or passenger vessels had already been overcome many years before monster tankers were seriously considered, and although the construction of a bulk carrier for liquid cargoes is not the same as the construction of a dry-cargo vessel or more particularly a passenger liner, no great difficulty has been experienced in developing suitable designs and techniques. In adopting designs for super-tankers shipowners are likely to be able to cut their operational costs by an amount which would take very many years to accomplish by a succession of small changes and improvements in design and construction.

As we have seen in Chapter 5, the anticipated reduction in operational cost is little short of revolutionary. The total cost of operating large tankers appears to be about the same as the prime cost of operating tankers one-third the size.[1]

A reduction of operating costs with increase in size is not confined to tankers; it applies to bulk carriers in general. Consequently, as we have seen, there is a tendency for all types of cargo ships to increase in size, the

---

[1] This view is based on figures given by H. F. Robinson, J. F. Roeske and A. C. Thaeler (1948), *Trans. American Soc. Naval Architects and Marine Engineers*, Vol. 56, pp. 422–47, and *The Financial Times*, 8 September 1956, p.4.

upper limit depending in the case of tankers or ore-carriers on the available loading or unloading facilities and for various other types on the certainty with which full cargoes can be obtained.

All these changes in the design of ships react on the shipbuilder. So far as engines are concerned he must be ready to build whatever type is proving to be the most satisfactory and economical; so far as size is concerned he must be ready to build and repair progressively larger ships as shipowners find them more economical to operate. No less the shipbuilder must be prepared to scrutinise the materials he uses in order to be sure that they continue to be the most satisfactory available for the various purposes for which they are used.

There has been no serious challenge to steel as the material most suitable and most economical for ship construction, but for some purposes aluminium is proving to be more satisfactory. The advantage of aluminium is that it combines great strength with light weight; its disadvantage is that it is more expensive than steel for most purposes. Broadly speaking, one-half ton of suitable aluminium alloys suffices to replace one ton of steel—ton per ton aluminium alloy is stronger than mild steel—but the prices of aluminium alloys per ton are roughly ten times the price of steel per ton. Even allowing for the fact that the reduced weight of aluminium used in hull construction means a saving in the power and size of engines needed to propel a vessel, it is still true that for most purposes aluminium costs too much to be used extensively. There are, however, exceptional circumstances when the almost exclusive use of aluminium may be justified, for example, for the construction of small vessels of shallow draught, and there are a number of uses for it in ship construction of a specialised kind. A cross-channel passenger ship constructed entirely of aluminium is one possibility. For this type of ship the bulk of the weight of the loaded vessel consists of its own structure rather than the cargo taken on board, and in consequence the proportionate reduction in weight from using aluminium is considerable.

Aluminium is being used increasingly in the fabrication of superstructures, particularly in passenger liners, where on stability grounds it is important to keep the centre of gravity of the ship low and so to reduce weight in the upper parts. Thus aluminium tends to be used in conjunction with steel construction, though its use in this way raises a number of difficulties. For one thing, aluminium and steel have different coefficients of expansion with heat and any union between them is likely to be a source of strain, and, for another, aluminium alloys which by themselves are comparatively corrosion-resistant (to the extent that no external protection is needed) are so no longer if brought into contact with steel. These difficulties can be overcome by the use of suitable joints and protection procedures at the expense of complication, and at the same time it is possible to make the alloys sufficiently heat-

111

resistant to avoid serious risks from fire. Aluminium alloys can be joined in much the same way as steel structures. They can be riveted and, with the development of inert gas welding, they can also be joined by this means, but some experience both in design and on the part of the workmen is needed if the best results are to be obtained and distortion avoided.

At present prices there is little likelihood of aluminium being used for major structural work, and if, as seems rather unlikely in view of the energy needed to prepare the metal, its price were reduced so as to bring it into near competition with steel for important uses, it is probable that new steel alloys of properties more nearly equivalent to aluminium alloys would be pressed on shipbuilders who so far have not considered it worth while to pay the additional cost of their production. This is not to say that in the future steel will necessarily continue to be the shipbuilding material *par excellence*; suitable plastics might be developed for large ships in the way that fibre glass has proved its value as a material for yachts or lifeboats, but at the present time nothing can be foreseen which is likely to alter the character of ship construction.

II

Shipbuilding techniques have undergone a spectacular change in the post-war period which has largely been associated with the introduction of welding as an almost universal method of making joints in place of riveting connections. Like all technical changes welding has a long history. Its first applications tended to be made outside shipbuilding, but towards the end of the First World War it was finding an application in the repair of ships, particularly in the repair of heavy engine parts. The first all-welded vessel of any size to be completed was the *Fullagar* built by Cammell Laird in 1920. This coasting vessel demonstrated the soundness of welded connections when it survived a period aground, subsequently being refloated with repairable damage. She was ultimately lost in a collision after 17 years of service. The example of the *Fullagar* was not, however, followed by any general move to welded ships and, until the 1930's, welding in shipbuilding languished. In the main the reason for the slow acceptance of welded ships was of a technical nature. The early welds tended to be brittle, and shipowners doubted (and with considerable justification) whether welded connections could stand up to the full strains to which they would be subjected in large ships. The ultimate reliability of any method of hull construction is demonstrable only after a number of ships have been proved over a span of life approaching the service life of a ship; that is to say, over 30 years or more. The reliability of test-pieces demonstrated by laboratory techniques is no guide to the performance of a complicated structure such as that of a ship, and it is understandable that the risk of failure is likely to rank higher in the mind of a shipowner than any potential economies in first cost that would arise through the adoption of a welded ship. There is thus a very real difficulty in gaining acceptance of new systems of construction when to be proved they must be used and to be used they must be proved. This impasse can generally be resolved only by a gradual approach of introducing modifications bit by bit and slowly building up to complete change over an extended period of time. Sometimes progressive shipowners well placed to stand the losses and reap the benefit of improved methods of construction may be ready to underwrite the cost of economic failure, and exceptionally war or government action may hasten change, but more normally when the safety of the ship is at stake, change is likely to be slow and sure.

By the early thirties, shipbuilders in this country were arguing on the basis of strength tests carried out on welded test-pieces that Lloyd's Register should be ready to accept an all-welded ship for more than experimental classification. Lloyd's Register felt, however, that too little was known about welding and welded structures at that time to justify giving an unqualified A 1 classification to a ship of wholly welded construction. Classification by Lloyd's Register is not obligatory but it is the hallmark of accepted practice, and without it shipowners were not prepared to go to the risk and expense of ordering ships of welded construction when the bulk of them were well satisfied with riveted ships and saw no reason to change. It must be agreed that Lloyd's Register were right in doubting the reliability of welded ships built at that time, but the fact remains that the development of welded ships in this country was held back in consequence.

Two happenings in the thirties combined to pave the way for the successful use of welding. The first was the development of the coated electrode in this country, which made possible for the first time a high degree of reliability of the weld; and the second was the incentive given by the London Naval Treaty to the use of welding in warship construction in order to save weight, a practice adopted first by Germany and later by this country. As the warship programmes were extended, more and more welders had to be trained and the requisite skills and welding techniques built up.

Even with these developments the application of welding to merchant ships was slow, and there can be no doubt that had it not been for the exigencies of war, welded construction would not have been so widely used as it is today. The construction of Liberty and Victory ships in the United States provided an opportunity to test the performance of wholly welded ships on a massive scale, for the alternative of building riveted ships in the numbers required was quite impracticable in the circumstances. The results of this enforced experiment in the adoption of all-welded ships was at one and the same time to confirm the views of the advocates and opponents of welded-ship construction. On the one hand, the mass-welded vessels proved to be generally successful; on the other hand, there were a large number of both major and minor failures in the welded structure, bringing home the dangers inherent in an over-hasty adoption of a new method of construction radically different from older and well-tried methods.

One wintry evening in 1943 a welded tanker, the *Schenectady*, lying quietly at her fitting-out pier at Portland, Oregon, having that day passed her acceptance trials, suddenly broke in two with a report that was heard for at least a mile. The deck and sides had fractured amidships and the vessel, held together only by her bottom-plating, jack-knifed so that the centre rose out of the water. In the world of shipbuilders and steelmakers the noise of this failure travelled far and lasted long, but was soon followed by others. Between 1942 and 1952, about 250 welded ships suffered one or more brittle fractures of such severity that they were lost or in a dangerous condition, and 1200 more suffered small brittle cracks dangerous but not disabling.

Between 1947 and 1952 there were 15 ships of between 2000 and 10,000 g.r.t. which broke in two after major structural failure; of these four were all-riveted and the rest of welded construction. . . .

As we have seen, brittle fracture has occurred alike in riveted and in welded structures; however, more failures by far come in the latter than the former class of structure. This general statement is not quite simple, since the total number of riveted and welded structures is unknown, and the number of welded ships built is now about four times as great as ships with riveted hulls and decks. However, it is clear that a large welded structure may be more liable to catastrophic damage than a similar large riveted one, since the former is more 'monolithic' and the high-speed brittle crack is therefore liable to be able to travel much farther and do more damage.[1]

This summary of the dangers inherent in welded construction brings home the difficulties likely to be met in pioneering new forms of ship construction. Why is it that, in spite of this, welded construction has been increasingly adopted in this and other shipbuilding countries to the extent that riveted connections are now exceptional? The answer lies first in the continuous improvement in welded structures that has taken place, and secondly in the fact that welded ships can be produced more cheaply than those of riveted design.

Improvements in welded structures have been brought about in a number of ways. The quality of the welds has an important bearing on the strength of the resultant structure, and a good deal still depends on the skill and practice of the welding operator. Slag inclusions, for example, result in discontinuities in the welded areas, and notches made by the striking of an arc or inadequate control of the electrode may make a joint liable to subsequent fracture. Many of these defects are impossible to detect by eye and are shown only in some form of X-ray photograph of the weld. Reliable welded connections depend first on the careful training of the welding operator and secondly on periodical checks of the quality of the work. It has been found that long experience is no guarantee of quality, and that it is

[1] F. A. Fox, 'The Brittle Fracture of Structural Steel', *Science News*, 36, pp. 76, 77 and 80.

desirable to check the quality of the work of all welding operatives before they are accepted as having the necessary skill. When automatic or semi-automatic welding machines can be used the resulting weld is likely to be of better quality than one formed manually.

The quality of the weld and the means to obtain consistently high performance in this respect are not, however, the whole story. It was noticed in the early stages of welding that it was often not the welds themselves that failed but other parts of the structure. This pointed to a number of other factors not directly related to the quality of the weld which influence the strength of a welded structure. There is, for example, the notch effect where discontinuities in the structure, ranging from minute irregularities or incisions in the surface of the metal (caused perhaps by the welds themselves or the processing of the metal) to major breaks such as hatch openings, become a source of weakness and result in the development of a crack. Good design provides against this happening by strengthening weak points so that the notch effect is overcome.

Design is important in other ways; in laying down, for example, a sequence of welding and assembly operations which enables locked-up stresses to be minimised. In the process of welding, the metal on either side of the weld is heated and expands, when it cools contraction takes place and the metal may distort or remain in a state of stress. Stresses can sometimes be removed by subsequent heat treatment, but this is not a practical proposition for the general run of work and it does not obviate the need to avoid locked-up stresses in the first place.

As a better understanding of the causes of welded failures has been arrived at, constructional techniques have been modified without, however, convincing all shipowners or all shipbuilders that the all-welded ship is as reliable as one of riveted construction. The idea that a riveted ship is more flexible than a welded ship, due to rivet slip, appears to have little foundation in fact. The experiments conducted by the Admiralty on two similar ships, one of welded and one of riveted construction, provided no support for this view. Since, however, cracks once started tend to spread through a continuous structure, it is common for welded ships to have some vertical and horizontal riveted connections on the outside shell, in order to break up the structure, and to take similar precautions at other places subject to unusual strain. Thus the main function of rivets in an otherwise all-welded ship is to serve as crack-arrestors, the cracks running to the rivet-holes and stopping there if the strain is sufficiently relieved.

Underlying these influences, however, is the liability of some types of steel to brittle fracture under certain conditions of load and temperature. The effect is not confined to ships but is evident in other structures and, for that matter, in other metals subject to fatigue. Attention has therefore been directed to the use of appropriate types of steel less susceptible to brittle fracture in those parts of a ship structure most liable to strain, and new rules specifying the use of special steel for some purposes were adopted by Lloyd's Register in 1955.

Without technical progress in all these directions there might have been a tendency after the war to revert to riveted construction, even though riveted ships might have been equally liable to brittle fracture. As it is, shipbuilders have been able to convince most shipowners of the essential soundness and reliability of welded ships, and there has been an opportunity for both sides to see that welded ships are more economical to run and cheaper to produce than their riveted counterparts.

One of the reasons why a welded ship is less costly to produce and operate is that it requires less steel and consequently is lighter and easier to drive through the water. With welded connections the various parts of the structure must overlap in order that the rivets can be driven through all the members to be joined together; with welding, however, butt-joints are used for plating so that overlaps are eliminated and welded rolled sections are used instead of flanges; there is also a minor saving in the steel used for rivets, since the weight of metal deposited for a welded connection is less than that of the rivets which it replaces. The proportion of steel saved by welding rather than riveting varies with the type of vessel considered. It has been estimated that in the construction of a liner 12 per cent of the steel required for riveted construction is saved by welding,[1] and this means either that a welded ship may be more economically powered because it is lighter, or can be loaded with a greater weight of cargo, or some combination of both these effects arranged.

At the same time power requirements are reduced because the smooth hull of a welded vessel offers less resistance to the water than one of riveted construction. Experiments on the *Lucy Ashton*, for example, demonstrated conclusively that with a given power and fuel consumption speeds could be quite considerably increased by fairing all joints and presenting a flush surface to the water. The effect is more marked the larger the ship concerned. Rivets on the hull of a 1000 ft. vessel reduce its speed for a given power by some 20 per cent, but even for smaller ships the reduction of speed may be 10 per cent or more.[2] Alternatively, for the same speed as much as 20 per cent of the fuel required may be saved.[3]

The direct saving of steel by the use of welding may reduce the total cost of construction of a ship by some 2–3 per cent. The saving of weight in a 15,000 d.w.t. ship means that with suitable cargoes it could earn as much

[1] L. Redshaw, 'Welding as applied to shipbuilding', *Welding Research*, 1949, vol. III, pp. 36r–46r.
[2] See *The Financial Times*, 29 May 1957.   [3] Ramsay Gebbie, *loc. cit.*

as one of 16,000 d.w.t.[1] In total, therefore, welded construction may reduce the cost of building a ship calculated to carry out a certain amount of transport by 10 per cent or more. This is not all, however, for welding is one step to the use of more economical production methods affecting nearly all aspects of shipyard construction, and it is only in relation to these consequential changes that the full significance of the change to welding can be appreciated These changes have been sufficiently drastic to justify comparison in the eyes of one eminent shipbuilder to the substitution of iron for wood in ship construction, and it is to the reorganisation of shipyards following the adoption of the welded ship that we turn in the next chapter.

[1] It might be thought at first sight that a reduction in the weight of steel by some percentage would increase the weight of cargo that could be carried also by the same percentage. This is not so. Generally the cargo weighs more than the ship, and it follows that a reduction in the weight of the ship in some proportion permits only a less than proportionate increase in the cargo.

CHAPTER 10

Shipyard Organisation and Technical Change

I

The mechanical aids in use in shipbuilding at the end of the nineteenth century were few, and this was nowhere more evident than on the berths themselves. The only lifting devices available were simple pole-derricks, visible in the photograph of John Brown's yard in 1889 above the staging (Pl. 1). Just before the First World War 45 derricks of a different pattern were erected to service five building berths, and although the maximum lifting power of the most powerful did not exceed 5 tons, they were sufficient for the *Aquitania* to be built in 1913 and the 'Queens' before the Second World War (Pl. 2). The last photograph of the sequence (Pl. 3) shows the yard as it is today. The derricks have disappeared and in their stead stand hammerhead cranes with a maximum lifting power of 40 tons at 70 ft., supplemented by three smaller cranes.

The evolution of the berth cranage accurately reflects the changes that have occurred in shipbuilding methods during the present century. At the beginning of the century mechanical aids were more of a means to carry out operations that could be only indifferently carried out by hand, than a means to economise in labour. Pole-derricks overcame the limited lifting power of labourers unaided, but they did not alter in any way a system of work in which, characteristically, each part of the ship was individually prepared, transported and hand-assembled on the stocks as the vessel grew out of the ground.

The method of construction was a natural one and it required the minimum organisational powers. Plans had to be prepared, but much of the detail could be filled out as construction proceeded. The difficult task of setting out the lines of the vessel and 'fairing' the various sections of the vessels, that is to say, ensuring that they are consistent, was solved by drawing out the plan full-scale on the loft floor, a procedure that is still widely used today though alternative methods may eventually supersede the practice. The plans drawn full-scale in this way could readily be made available either in the form of full-scale copies marked on scrieve boards, which could be transported to the frame benders to serve as a pattern for the frames (the ribs of the vessel), or in the form of templates in wood to give the information necessary for the preparation of plates. Failing this, the vessel itself was always available, and

118

the dimensions and shapes of difficult parts could be 'lifted' directly from it as construction proceeded.

The accessibility of plans and the vessel itself and the simple equipment in use meant that much of the work of construction could be farmed out to squad leaders contracting to carry out part of the construction of the ship, such as the preparation of the frames, deck-plating or other major tasks of hull fabrication—a system which is still in use, although it is of declining importance and tending to change its form as production methods alter.

By modern standards the whole system of construction was exceedingly wasteful of labour, but the sparsely equipped yards of the north-east coast, concentrating on the production of simple tramps and using few aids to assist the highly skilled shipyard workers, other than a plentiful supply of labouring helpers, were able to compete with more lavishly equipped yards in other countries. Paradoxically, as time went on the surfeit of skilled labour in the shipbuilding industry acted as a drag on efficiency. The Dutch shipyards could not muster skilled labour on the scale that was possible in the United Kingdom shipbuilding areas and, though the roots of the Dutch shipbuilding industry lay in United Kingdom practice, the squad system of construction proved to be impracticable in Dutch conditions when it was desired to increase output in the 1930's. With the squad system went the practice of lifting dimensions from the ship's structure. In its stead increased reliance was placed on managerial supervision which insisted on the maximum of economy in the use of direct labour and much more detailed planning of the ship's structure in advance of its construction. At the same time every effort was made to reduce unnecessary handling of materials, to reduce the amount of work carried out on the berth, where bad weather was always likely to interrupt construction, and to improve layouts and balance machinery requirements.

The impulse towards these changes in the Netherlands stemmed, as we have seen, from a shortage of labour and not as a consequence of a change from riveting to welding, and it is probably true to say that even without the introduction of welding in this country large alterations would have been necessary in the organisation of production, largely along the lines of those that have taken place ostensibly to fit the shipyards for welded construction. But welding hastened the change because it proceeds more easily under cover.

The construction of ships under cover is not a new idea. Although the provision of covered berths did not on the whole find ready acceptance in the United Kingdom shipyard techniques, some of the yards on the north-east coast, including that, for example, of Swan, Hunter & Wigham Richardson as early as 1894, were roofed-over to provide protection against the weather. There is, however, a radical change when the cover is provided not on the berth but in erection shops where large sections are prefabricated ready to be incorporated in the ship's structure. Although this procedure was sometimes used for isolated items with riveted construction, and probably would have been adopted on a larger scale in time, it needed the building of a long sequence of welded Liberty and Victory vessels in the United States, during the war, to bring out its full potentialities.

Joining the parts of a ship by welding leads naturally to indoor working and prefabrication. First, welding is much more easily carried out under cover than in the open. Indeed, for some types of welding, such as welding aluminium using a jacket of inert gas to prevent oxidisation, protection from air currents is essential, but all types of welding can be more efficiently performed in a shop rather than in the open. Secondly, although welding by hand can be performed in almost any direction and the welds may be vertical or horizontal, downhand or overhead, it is much easier to weld downhand than in any other way, and since machine welding can only be carried out if the machine can traverse the top of the work, it is desirable to be able to present the majority of connections in a position suitable for downhand welding. This means that it is necessary to turn over sections while they are under construction, so that, for example, deck-plates can be welded from above and then reversed for the attachment of strengthening bars and other connecting pieces. Operations of this kind can be carried out with ease in welding bays fitted with suitable cranes, but they become quite impossible if each individual member is secured, when it is ready, to the main structure of the ship on the berth.

Undercover construction of welded sections is also desirable on grounds of accuracy. Welded parts must fit within close tolerances; there is not an adjustable overlap to be taken up at every connection as there was with riveting when rivet-holes were reamed to fit and an appropriate size of rivet selected for tightness. Accuracy is best achieved in workshop conditions where machines are on the spot and close supervision can be given.

It may seem, at first sight, that the construction of large sections of a ship away from the berth is a small change in production procedure. This is not so. The decision to build under cover carries with it a vest sequence of alterations in every phase of shipyard organisation.

In the first place it gives rise to a complete change in the layout of the berths, cranes, buildings and storage grounds needed. Yet it is perhaps true to say that these physical changes are the least of those that are required in organisation, in managerial methods, and in attitudes to work.

The essentials of the layout needed for modern methods of shipyard construction can be simply set out. The sequence of production can be thought of as following the passage of the steel through the various transformations it undergoes. Thus the steel needs to be stored after delivery by rail or water, in appropriate grounds equipped with transport facilities and cranes, until it is needed for processing. The amount of ground needed for this purpose depends on the ease with which steel can be delivered in the amounts and of the type needed. In the United Kingdom the shipyards are well served in this respect and they do not need to carry the large stock, amounting to six months' or a year's consumption, that may be needed in Continental yards remote from sources of supply. When required, the steel must be transported to the platers' sheds, probably undergoing some preparatory processes in order to flatten and clean it before being marked for shape, size and connections, and cut or burned to the appropriate outline. While this is going on, the other parts of the structure, beams, bars, frames and so on, are being simultaneously prepared. When the appropriate parts have been made ready, the assembly or prefabrication of large sections of the ship can be carried out in erection bays supplied from the platers' sheds with the material required. These sections may range from part of a double bottom to a sternpost and quite exceptionally may weigh as much as 300 tons; at present, however, 30 tons is a much more usual weight, and with present techniques, larger sections are not generally thought to offer any advantage, although some shipbuilders looking to the future think that larger units will eventually prove to be more economic for prefabrication,[1] and the thicker steel needed for larger ships will increase the weight of typical sections irrespective of any change in constructional procedure.

When a section is completed it must be transported to the berth either for storage or for immediate erection. (Pl. 3 shows some sections in store in the foreground.) This again involves the provision of suitable cranes or transport systems. A large section may be lifted out through the roof of an erection shop by a suitably placed travelling crane of adequate capacity and transported direct to its final position on the berth or to store, or it may be removed on bogies and transferred into position by the cranes serving the ships. The latter method is more usual, but the former has been adopted by Connell's on the Clyde and the Lindholmens' yard in Sweden, and in suitable circumstances can effect economy in the provision of cranes and avoid double handling.

Ideally perhaps a straight-line flow of production from railhead to berths might be adopted, and this was typical of the layout of American shipyards operating during the war, but there is no reason why the production line should be straight if an uninterrupted sequence of operations can be arranged in other ways. In many older shipyards alterations in layout have had to take account of the limited amount of space available, the siting of existing berths and the need to continue production while reorganisation is in process.

Reconstruction of an existing shipyard is often a difficult undertaking when

[1] See Clement Stephenson, 'A Shipyard reorganisation for welded prefabricated construction', *Transactions of the Institute of Welding*, August 1952, p.101.

space is limited. More space is needed for the prefabrication and storage of sections which is a new process in the chain, but it is not only a matter of providing for this. Almost every phase of shipyard operations seems to require additional facilities to fit it for new production methods (the one exception is, perhaps, the mould loft which is being replaced by the drawing office), and new office accommodation is needed for the increasing number of supervisory personnel. It has been the almost invariable experience of shipbuilders that every reconstruction they have embarked on has been too small in one way or another. Buildings require great height if they are to be used for prefabrication of sections which necessitates having sufficient clearance to be able to turn them over; assembly areas are never large enough and, increasingly, the berths themselves are becoming far too small in length or breadth to accommodate the largest vessels. All this is becoming increasingly apparent as larger tankers are put under construction.

A good deal of ingenuity has been needed to make the best of available facilities not only in the United Kingdom but in other countries as well. In some cases congestion has been relieved by scrapping some existing berths and using the space released for other purposes. For example, in the reconstruction of the Doxford shipyard three building berths out of six were considered surplus to requirements and converted to the storage of subassemblies prior to erection;[1] in the reorganisation of Lobnitz's yard two berths out of five were dispensed with for the same reason;[2] and in the reorganisation of the Walker yard of Vickers-Armstrongs three small berths were sacrificed to make way for a new platers' shop.[3] None of these shipyards anticipated any reduction in their output in consequence of a reduction in the number of berths; speedier erection was expected to more than compensate for a reduction in the number of ships which could be laid down at any time.

Complete reorganisation of production facilities to fit a shipyard for welded prefabrication work may involve virtual reconstruction of the whole yard, which of necessity must be extended over several years as the yard continues to turn out ships while first one building is torn down to make way for new facilities and then another, until the whole reorganisation is apparently completed. At the same time as buildings and layout are altered to conform to modern practice, machinery and cranes have to be brought up-to-date. Welding has meant that many machines needed to prepare the steel for riveting had to be replaced by others suitable for welded construction. Thus the drills or punches required to make the rivet holes can be largely dispensed with, while mechanical means used to cut the metal have

[1] See Clement Stephenson, 'A shipyard reorganisation for welded prefabricated construction', *Transactions of the Institute of Welding*, August 1952, p. 101.
[2] H. H. Hagan, 'Shipyard layout and technique for welded construction', *Shipbuilding and Shipping Record*, 28 March 1946.
[3] See *The Shipbuilder and Marine Engine Builder*, 1949, p. 168.

tended increasingly to give way to burners which in a single operation burn the steel to size, and shape its edges ready to receive the V-shaped deposit of weld metal. After a plate or other part of the ship is marked out, burnt or shaped, it must be transported to the place of the next operation to be carried out and manoeuvred into position with the minimum of effort. It is here that rollers and cranes, generally an important item in the new equipment of the sheds, come into their own, reducing manhandling to a minimum and freeing manpower for other uses. The final stage of assembly is again carried out with new machines ranging from the automatic welders that progress along a plate, welding as they go with the minimum amount of attention, to the simple hand-welding sets, and between them they replace nearly all the riveting hammers previously used.

It is usual to find in the course of reconstruction that a number of ancillary services require to be improved. These may range from the provision of concrete floors in older buildings, new working facilities, or heating arrangements for sheds to the construction of roadways in the shipyard, the substitution of tyred vehicles for small locomotives and, if the yard is large, the introduction of a shipyard transport service to enable workers and executives to move quickly from one part of the yard to another.

II

The foregoing sketch may have given some idea of the vast scope of reorganisation which is needed to bring the majority of shipyards up-to-date from the inter-war period. There are few, if any, shipyards in this country which can claim to have brought themselves fully up-to-date in all respects, and the extent to which they have been able to do so has naturally varied for a number of reasons. Some shipyards received assistance with reorganisation from the Admiralty during the war, while others that were able to commence the reconstruction of their yards at an early date after the war were sometimes fortunate in securing investment licences, in having adequate financial means or in being able to sacrifice the completion of current ships to future demands; but no less they were quick to recognise that new equipment was required in order to bring down costs and produce modern ships. This view is not in doubt, and nearly all firms of standing in the industry have either modernised their yards or are carrying out radical alterations in order to bring production facilities up to date. Those companies starting late with their modernisation programmes may have gained something from those who led the way, and they may also be able to prepare for the succeeding stages of development which were less apparent even five years ago.

This is true, for example, of the need to provide berths to take super-tankers. When the first shipyards were reconstructed in the post-war period the modal size of tankers was about 18,000 d.w.t. and there were very few tankers of large size; it is now expected that tankers of 60,000 d.w.t. will be constructed in fair numbers and that there will be a demand for tankers of 100,000 d.w.t. There were probably only two shipyards in the country, that of Vickers-Armstrongs at Newcastle, and that of Harland & Wolff at Belfast, that could have built a 100,000 d.w.t. tanker in 1957 with their existing arrangements; and the larger shipyards have had to find ways and means to modify their yards in order to be able to build larger tankers. Major reconstruction schemes in hand in 1957 for a number of companies made provision for very large tankers. Those of Cammell Laird and Swan, Hunter & Wigham Richardson made provision for 100,000 d.w.t. tankers, while reconstruction by Fairfield, Lithgows and the Furness Co. was expected to fit them for 60,000 d.w.t. tankers with the possibility of greater capacity in the case of the Furness Co. at a later date. Other companies which had previously reorganised their yards were also preparing for large tankers. John Brown's, for example, decided to convert three smaller berths to two large ones and Hawthorn Leslie were also increasing the capacity of their berths.

A parallel movement was needed in the provision of dry docks and there have been a number constructed or put in hand in recent years. Between 1952 and 1958, however, only three new dry docks capable of taking 32,000 d.w.t. tankers were constructed in this country, and available dry docks were totally inadequate to take the largest size of tankers projected. The largest dry dock in London is only 750 ft. long and 110 ft. in breadth and might take a tanker of 50,000 d.w.t.; the largest available on the north-east coast area is 715 ft. long and 105 ft. wide; on the Clyde the largest is 660 ft. long and 85 ft. wide; Belfast is better provided with one of 886 ft. in length and 96 ft. wide; in Liverpool the largest dock is 1050 ft. in length and 120 ft. in breadth; the Port of Bristol owns a graving dock of 875 ft. in length and 100 ft. in width, and the Bailey Dock at Barry is 940 ft. in length by 86 ft. wide. But few of these are as large as is likely to be needed. The only dock in the country capable of taking a super-tanker at the present time is the King George V Dock at Southampton with a length of 1200 ft. and width of 135 ft., built for the 'Queens'. Since a 100,000 d.w.t. tanker has a length of 900 ft. and a beam of 132 ft., new dry docks are likely to be needed in all repairing centres and at the oil terminals. No less there is the problem of bringing existing docks fully up-to-date in the provision of all the facilities needed such as modern cranes, pure- and salt-water supplies, compressed air, canteens and wash-places, electric light and so on.

The reconstruction schemes so far undertaken by the various shipyards have cost large sums of money. One of the most important items included in the cost has been that of cranes. In the reorganisation, referred to above, of four berths of John Brown's shipyard to allow about 70 per cent welding and 30 per cent riveting to be carried out, the cost of installing the cranes accounted for over three-quarters of the total cost of £688,000 involved in that stage of reorganisation.

The cost of complete reorganisation of even a medium-sized shipyard is likely to involve the expenditure of at least one or two million pounds over a period of years. It may cost very much more if engine shops have to be extensively re-equipped as well as the shipyard, and if it is intended to extend facilities for repair and construct a large dry dock or docks £10 million may be spent in as many years. Large Dutch shipyards starting from almost total destruction have been spending something of the order of £1 million per annum, and Swedish yards have been spending only a little less. Cammell Laird's estimated that some £17 million would be needed in order to modernise their yards, increase their capacity and provide additional dry docks and repair facilities. It was originally hoped to carry this out in 8 years, but in 1958 it was announced that it would not be possible to proceed as quickly as had been hoped. This is by far the biggest scheme announced by British shipbuilders, but in 1957 Swan, Hunter & Wigham Richardson had capital commitments of the order of £2½ million and were likely to spend as much again before their plans would be completed. In total about £5 million per annum have been spent on gross investment in the shipbuilding and repairing industry since 1948 and about £1¼ million per annum by marine-engineering establishments. The rate of investment has been increasing and much larger sums are likely to be spent in the next few years if new plans are pushed ahead.

The justification for expenditure on this scale rests on the facts we have discussed above: a welded ship is more remunerative than a riveted one; shipyard efficiency can be increased by reorganisation, and larger tankers are proportionately less costly to build and operate than smaller ones. None of these facts is in doubt, yet it must be said that the capital expended in United Kingdom shipyards has not resulted in any indisputable rise in productivity, and its expenditure must be justified largely on the grounds that it has enabled better ships to be produced rather than that it has resulted in a reduction in real costs.

Unfortunately, little evidence is available as to the course of productivity in shipbuilding. It is possible to construct indices of the volume of production and employment in the shipbuilding and ship-repairing industries for the Census years of 1924, 1930 and 1935, but the indices of the volume of production rest on the revaluation of principal products at 1935 prices, and as such include both merchant and naval construction as well as repair and conversion work in various proportions. They do not, therefore, represent a satisfactory index of performance either of the output of the three major divisions of work or of the whole of the industry's output. The level of output in 1935 was, of course, much lower than that in either 1924 or 1930 and more heavily weighted with warship and repair work. It is likely, therefore, that a comparison of output at constant prices with employment tends to mask improvements in productivity between the earlier years and 1935. These reservations must be borne in mind in concluding from Table 16 that there is little evidence of any appreciable improvement in productivity in the inter-war period.

Table 16.—*Volume of shipbuilding output and manpower employed* (1924 = 100)

	Volume of production (output at 1935 prices)	Employment	Volume of production: employment
1924	100·0	100·0	100
1930	95·1	94·1	101
1935	58·4	57·8	101

It is difficult, if not impossible to link these figures to the post-war period. It may be estimated that the number of men employed on new merchant construction in the years 1936–9 averaged about 40,000[1] and that output averaged 850,000 g.r.t. per annum. In recent years average employment on new building must have been in the region of 65,000 men and output has averaged about 1,400,000 g.r.t. per annum. For what they are worth these figures do not indicate that there has been any marked improvement in productivity in new construction since before the war, but they cannot be taken very far because of changes in the proportions of various kinds of ships in the total and an increase in the amount of man-hours per ton of shipping needed in construction, because present-day ships are more complicated and better finished than those turned out before the war;[2] nor can the figures be taken to indicate that new methods of production have failed to increase output per man employed, for there is no means of comparing the comparative effort put into the work. Finally, it should be remembered that not all shipyards had reorganised their production methods in 1959 or re-equipped their yards.

Two calculations of the saving of manpower resulting from the reorganisation of individual shipyards for welded construction suggest, however, that considerable improvement could be made. Rannie's calculations, for example,

[1] See the graph of employment reproduced in the *Shipbuilding and Shipping Record*, 26 April 1945, p. 397, from a paper given by Sir Amos Ayre to the Institution of Naval Architects.

[2] It is estimated, for example, that the cost of building the 9,000 d.w.t. ship introduced in 1956 by *Fairplay* as the basis of their cost series in place of an earlier ship to a 1945 specification had the effect of increasing the cost by 7 per cent per ton owing to improvements to meet current trends and comply with regulations, for example, in new accommodation. (Information contained in a letter from the Editor.)

showed a reduction in the cost of construction and installation of welded and riveted bulkheads of 20 per cent. Three-quarters of the absolute reduction in costs, however, was accounted for by savings in the material necessary and only one-quarter by savings in wage costs. Wage costs were, however, reduced by about 28 per cent, in spite of the fact that wage-rates are somewhat higher for welders than for riveters. This, however, was at a comparatively early stage in the development of welding. The full benefit is reaped only after management and labour have got accustomed to the new way of working, and it has not been unusual to find in the first stages that welded construction is more expensive than riveted construction. In the view of Mr Hagan 8–10 years' gradual development of welded construction is necessary before management, draughtsmen and workers have sufficient experience for welding to be decisively less expensive than riveting. Figures quoted by Mr Hagan,[1] however, confirm that the saving in manpower may ultimately be considerable. In the particular instance quoted the number of tons of steel worked per man employed in the steelworking trades and in the shipwrights' department, including the mould loft, was 10·25 t. per year in 1937 (when abnormally heavy steel was worked) and 6·60 t. in 1938. In both these years construction was almost entirely riveted. In 1947, when all output was welded, output per man was 12·35 t. Output per man in 1947 reflected increased mechanisation as well as the use of welding. Such figures are, of course, extremely difficult to interpret, suggesting as they do that welding in conjunction with extensive reorganisation may have resulted in an improvement between 20 and 50 per cent. It is difficult to narrow this range with the object of giving a more precise assessment of productivity improvements resulting from the adoption of new methods, particularly as experience varies a good deal. Figures published by Mr Redshaw, for example, suggested an improvement in productivity in the steel trades of only 12 per cent.[2] On the other hand, inquiries from other shipbuilders suggest that in these trades output per man may have been increased by perhaps one-third following modernisation. This could be consistent with another estimate prepared by Dr J. Ramsay Gebbie,[3] suggesting that excluding establishment costs a welded ship could be produced at 13 per cent less cost in manpower in total than a comparable one of riveted construction.

It cannot be pretended that the present level of productivity in the industry is satisfactory or that it compares with the best that can be achieved abroad. Indeed, while productivity in this country has been standing still it has undoubtedly been improving overseas. It is important, therefore, briefly to look to the future and see what factors on the side of the organisation of production are likely to influence performance as technical methods change.

[1] 'The economic construction of moderate sized all-welded ships', *Welding Research*, vol. III, June 1949, no. 3.   [2] L. Redshaw, *loc. cit.*   [3] Ramsay Gebbie, *loc. cit.*

Perhaps the most important change that has been taking place on the organisational side is the increasing importance being assumed by the drawing office. More and more plans are required for the construction of a vessel. With prefabrication the various units must be planned to fit, and it is not possible to decide the place of such things as hatch openings on the vessel as construction proceeds; all details must be provided for in advance of erection if difficulties are to be avoided. But more important, the drawing office must relate design to the actual process of construction. Thus the drawings must provide for a balanced welding sequence to avoid distortion, for the use of standard plates wherever possible and for simple erection on the berth. Increasingly the whole business of production must be decided at the drawing office stage and not on the shop floor. This means that the drawing office must be familiar with the facilities of the shipyard and with the various problems met with in welded construction.

The drawing office is thus the key to future developments in shipbuilding techniques designed to reduce production costs, and it is progressively replacing the loft as controlling centre of production. In some Swedish and German yards, and more recently in some shipyards in this country, drawings have become the basis of an optical system of marking the shipyard plates. With this system plans of various plates or other components are prepared on special drawing paper to a scale of 1 : 10. They are then photographed and a photographic plate prepared. This is then inserted in a projector placed above a marking table housed in a darkened room or tent and the image of the markings on the original plan are cast on to the ship's plate to be marked. As each plate is marked it is sent on its way and a new plate is introduced into the tent.[1]

The system has not found favour in British shipyards for a variety of reasons. Its main advantage appears to have been that it enabled space to be saved which would otherwise have been needed for the mould loft, and in the case of the Stülcken shipyard in Germany, where the loft had been destroyed, it enabled rebuilding to be dispensed with and capital to be saved. There is probably some saving of labour in the marking of the plates, but this is of negligible importance when plates are to be welded and there is no need to mark individual rivet-holes. The importance of the method lies not in the improvements it has effected so much as in the fact that it prepared the way for the preparation of drawings of sufficient accuracy to make it possible to use them as the basis for cutting plates to shape by means of suitably controlled automatic machines. The Schichau Monopol process, developed in Germany, carries this into effect. In this process a photograph

[1] See the reprint of a paper by Johann Köhnenkamp from the *Proceedings of the German Naval Technical Society*, 1951. English translation reprinted by Ampower Corporation, New York.

I. John Brown's shipyard in 1899
(Ship in background believed to be *S.S. Friesland*)

II. John Brown's shipyard in 1913. (*Aquitania*)

III. John Brown's shipyard in 1956

of the plan of a plate is prepared and inserted in a machine which can follow the outline of the plan and burn the plate to the required shape. In 1957 the machine was in its infancy, but it was already on trial in some Continental shipyards and it is now in use in this country. There have also been important British developments in this field by Ferranti, which ultimately could offer the possibility of a direct link between the mathematical design of a vessel and the fabrication of its structural parts. A large computer-controlled oxy-acetylene cutting machine has been built by the British Oxygen Company in conjunction with Ferranti. It was estimated that the cost of preparing curvilinear plates might be reduced by this means from £5 a ton to as little as £3 a ton.[1] It remains to be seen whether it will prove worth while to develop machines of this kind for shipyard use, but the preliminary experience of Bartram's shipyard with the Schichau Monopol process suggests that it may pay to substitute capital for labour in order to be able to increase output per man or introduce unskilled labour.

A good deal of the preparation of plates and other structural parts for ships is likely to be done by semi-automatic means in the future, but it will still be necessary to exercise close control over shipyard operations. Indeed, control is every bit as important as having the right capital equipment. One shipyard in the Netherlands found, for example, that a simple system of control consisting of no more than a number of pieces of coloured cardboard representing the plates and sections under preparation in the sheds enabled a very large saving to be made in the labour required. The main reason for this was that it encouraged the management to work out labour requirements with care, to study them and to plan the work so that there was no rush to meet dates for launching the vessels with a consequent waste of manpower. It was thought that this had improved production output by about a third.

III

The basis of good organisation can be set down in a few words: it is to work out the best methods of doing the job, to set the right norms and to see that they are kept to. But the organisational problem is immense and calls for a wide experience of production methods both within shipbuilding and preferably outside the industry as well. The reorganisation of a shipyard with the many problems associated with it may often exceed the resources of its existing staff, burdened as they are with the day-to-day effort of administration. It is becoming increasingly common in shipyards to call in consultants to assist with reorganisation. This practice is not confined to the weaker firms in the industry; rather the reverse is true. Some of the most efficient

---

[1] *Investors Chronicle*, 7 November 1958, p. 401.

shipbuilding companies in the world make a practice of calling in consultants from time to time in order to get a fresh look at their arrangements and very often the view of another industry. There are, of course, limits to what can be achieved in this way. On occasion the improvement effected may, however, be considerable: one of the smaller British yards noted for tackling unusual jobs was work-studied, and as a result there was an improvement of productivity over-all of 40 per cent; in many departments the improvement was greater than this and in one department output was boosted by 70 per cent.[1] This, no doubt, was an extreme example of successful reorganisation, but 'It is not unreasonable to suggest that British shipyard production could be increased by 15–20 per cent . . . by intensifying the production effort on modern lines of control and by seeking more automatic aid for the present well-tried methods of welded prefabrication . . . in the United Kingdom the outstanding fact is the lack of experienced managerial personnel to undertake the onerous tasks of either organising new departments or reorganising the old ones.'[2]

If there were unanimity in this view it is possible that greater efforts would be made to recruit additional managers to shipbuilding. There is, of course, always a danger that management will become top-heavy, but it may be noted that in Sweden, where the most efficient shipyards in the world are to be found, the ratio of staff to operatives is very high, and it is not unusual to find one staff to every five operators. In this country the ratio is less than one to ten.

In the past the industry has tended to rely on managers trained within the industry, and the view is frequently held that it is only by serving as an apprentice in the yard and by learning shipbuilding from the bottom up that good managers are made. It is said, in particular, that only in this way will future shipbuilding managers learn to understand their labour force. So firmly are these views held that there is resistance to recruiting managers from outside the industry, although the introduction of new blood from other industries has obvious advantages in promoting interchange of ideas and the adoption of practices which have proved their worth in other connections.

The recruitment of a large number of managers from within the ranks of shipbuilding is not without its advantages provided that they can be given a wide enough training, be kept up-to-date with modern practice and given a high level of technical knowledge where this is needed. The works-trained manager often does not show the reluctance to undertake the junior tasks of management as part of his training and promotion, which is the usual

[1] *Shipbuilding and Shipping Record*, 19 July 1956.
[2] *Journal of Commerce, Shipbuilding and Engineering Edition*, 7 March 1957.

complaint against the university graduate by shipyards in the United Kingdom and on the Continent; and if, as often happens, he has missed the net of advanced technical education there is likely to be every readiness on the part of the firm employing him to provide for his education by sandwich courses or other means. In this way he will not find himself at the age of 27 taking up a job of work for the first time, as so often happens to the highly educated Continental graduate; nor will he feel that a shipyard offers little scope for his activities and gravitate to the research associations, Lloyd's Register or similar bodies, as is frequently the lot of the university-trained naval architect or engineer. It is true also that in the individual shipyard it is important that the technically trained manager should not be too technically minded; often his main task is to co-ordinate production, and a knowledge of workshop practice, of costs and psychology may be no less important than scientific or technical knowledge. But there is still some research to be carried out in the individual firm; it has not all been transferred to research institutions or professional bodies, and there is vast scope for the application of laboratory results to the practical design of ships, which requires considerable training if it is to be carried out with success. Still more if shipbuilding included more graduates in its ranks instead of the comparatively few (no more than 0·4 per cent of the total employed according to a Report on Scientific and Engineering Manpower in Great Britain[1]) in the industry, it would probably become more aware of the contribution that can be made by the university-trained mind in industry if it is properly directed and catered for.

While it is natural to think first of graduates trained in engineering, science or technology, there can be no doubt that the arts man has often the mental equipment and outlook which can contribute greatly to industrial administration. There are a great many necessary functions in shipbuilding that do not require technical qualification so much as the ability to formulate a problem and seek solutions to it. But whether the shipbuilding industry views the graduate with favour or disfavour it will lose some of the most capable recruits to industry if in an age in which more and more able men will be given a university education it does not look to the universities for its potential managers.

The future of any industry depends on its ability to recruit young managers of high quality on an adequate scale. There have been some signs of uneasiness on this score in shipbuilding. 'Materially Britain's shipyards are being brought up in the best way of the best manners of intensive planned control methods, but there is a great risk that there will not be enough trained men to go round to keep the "pot" of planned production continuously on the simmer. . . . The technological staffs of the shipyards also need to be

[1] H.M.S.O., 1956.

131

raised to a higher status at least comparable with their opposite numbers in the new oil and atomic industries which use comparable amounts of the planned production of welded prefabrication.'[1]

It has also been suggested in some quarters that one of the reasons for difficulty in getting recruits of good quality is that technical staff appear to be underpaid in relation to other industries. 'There is a strong feeling—and perhaps with some justification—that they order these things better abroad. Young men with technical knowledge start on a better footing and have greater opportunities for genuine promotion.'[2] It is difficult to judge how far this is true. There does not seem to be any great difference in the treatment or the salary of graduates starting work in the United Kingdom or in the northern Continental shipbuilding centres; as a general rule a newly qualified graduate is worth about as much as a skilled worker; but it may be true that the prospects for graduates are better. The shipbuilding industry, however, cannot afford to take chances; too much depends on getting the right type of managers for recruitment to be neglected.

[1] *Journal of Commerce, Shipbuilding and Engineering Edition.* 1 August 1957.
[2] *Shipbuilding and Shipping Record*, 17 February 1955, p. 217.

CHAPTER 11

Industrial Organisation

I

It is clear from the foregoing that vast technical changes have been taking place in every aspect of shipbuilding, and that the future of the industry will depend on its ability both to develop new designs of ships and engines and to apply what is known to actual construction. It is still possible for individual shipbuilding companies to pioneer both research and innovation. In the United Kingdom it is possible to point, for example, to the Denny Brown Stabiliser, to the steam catapult for aircraft carriers and to other technical devices as examples of the innovations that can be made by individual companies. In marine engineering there is also scope for the pioneer work of the large builders, both in improving their existing designs and developing new ones; and in research into hydrodynamics no fewer than three testing tanks are owned by firms in the industry, that of Denny's built in 1882, that of Vickers-Armstrongs' at St Albans and that of John Brown's. Some aspects of research, however, require industrial or national endeavour. National facilities have been available for model testing and research for a great many years in addition to those owned by shipbuilders. Froude was given a grant by the Admiralty to build a tank completed in 1871, and this was replaced by a new tank at Haslar in 1886. The first tank operated by the National Physical Laboratory was opened in 1911; additional facilities were provided in 1931–2 and in 1936, and a new tank is expected to be working in 1959.

At the end of the war two new research bodies were set up: the Parsons and Marine Engineering Turbine Research and Development Association (Pametrada) and the British Shipbuilding Research Association (B.S.R.A.). The former was an extension of the arrangement made by a limited number of shipbuilders before the war with the Parsons Marine Steam Turbine Co. to develop steam-turbine engines. The work of Pametrada has continued the development of turbine engines, both steam turbine and gas turbine, on a co-operative basis, and it is in a position both to provide designs for special engines required by shipbuilders and allow the use of existing designs under licence abroad as well as in the United Kingdom.

B.S.R.A. is a joint government and industrial venture. It was established in 1944 and is financed partly by grants from the Department of Scientific and Industrial Research and partly from sums raised by the industry. The activities of B.S.R.A. have been complementary to those carried out by Pametrada, and apart from marine-turbine research nearly every other subject of shipbuilding research, including diesel engines, is covered. Much of the work of the Association is organisational in character, and it is concerned with drawing up research programmes of a kind designed to meet the needs of the industry and arranging for experimental investigations to be put in hand in various laboratories, including those of shipyards throughout the country. The research supervised by the Association has been of a varied character, ranging from tank testing in connection with hydrodynamic studies to research into ship structures, and from engines and boilers to materials testing. One of the functions of the B.S.R.A. is to act as an intelligence section surveying technical developments throughout the world and bringing them to the attention of British industry. It can be claimed that the United Kingdom was the first country to provide for shipbuilding research by institutional arrangements on the scale of those discussed above, but other countries have now also established co-operative research organisations similar to B.S.R.A. These include Belgium, France, Holland, Japan, Norway and Sweden; in Germany the Hamburg Ship Research Institute is being strengthened to enable it to undertake similar work, while the Society of Naval Architects and Marine Engineers in New York has established a series of committees to encourage and sponsor research.

Shipbuilding, of course, benefits from research done by a variety of other organisations outside shipbuilding, such as the British Iron and Steel Research Association, the British Welding Research Association, the British Ceramic Research Association and the British Cast Iron Research Association as well as others in this country. Lloyd's Register also conducts important researches, mainly concerned with strength, and the Admiralty, researches directed to naval requirements. One major undertaking of wide general interest undertaken by the Admiralty was the testing of two similar ships, one of riveted and one of welded construction, in order to appraise the comparative performance of the two methods of construction. Another interesting development was the assistance given by the Admiralty to the P. & O. Co. in the design of machinery for a new passenger liner. This arose indirectly as a result of an Admiralty decision in 1943 to set up a Committee to investigate steam-turbine machinery for warships. Certain land engine-producing companies were included on the Committee which decided to seek alternatives to the traditional Parsons machinery for installation in the Daring Class ship then projected; the new designs included one by British Thompson Houston as well as one by Pametrada. In 1945 Yarrow's installed an English Electric Turbine in one of the Daring ships, and as a result close collaboration was developed between the firms. A year or two later the Admiralty arranged with Yarrow's to run a joint research unit to carry out fundamental investigations into all aspects of naval engineering design, and there is now a staff of some 60 design engineers and assistants under the management of Yarrow but supported by Admiralty finance.[1]

For research into atomic power the shipbuilding industry has naturally been dependent to a large extent on the work done by the Atomic Energy Authority, which organised in 1956 a conference at which shipbuilders were able to discuss the state of knowledge at the time and anticipated developments. Since then, as we have seen, the Admiralty has been able to encourage and co-ordinate the preparation by a number of companies of reactor designs suitable for merchant ship propulsion, and, of course, to set in hand a parallel naval programme.[2]

Industrial Research was organised at the end of the war in order to give the United Kingdom industry an opportunity to make good the lead in the design of ships which had been lost in the inter-war period, particularly in the field of engine development. It is difficult to judge whether in the space of the ten years it has been running it has compared well with Continental progress. Doubt as to this has been cast recently by a report of the Advisory Council on Scientific Policy. The report stated that in some industries, including the shipbuilding industry, 'the research effort falls considerably short of the best standards in other countries'. Against this it has been claimed that, measured either in terms of the scientific manpower employed or by the expenditure incurred, none of the organisations similar to B.S.R.A. set up overseas is in any way comparable with the British effort, and that research undertaken directly by firms themselves in Britain exceeds that of any other shipbuilding country.[3] Quantity, of course, is no substitute for quality, but it is not for a layman to judge a technical issue beyond saying that British research is well regarded on the Continent.

II

Joint research organisations are only one of the ways in which firms must co-operate if they are to achieve the best results. It is a well-known piece of economic argument that there are both advantages and disadvantages in increasing the size of the firm, and shipbuilding is no exception. For some purposes the existing size of individual companies may seem to be optimum, for other purposes it frequently happens that it is necessary to co-operate with other firms in order to co-ordinate policies and actions and benefit from the economies of scale. Two industrial bodies exist for this purpose: the

---

[1] See *Shipbuilding and Shipping Record*, 8 August 1957, p. 173.

[2] See *The Financial Times*, 25 September 1956, for an account of the organisation of research into the design of atomic-powered ships.

[3] This was stated by Mr J. A. Milne, President of the Shipbuilding Conference. See the *Glasgow Herald*, 1 November 1957.

Shipbuilding Employers' Federation and the Shipbuilding Conference. The former association is the older one and it came into being in 1899. The Shipbuilding Conference is much more recent, being formed in 1928. The foundation of the Conference was the fruit of adversity and the need that was felt to deal with the 'rather uncoordinated state of the industry on the commercial and economic side . . . which in the grievous economic circumstances of the time, both existing and imminent, threatened grave danger to units and sections of the shipbuilding trade; and indeed to the industry as a whole'.[1]

Such a task is, of course, one of great difficulty, and it is doubtful if an industrial association can be expected to carry it through in all its implications. It is unusual for an employers' association to be given any control over the internal functioning of firms, and the Shipbuilding Conference has been no exception. The shipbuilding companies were certainly not prepared in the inter-war period to subordinate their individualism to the implementation of any industrial policy. The formation of National Shipbuilders' Security, the company established by the industry in the 1930's to reduce capacity, was no exception. It had no powers of compulsion to buy up redundant shipyards, but acted on a voluntary basis, offering compensation in return for the sterilisation of the shipyards. Much of what it accomplished would in any case have taken place by natural attrition, though it probably succeeded in bringing it about in a shorter time. While this course of action was valuable, it was not possible to follow it up with what was needed at least as much; the concentration of production in the most efficient yards, the re-equipment of a limited number of yards to bring production costs down, and increased specialisation. The Shipbuilding Conference was not constituted to carry out action of this kind, and even if it had been, the conditions of the 1930's were scarcely propitious for new departures. The most that could be expected of it was to put before the members of the industry what was needed to re-establish it on a sound basis; to suggest how production methods could be improved in individual cases; to outline schemes for greater specialisation in the industry; and for the rest to do what it could to improve prices by seeking agreements amongst shipbuilders nationally and internationally. This it probably did to the best of its ability, and it cannot be blamed if at the end of the 1930's, or for that matter ten years after the Second World War, the basic structure of the firms in the industry was as uncoordinated as ever and there was insufficient specialisation and too few 'runs' of similar ships from individual shipyards for efficient production—a point to which we return later on.

[1] Sir Maurice Denny, 'Amos Ayre, the man and his work', *Proceedings of the Institution of Naval Architects*, 1955.

In certain directions, however, it has been possible to co-ordinate activities on the commercial and economic side, though not always with the results desired. The steel shortage is a case in point. Since this involved government decisions on export policy and government assistance in other ways, it would be natural for the Shipbuilding Conference to act as a negotiator for the industry, putting its needs to the authorities. In the same way the Shipbuilding Conference can represent to government departments industrial views on such matters as the rate of expansion of capacity that is desirable, the placing of naval orders, and foreign subsidies —in short, deal with matters of general and industrial concern.

Another important function of the Shipbuilding Conference is that of making sure that its actions and those of its members are properly understood by the public and policy-makers. In order to do this it has to be properly informed, and for this purpose it collects a variety of information from its members, which also assists in the formation of industrial policy.

All these functions involve very little interference with the normal working of a shipyard, and since the interests of the individual firms in the industry in relation to outside interests may often coincide, they are not likely to give rise to contention. It is not part of the activities of the Shipbuilding Conference as it is organised and functioning at the present time to influence the placing of orders or the prices charged by shipbuilders.

Apart from industrial co-operation between firms through the Shipbuilding Conference there is probably a great need for co-operation between individual firms in order to increase productivity. There is no doubt that there are very wide differences in the comparative experiences of different firms, and there is considerable room for an exchange of ideas and practices between the efficient and inefficient of a more thoroughgoing kind than results from informal contact between fellow-managers, in order to bring productivity in the least efficient firms nearer to the standards of the best. It is a curious fact that the flow of technical information within the industry is generally untrammelled, while economic data is generally closely guarded. In fact, a free flow of technical information is essential if products are to be sold. It is quite impossible to sell an engine without giving some fairly precise data of its performance; the makers of a new type of steel will wish to make clear and perhaps extol its virtues; naval architects will not fail to draw attention to the economies that their vessels promise; and there is a tradition of not concealing technical information which will in any case eventually be revealed in service.

While, however, technical information is common property—at least as soon as a product enters the market—economic information is jealously guarded for fear of giving an advantage to a competitor by enabling him to estimate the production costs of his rivals and cut his prices below theirs at some opportune moment. It is unfortunate that this is so, for nothing is more likely to promote efficiency than a rigorous comparison of costs, and this is not likely to be made perforce in the market, by one or another competitor finding that he is outpriced, so long as demand is high enough to give employment to all shipyards, good and bad alike.

It might seem, therefore, in the circumstances, that it would be at least as useful to assemble a body of economic knowledge to do with shipyard practice and production costs on which all firms in the industry could draw, as to pool resources for the purposes of technical research. The idea has been tried on occasion between firms in the same locality in the hope that an interchange of knowledge between them would be to their common advantage. But the difficulty of such an informal arrangement is that the exchange of ideas is likely, unless the firms concerned are very evenly balanced, to be all one way, and on this basis breakdown is inevitable after a period of time. An industrial service, on the other hand, although it would still be largely of benefit to the lame ducks in the industry, would make it possible for even the most efficient firms to have some chance of benefiting from their rival's experience. In this connection the finding of a study of welding practice in three shipyards is apposite. It was found that each firm could increase productivity by 70 per cent by adopting the best practice in the three firms for each factor influencing productivity. And it is significant perhaps that the differences in productivity measured for the shipyards was due to design not labour.[1]

It may be argued that such an exchange of ideas and information is becoming increasingly unnecessary, as it is more usual for shipyards to employ outside consultants from time to time to check on their performance and to seek to improve it. Eventually this may be true, but not all firms employ industrial consultants, and although the consultants themselves are able to bring to bear in shipbuilding problems a wide knowledge of practices and developments in other industries, there may still be a case for setting up a specialist body within the industry, concentrating on the production problems that are peculiar to it. Not least of the advantages of such an arrangement would be that it would be possible to develop a higher level of management within the industry and provide both opportunities of promotion for outstanding shipyard production engineers and a training ground for those wishing to improve their managerial knowledge and fit themselves for higher posts in the industry.

[1] See the *Journal of Commerce, Shipbuilding Engineering Edition*, 1 August 1957.

III

We turn now to what is essentially another aspect of industrial organisation: that of encouraging standardisation of ships and components in order to facilitate longer runs in shipyards and marine-engineering shops, so as to reduce production costs.

There have always been divergent views on the merits and demerits of standardisation and the possibilities of channeling orders within the industry to specialist producers. It is often assumed that ships cannot be standardised without impairing their usefulness to owners, and that in any case they are required in insufficient numbers for standardisation to have much effect on production costs. This view cannot be accepted without question. It is at the most a half-truth, and detailed examination is needed to unravel the advantages to be gained from either complete standardisation of certain types of ships, or from standardisation of certain features about them, including standardisation of components. Moreover the comparative advantages of specialisation are not invariable over time, or independent of the state of development of the shipbuilding industry in particular countries, or of the production techniques which are employed, or of the organisation of the shipping and shipbuilding industries, so that the rejection of specialisation at one epoch is not conclusive evidence that it will not be advantageous at other times.

Historically, standardisation in shipbuilding has found favour in three different sets of circumstances: during war, at the start of a shipyard's operation and in the exploitation of an unusually successful design. The First World War saw the first attempt in this country to turn virtually the whole of the shipbuilding industry over to the production of a limited number of standard types of ship. The arguments advanced in favour of standardisation stemmed largely from wartime needs: the necessity to subordinate commercial considerations to war requirements, the need for economy by eliminating inessential details, and the desirability of ensuring interchangeability of parts and machinery so that, for example, the completion of a hull would not be delayed for want of an engine of some particular type when another of different pattern was unused for want of a suitable hull. These arguments would not necessarily hold with the same force in peacetime, when commercial consideration would be uppermost and production programmes more easily integrated. But other arguments were equally applicable in peace and war though not necessarily as acceptable. It is, for example, important at all times to minimise the change of rolls required at the steelworks in order to produce suitable sections as cheaply as possible, and it is desirable to make the best possible use of unskilled labour; similarly, simplification of constructional details required in wartime to harness construc-

139

tional engineering firms to shipbuilding production is no less important in other circumstances.

From the start, however, the proposal to construct standard ships evoked a great deal of opposition. It was argued, for example, that it was often better to allow builders to work on plans and specifications with which they were familiar rather than to enforce a rigid scheme of universal standardisation, and in the minds of many standardisation must have been inseparable from the establishment of national shipyards, and the proposal to use prisoners-of-war on new ship construction at a time when available materials were inadequate to keep the existing shipyards at work. It was also felt that a limited number of types of vessels could not meet even wartime needs and did not provide for the post-war requirements of the liner companies. The five types of ocean-going vessels originally approved had to be expanded to a dozen, including two which had originally been laid down without authorisation to meet the requirements of the liner companies.[1]

Even as a means to increasing shipyard output in wartime standard ships were not an unqualified success, though more experience with them might have brought their advantages greater to the fore. The experiment of producing standard ships was not repeated in the Second World War. It was decided 'not to standardise hulls in the national sense but rather to standardise their machinery and equipment. The vessel usually selected as the prototype in a particular yard was in many cases one that was in current production and of structural design most economically and expeditiously applicable to the plant.'[2] This decision made it possible to combine a degree of standardisation of the ships produced in individual yards with sufficient flexibility in the prototypes selected to meet the production facilities and experience of those yards, and at the same time to provide some necessary variety in output; but greater standardisation might have been desirable if it had not been for the complementary programmes of the United States.

In the United States different considerations were involved. It was not so much a question of using existing establishments to the best advantage as of creating new shipyards and building a type of ship which could be easily produced by newly trained labour and a limited number of design and managerial staffs experienced in shipbuilding. This alone would have dictated concentration on a limited number of types of ships in the initial stage. But, in addition, radically different methods of shipbuilding were possible in the greenfield sites of the shipyards. There was space for the organisation of a production flow and the opportunity to use fully machines

[1] For an account of standard ship production see C. E. Fayle, *The War and The Shipping Industry*, chap. xv.

[2] Sir Amos Ayre, paper read before the Institution of Naval Architects, April 1945. Note that partly as a consequence of better information and production programmes Sir Amos Ayre claimed that productivity had been 50–75 per cent higher than in 1917.

designed for particular circumstances. If it was right to permit variety in United Kingdom output it was no less correct to insist on standardisation in United States conditions.

It is, however, a far step to argue from wartime experience when ships are needed in great numbers with the minimum of delay, when the service expected from shipping itself is standardised in large measure, and when gross tons of shipping outweigh commercial considerations of many kinds, that what applies in war should also apply in peace. The experience of producing standard ships during two world wars has done little to encourage the production of standard ships in this country.

Why is this? The most ready explanation is, of course, that the advantages of having individually designed ships specially suited for their trades outweigh any economies which result from the production of ships of basically standard design. Yet the answer is not really so simple as this statement might imply, for surprisingly little is known about the extent to which costs can be reduced by systematic concentration on the production of standard vessels and little more about the extent of the gains from using vessels of individual design, and the issue is obscured by many factors of an institutional character; nor should it be forgotten that the general-purpose ship has a value simply because it is not specialised in operation. 'In times of growing specialisation, in tramp shipping as elsewhere, the Liberty (ship) has turned out to be an inspired compromise, not competitive with the specialised ship in any of the specialist trades, perhaps, but able to take a slice of any trade if the market is above a certain level.'[1]

The view remains, however, that there is no market for standard ships, and shipbuilders are quick to point out that no two ships they build are ever exactly alike. Sister ships are so named because they have a family resemblance, not because they are identical in all respects. It is true, of course, that a year's output of ships will include many different kinds ranging from large passenger liners and giant tankers to small coasters, and that a variety of highly specialised vessels such as ore-carriers, refrigerated vessels and train ferries will be ordered in their ones and twos. But for a number of types of vessels with common characteristics the distinction between them is one of degree and not one of kind. 'It cannot be denied . . . that there are so many tramps of certain deadweights as to very closely approximate standardisation . . . a type (of vessel) proves satisfactory in service and may be repeated in groups as many as 15 or 20 times with only minor and detail changes.'[2] In more recent years it is also evident that tramps have tended to cluster about characteristic sizes and speeds; 48 produced in the years 1952 and 1953

---

[1] *The Times*, 11 December 1957.
[2] E. H. Rigg, paper read at the Thirtieth General Meeting of the Society of Naval Architects and Marine Engineers, New York, November 1922.

were within the range 7500–11,500 d.w.t. and half of these were between 9500 and 10,500 d.w.t., while characteristic speeds were 13–14 knots.[1]

The growing tanker market provides a similar illustration of the existence of characteristic sizes. Of some 180 tankers constructed in the years 1952–4 over 70 per cent were between 10,000 and 15,000 g.r.t. and most of these were about 12,000 g.r.t. Although the size of tankers most in demand has continued to move upwards in post-war years it is to be expected that there will continue to be substantial numbers grouped about characteristic tonnages, and it is of interest that a move is now on foot to standardise the 65,000 d.w.t. tankers that are expected to be built in fair quantities.

Similarities are evident in other types of vessels. A statistical investigation by Mr H. H. Hagan showed that with five or six standard designs the requirements of most trawler owners could be fulfilled.[2] In an apparently much less promising field, that of ore-carriers where the largest ships are the most economical but size is limited by the capacity of the individual ports used for loading or unloading ore, it has been shown that United Kingdom requirements can be met by three sizes capable of transporting 8000, 14,000 and 20,000 t. of ore respectively.[3]

The above analysis suggests that in spite of the variety of ships needed to carry the world's traffic of passengers, liquid and dry cargoes between innumerable ports and in greatly varying conditions, a substantial block of the demand for ships could be met by standard designs varied perhaps in detail and modified intermittently on a more comprehensive scale to take account of new developments. It seems useful, therefore, to consider whether production costs can be reduced when individual shipyards concentrate their output on standard types of vessels.

The economies which can be achieved within a single shipyard from producing a succession of essentially similar vessels have not been discussed in a sufficiently quantitative manner by those most familiar with shipyard operation to enable any definitive opinion to be formed as to the merits of batch production. In the absence of detailed information the most that can be done is to indicate the nature of the economies which might be expected to follow from batch production.

Some economy should result in the preparation of plans and specifications. The cost of designing a vessel probably amounts to only about 1 or 2 per cent of the total cost of construction, and the scope for saving in this direction is therefore limited. But drawing-office costs have been rising over the past years as a result of continuing improvements in ships' designs, changes in

[1] See an article by Mr. James Lenaghan in the *Shipbuilding and Shipping Record*, 1955, p. 11.
[2] *Shipbuilding and Shipping Record*, 'Observations on trawler design', 1 August 1935, p. 119.
[3] See Sir Charles Goodeve and J. S. Terrington, 'Iron ore-carriers for Britain', *The Shipping World*, 19 October 1955, p. 376.

the Ministry of Transport's and Lloyd's Register's rules and the greater use of welding. Moreover, more work is being carried out in drawing offices as an aid to better planning and production control. In consequence, the preparation of plans is likely to be a more costly item in the future and sufficiently integrated with production control to make the savings from using one set of plans for two or more vessels worth while.

Apart from this, intangible advantages arise from the concentration of design work on a limited number of vessels. It allows technical staffs in the shipyards to devote more time to the improvement of designs and, equally important, building techniques. Generally the technical resources of the industry are less thinly spread and there is better opportunity to use extensively designs of proved merit.

We may note as an illustration of the economies possible in design work that the plans of ships building for the United States Maritime Commission during the war were prepared by one firm in New York which distributed them to 70 shipyards. In addition, in this case it was also possible to undertake centralised ordering of materials.[1]

In the processing of hull material considerable savings can be achieved through batch production, though the economies may be less for welded ships than those of riveted construction. Calculations made in 1918 suggested that with a multiple punch and plates of uniform size 'it would be possible to pass through such a machine 100 plates per day, but if the same plates were marked from a loft template, and manhandled at the punching machine 40–50 plates per week would admittedly be an excellent output'.[2] One reason for the high productivity of labour in Swedish shipyards given by a United Kingdom shipbuilder was that the production of similar vessels made it possible to process large numbers of plates, perhaps as many as 2000, of the same dimensions and markings.

The elimination of rivet-holes in most plates with the adoption of welding has reduced the amount of marking and processing required, and as a result it may be less difficult to process plates individually. The possibility in the future of processing plates of individual dimensions semi-automatically by means of machines easily set to perform a variety of operations might at first sight appear to reduce the advantage of organised repetition work. But this does not necessarily appear to be the case. The Schichau Monopol process, for example, described above (Chapter 10) is specifically designed to deal with similar parts and shapes as a group, and standardisation is desirable in order to facilitate this.

---

[1] Russian plans before the war also were prepared in a central office at Leningrad (see *Shipbuilding and Shipping Record*, 3 March 1938, p. 274.)

[2] Mr John Craig, 'Effects of war on merchant shipbuilding'; paper given before the Institution of Engineers and Shipbuilders in Scotland, March 1918.

The same end of simplifying production methods while producing plates for a variety of types of vessels could be attained if standard plate sizes were introduced and used in most types of vessels. If this were done the difference in template work between the standard ship and the 'tailor-made' standard-plate ship would be substantially reduced. We shall return to a more general consideration of this kind of approach at a later stage.

Much of what has been said applies to the preparation of frames. The number of similar dimensions in a ship requiring a similar degree of curvature is not large, but if the number could be increased by producing standard ships a greater element of repetition could be introduced and more mechanical means of processing used than at present appear possible.[1]

Thus standardisation and production methods interplay the one with the other, and it sometimes happens that the degree of standardisation possible dictates the most economical method of production. For instance, small quantities of bollards are best fabricated by welding and shaping steel plates; if, however, large quantities are required, for example, for a number of tankers, the cheapest method is to cast them from a single mould.

In the assembly, as opposed to the fabrication, of the members of a ship's steel structure, batch production offers considerable advantages. It is common experience that each ship presents particular problems, and that difficulties arising in the construction of a single ship can be anticipated and eliminated when the design is repeated. Unless plans are exceptionally detailed a number of constructional problems must be solved in course of erection, and in most cases alternative procedures come to light which can be adopted with advantage in the construction of subsequent ships of the same design. Amongst shipbuilders there is general agreement that repetition serves to eliminate many of the teething troubles experienced in the 'one-off' job.

Concentration on the construction of similar ships would make possible a production layout specially designed for the work in hand. It should help also in organising a smooth flow of production and in balancing the capacity needed in one section against that in another and so permit a fuller utilisation of available machines.

So far we have been concerned with the possibility of increasing the efficiency of hull production with the adoption of batch output. It is no less important to consider the effect on machinery installation and the provision of auxiliary fittings.

There is a very great variety in the types of engines fitted to merchant ships. Steam-reciprocating, steam-turbine, gas-turbine, free-piston and diesel engines are alternative methods of propulsion, each more suited than the others for particular applications; and further developments are likely to

---

[1] Straight-framed ships have been advocated as a means to simplifying production, but although examples of such ships have been constructed they have not proved their worth.

add atomic-power plants to this range. We have seen that marine-engine works attached to shipbuilding establishments tend to build most of the engines required for the parent yard. In consequence a vast number of types are produced, and there are great divergencies in size and detail of engines of even the same type. There is thus little opportunity for specialisation in the average engine works, and a number of different engines tend to be under construction at the same time.

In practice shipowners find that they can always insist on having the kind of machinery they require, and there is full play for every individual preference of marine engineers attached to the various shipowning companies. It may be doubted if so wide a choice of propelling machinery is really advantageous. In 1923 a questionnaire sent by the North-east Coast Institution of Engineers and Shipbuilders to leading shipbuilding and marine-engineering firms asked what engines would be specified for a motorship of given dimensions. Each of the firms considered that it produced a suitable engine, though all the engines specified differed greatly in design. Possibly one was more suitable than the rest though all may have been equally effective, but it would be reasonable to suppose that the range of types offered could have been drastically reduced while still giving shipowners satisfactory engines.

That from the production point of view there is advantage in limiting the types of engines in production has long been recognised; 'carrying on the manufacture of diesel engines on a sound commercial basis means standardisation, owing to the considerable outlay on patterns, jigs and special tools required for the different types'.[1] Deutsche Werft concentrated on the production of Burmeister & Wain engines when they commenced building and, using only two sizes of cylinder diameter in units of six or eight cylinders, they were able to power all manner of types and sizes of vessels ranging from 4000 to 21,000 d.w.t. The influence of this practice on the competitive position was readily traced.[2]

In spite of the widely held belief that standardisation of engines leads to reductions in costs and the added advantage from the shipowner's point of view that servicing and the supply of spare parts is facilitated, it has proved difficult to put into practice. Amongst shipbuilders it is feared that efforts to standardise machinery might stultify development and impede the search for economies in fuel consumption. There is no real reason, however, why both should not be compatible.

These general observations lead to no certain conclusions as to the extent of the economies in production costs which arise from batch production of

---

[1] Mr H. H. Blake, paper read before the Institution of Engineers and Shipbuilders in Scotland, February 1925.
[2] *Shipbuilding and Shipping Record*, 12 March 1925, p. 304.

engines and hulls. They do not enable us to estimate, for instance, how much more cheaply a dozen ships of the same design could be produced than a number of different ships of the same value to shipowners.

The United States' experience of producing large numbers of standard ships during the Second World War throws very little light on the question. It was carried out in conditions far removed from those encountered by shipowners and shipbuilders in peacetime, and it appeared to be much more extravagant in the use of direct labour than could be justified in normal conditions. This was to be expected. The emphasis in United States production was not on obtaining the highest output per head, but on speed of construction and maximum output. Such conditions are not conducive to high labour productivity, even when production is highly standardised and divided into simple repetitive operations. Nor was the labour force highly skilled or experienced. Thus it is not surprising that the number of man-hours required to construct a ship in the United States was often 50–100 per cent greater than the number required in the United Kingdom for a similar vessel. But there were great variations in the performance of the individual shipyards, and the United States Maritime Commission felt able to claim, though on rather uncertain evidence, that the best shipyards were exceeding the British standard of performance.[1]

In default of recorded experimental evidence, it is instructive to sound the opinion of shipbuilders on the matter. For practical men this would seem both a simple and conclusive means of putting the virtues of standardisation to the test, but few shipbuilders have had the opportunity of construtcing a series of vessels of essentially similar design in a shipyard laid out and organised for repetition production, and their views founded on their own experience must consequently be treated with reserve. From the result of a score or so inquiries at European shipyards it may be said that at those yards producing a variety of different types of ships the opinion is usually held that sister ships can generally be produced 1 or 2 per cent more cheaply than the first ship off the scrieve, largely because the cost of preparing the plans and templates can be spread over a larger number of vessels; occasionally it may be conceded that if a longer run could be secured it might be possible to save up to 5 per cent; but it is only at the few yards producing standard ships in quantities up to a score that there has been opportunity to appreciate the full savings resulting from batch production; and here it may be said that on the basis of experience it has been found that costs fall fairly steadily as each successive ship is built, and that for numbers approaching a score shipyard costs may be cut progressively by as much as $\frac{3}{4}$ per cent a ship. It is scarcely surprising that in such yards the non-standard ship is accepted

---

[1] See the *Shipbuilding and Shipping Record*, 5 August 1942, p. 133.

only with reluctance and at a penal price, or refused for fear of upsetting the production flow so long as standard ships are in demand.

Much the same can be said about the cost of producing engines. It has been found in practice by those who have observed it that concentrating on the production of no more than one or two sizes of diesel engine of the same type, and incorporating the same cylinders and components wherever possible, reduces costs in no uncertain fashion. Specialisation in this way can reduce the cost of producing a run of half a dozen engines by 30 per cent, and in a long run half the man-hours needed for the 'one-off' engine can be saved.

If we are right in thinking that there is a market for standard ships and in concluding that concentration on the production of such ships would reduce costs very considerably, we are led to inquire why batch production is not the characteristic feature of United Kingdom production today. Part of the explanation is historical; we have already seen that the experience of producing standard ships during the war left no lasting impressions on the shipping industry of the virtue of such arrangements. Lord Inchcape, for example, held that under ordinary conditions there was nothing to recommend the mass production of ships: '. . . in laying down the plans of a ship once the broad principles of her constitution . . . have been conceded there the similarity of ship to ship, or at least type to type, must terminate and the region be entered in which lies the widest imaginable diversity of detail and assembly, and from which have been produced the hundred and one excellences of the shipbuilder's art and craft which are afloat today'.[1]

Lord Inchcape's views, however, were not applicable to all shipowners. We have already seen that there was in fact a market for standard ships, which shipbuilders had been able to exploit from time to time with outstanding success. The Doxford turret ships introduced in 1893 combined a novel system of construction with the advantage of a high carrying capacity which was so successful that 178 steamers of the type were ordered between 1893 and 1911, including 30 for the Clan Line. The Northumberland Shipbuilding Co. (no longer in operation) concentrated from the start on building to standard design in order to cut costs; 45 basically similar vessels admitting of some variation in the details of deck assembly and machinery were produced in its first nine years of operation before it was necessary to amend the original design.

The impact of wartime experience affected the plans of newly created shipyards even if it found little reflection in the attitude of shipowners. The Burntisland shipyard established by the Ayre brothers was designed for the production of economy ships, not necessarily the same in detail but sufficiently similar to reap some economies of repetition. Likewise the Furness yard, which commenced its work as an assembly yard, built strongly on the

---

[1] Lord Inchcape, *Brassey's Naval and Shipping Annual*, 1923, p. 229.

principle that economy comes from concentration on a limited range of vessels. The Blythswood Shipbuilding Co. also built largely one type of tanker in their early days, and Lord Pirrie, extending the interests of Harland & Wolff on the Clyde, had in mind the advantages of concentrating on a limited range of output.

As the shipbuilding and shipowning industries are organised at present batch production can occur in two ways. Shipyards can produce their own standard ships either as a speculative venture or to order; and shipowners can concentrate on a standard design for the various units in their fleet. Thus, as we have seen, it is not uncommon for shipbuilders to produce a series of similar vessels finding their market amongst a number of shipowners; and shipowners may also order a number of sister ships from the same shipbuilder. Small shipowners are not, of course, able to put this into effect on any appreciable scale, but the larger companies, particularly the larger tanker companies, who place orders for numbers of ships at one time, often have their own designs and stick to them closely.

This could be a useful contribution towards greater standardisation, but as we shall see it has not prevented a large number of similar orders being widely scattered amongst shipbuilders. Nor has there been any universal tendency amongst shipbuilders to concentrate their attention on producing a narrow range of vessels. As we have seen in Chapter 2 most shipbuilding firms are comparatively unspecialised, and if their facilities are adequate they tend to build a large range of vessels. The reason for this must largely be sought in the uncertain nature of the market which the shipbuilding industry serves. In the most depressed years of the 1930's, the demand for new tonnage was no greater than would have been necessary to occupy fully two of the largest shipyards, and it was too small and too diversified to permit batch production of similar vessels. The ability of shipyards to secure orders depended on their being able to supply the type of tonnage in demand; in this respect specialisation was disadvantageous, for it automatically excluded some yards from tendering for orders for vessels which they were not equipped to produce at a time when there was little chance of securing sufficient orders to realise the economies of batch production.

The very variable nature of the market, both in amount of tonnage demanded and even more in the kind of tonnage demanded, is a considerable deterrent to narrow specialisation. There may be violent swings in demand between tanker and non-tanker construction, between passenger and non-passenger vessels; between specialised ore-carriers, banana-carriers and vessels for bulk transport of miscellaneous cargoes; and not least between naval and merchant work. This is one reason why shipbuilders are reluctant to concentrate too much on producing a limited range of vessels for which demand may be fickle and why those shipbuilders who tend towards concentration on a limited range of vessels are often small or of medium size.

When, in contrast to the early years of the 1930's, demand is high and a sufficient number of similar vessels are ordered to make possible greater specialisation and even batch production, the factor of uncertainty as to the future composition of shipbuilding orders still operates and makes many shipbuilders reluctant to narrow their order books. More important than this, however, is the fact that when demand is high many shipbuilders are booked for years ahead, and for a shipowner to place an order for several sister vessels with one shipbuilder would be to delay delivery of some of the vessels included in the batch. Speedier delivery is obtained by spreading orders amongst a number of shipbuilders, so that the turn of one vessel will not wait on the completion of another. When freights are high and shipbuilding costs rising continuously delivery delays are more important than the prospect of saving 5 per cent or even 10 per cent of construction costs through batch production.

The most propitious conditions for batch production arise when demand is high enough to include a sufficient number of similar vessels without causing serious delays in delivery. In the less depressed years of the 1930's the dispersion of similar tonnage amongst shipbuilders appears to have been less marked than it is at present. The year 1938, for example, was notable for the number of sister ships launched from the same shipyards; in the years 1936–8 Doxford's achieved a remarkable run of economy ships of similar design and size; and 1930 was notable for the launching of two batches of six and four sister ships respectively from the Belfast shipyards of Harland & Wolff. Again in 1928 and 1929, the production of a series of vessels by several shipyards was much in evidence, and to a lesser extent in other years of comparative prosperity in the 1920's.

In post-war years batch production appears to have been much less marked than would be possible with a rearrangement of orders. For example, 25 ore-carriers on order in January 1956 were shared between ten firms, some of whom were fortunate to secure orders for two or three sister ships. Included in the total were nine ships of about 14,000 d.w.t. spread between four shipbuilders. At the same date Shell Tankers had on order 22 tankers spread amongst ten producers of which 15 of 18,000 d.w.t. were placed in four yards. A casual glance at the post-war programme of a typical tramp shipyard revealed that it covered a range of ships with six different over-all dimensions. But the difference in tonnage was only 1000 d.w.t. and the difference in speeds a little over 1 knot. 'It might have been more advantageous and in the interests of both parties if the different owners concerned had mutually agreed on the acceptance of the standard ship produced in that particular yard.'[1]

[1] Mr James Lenaghan, *loc. cit.*

In present circumstances it is difficult to see how the distribution of orders can be improved without some changes in the organisation of shipbuilding and shipowning. It is the character of the market more than any other single factor which weights the scales against further specialisation and standardisation in shipbuilding. There is no question that it is more economical to build similar ships today than it was half a century ago when skilled labour was abundant and ships were largely hand-assembled on the stocks. The prospects of getting a sufficiency of orders are at least as good. Yet it appears unlikely that further specialisation and standardisation will result unless shipowners and shipbuilders concert their efforts to concentrate demand and production on as limited a range of types and sizes of vessels as is consistent with the real differences in the requirements of various trades.

The production of standard ships on a national basis might be one way of achieving this end, but it would be a very drastic and more far-reaching solution than would be justified by the importance of the issue. An alternative approach is through the voluntary co-ordination of the type and flow of orders between shipowners and shipbuilders.

This would not be easy to achieve. Shipowners will not be readily convinced that greater standardisation is possible or desirable. Shipowners are individualists, and it is difficult for shipbuilders to persuade long-established owners to accept standard ships except as a means to speedier delivery. Some Continental shipbuilders have been able to use this argument to push owners into accepting standard ships during recent years, and the provision of credit purchases has sometimes been tied up with the acceptance of a standard ship. 'Principal Swedish shipyards developed a number of "standard" designs of dry-cargo and tanker ships which they reckoned would suit a large number of clients, and they were able to offer them at prices which took full advantage of the economies involved in this "standardisation". These designs cover a wide range of ships, including tankers of 18,000 to 32,000 tons, combined oil- and ore-carriers (which are a special feature of Swedish shipping) bulk carriers, and fast cargo liners of up to 20 knots speed.'[1] But shipbuilders in this country prefer for the most part to maintain their reputation of being ready to produce exactly what the owner requires and to leave the owner to determine whether he is prepared to pay the price for an individual design.

Nevertheless, an owner's choice is not always certain to be wise in the event, and it is restricted by the fact that few shipyards at the present time are producing sufficiently long runs of similar vessels to offer a standard ship at the lowest price that could be achieved. There can be little doubt

[1] Peter Duff, 'Britain's shipbuilding rivals', *The Financial Times*, 25 April 1957.

that owners are inclined to over-emphasise the advantages of the special ship. The readiness with which the Liberty or Victory vessels are bought at inflated prices when freights are high illustrates that standard ships command a wide market. No less, there is clearly no need for an infinite selection of vessels to fit the needs of every trade. The larger tanker owners have found that there is no need, for example, for an infinite variation in the size of the tankers they require, although that is what now occurs. 'The *Hemisinus* is a general-purpose tanker designed for product distribution. Our main British competitor is also building ships very similar; they are 5 feet longer, 2 feet wider and 2 feet deeper, but the speed and the power are about the same. Similarily a large independent company, newly entering the field has ordered ships 3 feet longer, 2 feet wider and the same depth; again speed and power are about the same.'[1] In January 1956 Shell Tankers had on order a large number of vessels of 18,000 and 31,000 d.w.t. British Tankers had on order 8 tankers of 32,000 d.w.t. and 10 of 34,500 d.w.t. No doubt there were many differences in design other than that of size between these blocks of orders. But it is possible that with greater co-ordination the different sizes of tankers required by these two companies could have been brought together and a design evolved acceptable to both companies and to other tanker operators on the same routes. Given the trend to larger tankers, it can be said that the choice of building a tanker of 31,000 d.w.t. or one of 32,000 d.w.t. is probably of minor importance compared with the choice of building tankers of about this size or ones of vastly greater capacity. Since tankers on the British Register are owned by relatively few independent companies, and since many of those owned by other tanker operators are on charter to the major oil companies, any measures to standardise on a limited number of types would have a good chance of success.

The opportunity to standardise other types of vessels is no doubt less. It is unlikely that large passenger liners will ever be standardised. There has, however, always been a market 'for a large number of ships almost exactly alike' which could be extended if the few owners of dry-cargo vessels considered it worth while to examine their designs with a view to greater standardisation. The standards accepted by the few dominant companies would find a ready application amongst other owners, particularly if greater application of design facilities to a limited number of types of vessels resulted in marked technical improvement.

But if shipowners consider that they have little to gain and much to lose by concentrating their demands on standard ships, it would still be possible to increase productive efficiency if orders for individual ships could be sifted so as to permit longer runs on ships of basically similar type. This could not,

[1] J. H. Kirby, a director of Shell Tankers, *Journal of Commerce and Shipbuilding*, 21 February 1957.

however, occur without some interference with normal marketing arrangements either by the establishment of some central agency governing the placing of orders amongst shipyards or by outright amalgamation. The Dutch dredger builders have not hesitated to co-ordinate their activities and although the main reason for this may have been to subdue competition it has led to a degree of integration in their building programmes.

The production of standard ships or greater emphasis on specialist construction by individual shipbuilders might lead to amalgamation for another reason: if the maximum economies are to be obtained from batch production the output of individual shipyards will need to be large. An output of 100,000 g.r.t. or more a year might be typical of a shipyard concentrating on the production of batches of standard vessels. The output of the Furness shipyard in this country or the Eriksberg shipyard in Sweden, both of which tend to concentrate on the production of standard types, has been of this order of magnitude.

No one familiar with the character and organisation of shipbuilding and shipowning can be at all optimistic about the possibility of some central organisation attempting to rationalise the type and flow of orders to shipbuilders in the interests of achieving longer runs. Concentration of the production of similar vessels in yards specially adapted for the purpose is likely to continue to be more a matter of market accident than industrial policy. There may, however, still be scope for the standardisation of specifications, components and materials in the interests of cutting costs. The number of similar ships which can be produced at any one time is likely to be small, but component parts such as steel sections, pipes and valves of various dimensions, for example, are used in profusion in shipbuilding and often in other industries as well.

The advantages and possibilities of standardising components have long been recognised. In 1917 the North-east Coast Institution of Engineers and Shipbuilders set up a special committee to prepare standards for all eligible details of ships' equipment, and it was able to recommend standards for bollards, fairleads, mooring pipes and hawse pipes.[1] The work was taken up by the British Engineering Standards Association, which prepared standard specifications for materials used in components, for the design of components and for tolerances. A wide range of items was considered including rigging screws and gear, pipes and pipe flanges, cocks and valves, condenser tubes and ferrules, shafting and propeller bosses, bilge, ballast and ship side fittings.[2] Progress towards standardisation was entirely voluntary; in 1927 the necessary steps to bring it to fruition had still to be taken;[3] and, frustrated

[1] *Shipbuilding and Shipping Record*, 10 June 1920, p.771.
[2] *Ibid.* October 1921, p. 465.
[3] *Ibid.* June 1927, p. 757.

by the British love of individuality, standardisation of such things as port-holes, fairleads and rails was still an open issue in 1944.[1]

Perhaps the major difficulty in securing standardisation of small components is the large number of shipowners, shipbuilders and component producers who need to agree on standards and push their adoption. The saving in every individual case is likely to be small and intangible, yet savings for the industry as a whole could well be considerable. And not least important is the greater ease of servicing and repairing ships in which standard components predominate. Moreover, when demand is high, standardisation enables the production of bought-in components to be increased more readily and the shipyards to be supplied without delay.

The main object of standardising components is to reduce their cost of production. But at the same time standardisation of components can lead the way to simpler types of construction and increase the amount of repetition work involved in vessels of different size and even character. In an article in the *Glasgow Herald Trade Review* 1918, Mr (later Sir) Amos Ayre (then jointly directing the activities of the Burntisland shipyard) expressed the opinion that standard frames and rivet spacings, standard lengths and widths of plate and a uniform depth of double bottom could be used to build ships ranging from 4000 to 6000 d.w.t., 'By careful and efficient organisation and a reasonably large demand for standard structural parts so produced—which would approach the system of manufacture obtaining in other industries—the cost and rate of production should become more economical.' It may still be 'to the advantage of British firms individually or in combination, to consider closely the benefits to be obtained by standardising structural parts, particularly in connection with the system of fabrication from establishments where a speciality in a single or a few parts can be made'. It should not be forgotten that it was by standardisation, not by producing luxury liners, that the United Kingdom's reputation was made.

'The advantage British shipbuilders have over others is that they can build according to standard type. It may be taken for granted that 90 per cent of the ships built consist of the average freight steamers and freight passenger steamers and belong to one or other of these types. The great demand in this country for this class of ship and the desire for such from shipowners abroad, and upon whom British shipbuilders impose their different types, has enabled the latter to push standardisation of type to an extremely advantageous degree. This means particularly the wholesale manufacture of individual parts of ships and the consequent economy for both the shipbuilder and the supplier of machinery. . . . A shipbuilding yard with stocks for, say, three ships with another ready for installation of machinery lying in the water . . . can from this cause alone, undersell any foreign competitors from by 5 per cent to 10 per cent.'[2]

That was in 1913.

[1] *Ibid.* September 1955 p. 291.   [2] *Ibid.* 24 April 1913, p. 139.

CHAPTER 12

Labour

I

We turn now to the examination of another aspect of industrial organisation, that of labour, covered so far as the employers are concerned by the Shipbuilding Employers' Federation, which deals exclusively with labour questions of an industrial kind. The Shipbuilding Employers' Federation is a voluntary organisation representing about 95 per cent of the shipbuilding and ship-repairing firms in the country. It does not represent the boat builders who have an organisation of their own, nor does it include Admiralty establishments, but the attitude of the Federation is bound to set the tune for the whole industry. The headquarters of the Federation is in London; there are, however, local organisations in each main shipbuilding centre dealing with issues which can be settled on the spot by negotiation between employers and unions.

On the union side the organisational structure is complex. Many and diverse crafts are employed in shipbuilding as well as semi-skilled and unskilled workers, and this has tended to dominate union organisation. An idea of the proportions employed in the various trades can be obtained from Table 17 which brings out the importance of the black-squad workers —platers, welders, riveters, caulkers and burners.

On the Clyde there are sixteen unions—seventeen if draughtsmen are included. The United Society of Boilermakers, Shipbuilders and Structural Workers, with its numerous sections of black-squad workers, and the Ship Constructors' and Shipwrights' Association represent the major shipbuilding crafts. The latter, which includes drillers within its orbit, can be regarded as almost exclusively a shipbuilding union, in contrast to the finishing trades whose services are predominantly in demand elsewhere. These other crafts are represented by a number of unions ranging from the Amalgamated Society of Woodworkers to the Plumbing Trades Union, while semi-skilled and unskilled workers fall into the orbit of the 'General' unions. The main shipbuilding unions are affiliated to the Confederation of Shipbuilding and Engineering Unions for a number of purposes including national negotiations, though within the Confederation there are separate shipbuilding and engineering committees to deal with negotiations in the two industries. In its present form, the Confederation is of recent origin (it was not until 1946 that a way was found to balance the voting strength and representation of the Amalgamated Engineering Union in the Confederation to the satisfaction of all parties), although its predecessor, the Federation of Engineering and Shipbuilding Trades, was founded in 1890 and after considerable vicissitudes was reorganised in 1926.

The historical changes in union organisation and the continued independence of the constituent unions of the Confederation in many matters have resulted in an untidy system of interrelations both between the unions themselves and between the unions and the employers. Not all unions are parties to the same agreements with the employers. The shipbuilding procedure

Table 17.—*Shipyard trades and unskilled workers on the Clyde*
(*percentage of total shipyard employment*)

Skilled	
Platers	10
Welders	7
Riveters	2
Caulkers	2
Burners	1
Shipwrights	5
Drillers	1½
Joiners	6
Electricians	3
Plumbers	3
Engineers	2
Sheet-iron workers	2
Blacksmiths	½
	45
Semi-skilled	5
Unskilled	50
	100

governing negotiations between the Employers' Federation and eleven of the shipyard unions on general wage fluctuations was laid down by agreement in 1913, but some shipbuilding unions, of which the most important was the Boilermakers' Society, were not a party to that agreement. Similarly, the boilermakers are not a party to the agreement reached between the Employers' Federation and the Confederation of Unions, dated February 1943, which provides that the Confederation will act only in connection with general questions raised locally which are common to affiliated unions which are parties to the Provisions for Avoiding Disputes; and the boilermakers did not join the National Agreement of 1912 providing for the settlement of demarcation questions. Since the Boilermakers' Society is the largest union in shipbuilding it happens that negotiations are dominated by the boiler-makers, although they proceed under arrangements to which the boilermakers are not parties. It is fortunate in the absence of written agreements between the employers and the boilermakers that the written procedures laid down between the employers and other unions are the accepted procedure for negotiations.

The relations between employers and unions take place at various levels. An industrial claim may be initiated by the Confederation of Unions, but local claims for higher wages or better conditions and demarcation disputes, which are always of local origin, are discussed first by the local branches of the unions concerned with the employers and only if there is failure to agree does the matter get discussed between the Unions' national representatives matched by the Employers' Federation at the same level. While this has its administrative conveniences, it means in practice that national wage agree-ments tend to be imposed on local arrangements, and that national agree-ments are variously interpreted in relation to branch conditions. We shall return to a discussion of the consequences of interaction between national and local agreements.

Labour relations in the shipbuilding industry can only be described as troublesome, and there can be no doubt that they occupy far too much time and thought of management which could be better devoted to other matters. The incidence of strikes is not a full indication of the extent of the difficulties that are experienced in the industry, but they indicate that shipbuilding has a worse record than any other industry in the country. Figures in the *International Labour Review* for July 1955 showed that between 1947 and 1954, in comparison with other countries, the United Kingdom had very few days lost by strikes per thousand persons engaged in mining, manu-facturing, construction and transport. The number of days lost in 1950–6 in the shipbuilding and ship-repairing industry, however, averaged 970 per 1000 persons against only 84 in engineering (excluding vehicle) manu-facture. The Court of Inquiry into the wages dispute between employers and unions in 1957[1] took the view that this pointed to the conclusion that the procedure for the settlement of disputes in shipbuilding and ship-repairing was not satisfactory or not operated in a proper manner. This may be true, and we have already briefly indicated some complexities of the matter, but it is not the whole story.

There are a number of factors—some mainly of historical importance—

[1] *Report of a Court of Inquiry into the wages dispute between . . . the Shipbuilding Employers' Federation and . . . the Confederation of Shipbuilding and Engineering Unions*, Cmd, 160.

which have contributed to difficulties in labour relations, and it may be desirable to list them in passing. Relatively to foreign countries the industry has been steadily losing ground over the years. In the inter-war period its output fell not only relatively to other countries but absolutely, and the years of depression were both severe and at times prolonged as the industry lost the commanding position it had built up in the nineteenth century and was increasingly subjected to the buffetings of growing industrialisation in other countries, and to foreign competition. The force of the ups and downs in the output of the industry and the years of depression fell on a shipbuilding community highly concentrated geographically, not just in the depressed areas, but in streets and closely knit communities within those areas. Unemployment in a widely scattered industry is a far less potent influence on industrial attitudes than when it is concentrated on a narrow river bank, and it is likely to be less serious also when there are opportunities to find employment in other industries within the reach of labour and craft mobility. The instability experienced by the industry did not affect a labour force of casual skills and accomplishments but one predominantly highly trained, time-served and craft-differentiated to an unusual degree, and it is not surprising that it aggravated the problem of craft demarcation, which is a device to protect sectional interests.

There have been nearly 20 years of full employment in shipbuilding since the depression ended and more than 10 years of peacetime working. Yet the memories of the thirties, though they can be fresh in the minds of only a few workers in the industry, are not easily extinguished and tend to be preserved from generation to generation by word of mouth. As one young shipbuilding manager put it, 'When I started my apprenticeship I had not even heard of the depression. But after the first week at work I knew all about it, about the dole years, making meals out of bones, and all the rest of it.' It is in this way that a feeling of insecurity continues to be a factor making for disturbed labour relations.

II

Traditionally shipbuilding workers have been highly mobile, and a high degree of labour turnover is still characteristic of the employment of certain trades in shipbuilding for which demand is irregular even in the largest shipyards. In 1955, for example, a large number of men had to be paid off in Harland & Wolff's Belfast yard because a break in the construction of passenger liners meant that there was no work for them to do.

A detailed study of labour turnover in one shipyard during 1952 has been made by Mr D. J. Robertson.[1] His statistical investigations showed that there

---

[1] *Scottish Journal of Political Economy*, March 1954.

were marked differences between the maximum and minimum employment during the year in the numbers employed in all trades in the shipyard. Turnover was greatest for the finishing trades (joiners, electricians, plumbers, sheet-iron workers), and with the exception of shipwrights much lower for metalworking trades engaged in fabricating the hull. Turnover of the semi-skilled group of redleaders, cranemen and stagers was also comparatively low.

In general, high turnover was associated with variation in total employment, indicating that an important cause of turnover was the varying demand for certain kinds of labour and that it was not just, as may be the case for 'helpers', due primarily to high voluntary turnover.

Table 18.—*Labour turnover in a shipyard in* 1952

Occupation	Variations in employment in 1952 as percentage of average		Annual average of weekly turnover (%)
	Maximum	Minimum	
Joiners	130	84	51
Electricians	123	74	60
Plumbers	109	84	48
Sheet-iron workers	125	83	49
Welders	113	83	32
Shipwrights	111	91	56
Smiths and Riveters	112	84	17
Platers	106	93	30
Other skilled trades	117	86	26
Redleaders, Cranemen and Stagers	109	89	23
Platers' helpers	111	91	28
Unskilled	105	92	39*
Boys and Apprentices	110	83	26*

Source: D. J. Robertson, *loc. cit.* p. 23. For further details and statistical explanations see the article.

* May be on a slightly different basis from other figures.

The variations in employment in the various trades during the year reflect in the main the changing labour requirements as a ship is under construction. The sequence of construction is planning, hull fabrication and finishing. By the time the finishing trades are required the bulk of the vessel has been completed, and it is desirable to proceed with its completion as quickly as possible in order to put the ship into service. Large numbers of joiners, electricians and so on are required, therefore, for a comparatively short period of time. In a medium shipyard with perhaps five or fewer occupied berths, it is unlikely that the run-down of employment in the ship will correspond fully with the build-up of finishing trades on the next most complete vessel, and there will be a gap when the labour force will have to be reduced well below average requirements. The greater the amount of finishing work involved in individual vessels the more serious is this gap likely to be.

Labour turnover is likely to be at its greatest when a shipyard is catering intermittently for passenger liners or other work requiring a high finish or specialised equipment in unusual quantity. It will tend to be smaller when the work of the shipyard can be easily balanced between the various skills required, when the output of the yard is large and, of course, when the flow of orders is both adequate fully to employ the yard and enable it to pick those orders which are most appropriate to its programme and its labour force. Labour requirements may also be balanced in some cases by regulating the amount of subcontracting to outside firms. A considerable amount of finishing is capable of being put out to subcontract, including, for example, plumbing, refrigerating equipment and furnishing.

Although no figures are available it seems likely that the incidence of labour turnover varies considerably from shipyard to shipyard, being least when there is a degree of geographical isolation and greatest when several firms are crowded together. From the shipyards' point of view the drawback of labour turnover rests in the difficulty of maintaining an attached labour force, a better team spirit and higher productivity. But, at the same time, stability may also be desired in order to give a greater opportunity to do more for the men by establishing a nucleus qualifying for staff status. There can be no doubt also that, since labour turnover is not confined within the shipbuilding industry but extends to the loss of men to other industries without any corresponding intake, training costs are increased.

It is the constant complaint of shipyards which run training schools for apprentices that they have to train far more than are required to meet their own needs, for the well-trained journeyman is in demand both in neighbouring shipyards and in other industries outside the industry. It seems that there is a steady loss of skilled men from the shipyards to other occupations. The boilermakers appear to countenance a ratio of one apprentice to every five journeymen, and some other unions a ratio of one to three, which, if it were fully taken up, would refurnish the labour force every 25 or 15 years, with a 5-year period of training, against a working life of nearly 50 years. But it is doubtful if, in practice, wastage is more than made good. The loss is not confined to the finishing trades, where a movement between shipbuilding and other industries is most to be expected, but includes many of the shipyard trades—the workers employed in the black squads.

Mr Robertson's figures throw some light on the interchange of personnel between shipbuilding and other industries. Two samples of workers employed by a shipbuilding firm taken for 1952 and 1953 showed that about one-third of the labour force of welders, shipwrights,[1] smiths, riveters and platers had been recruited from other industries. The definitions used, however, were very narrow, and some of the outside firms from which the members of the black squads were recruited must have been closely connected with the shipbuilding industry, and there can be no doubt that many of the men must have been returning to their original occupation of shipbuilding. Nevertheless, the fact remains that black-squad workers, and particularly welders, interchanged employment with other industries not at all closely connected with shipbuilding, including the construction of oil refineries. And it may, perhaps, be concluded on the basis of Mr Robertson's figures that so long as employment remains high in industries situated in the shipbuilding areas there will be a reasonable chance of shipbuilding workers finding employment outside shipbuilding, should the demand for ships fail.

III

Few issues have attracted more attention in shipbuilding than that of demarcation. This can be described as the insistence of certain trades that they, and they only, should carry out various tasks to the exclusion of all others who might be competent to do them.

The historical origins of the demarcation problem can be traced to a change in labour requirements as ships built in iron and steel began to replace ships built of wood. The shipwrights, who had been the most important trade in shipbuilding, were woodworkers and, apart from those employed in the naval dockyards and some others employed in the less important centres of shipbuilding, they did not take over the fashioning of iron and steel. There does not appear to have been any question of demarcation amongst shipwrights at this time, but the issue was not unknown between other woodworking trades. A document drawn up in 1737 sets out a schedule of the several sorts of work belonging to each of the companies of house carpenters and joiners. This attitude may have had some influence in conditioning shipwrights to their own trade, but there is a vast difference between the techniques of wood- and metalworking, and it must have seemed both sensible and natural to leave metalworking to boilermakers, smiths and engine builders, whose trade it was. In any case the introduction of metal proceeded gradually, and in the early stage of this development there was no sudden substitution of boilermakers for shipwrights; when iron was used in composite vessels, wood attached to iron frames was used as the outer skin

---

[1] It is interesting that shipwrights, who are first and foremost shipyard workers, were no exception to the general conclusions.

of the vessel and the shipwrights continued to predominate in construction. Moreover, there were new opportunities for them as the total construction of ships increased rapidly. As iron and steel ships became more common the relative importance of the shipwrights declined, but they were not deposed from the shipyards, first, because they continued to work in wood and to carry out such tasks as laying the decks, constructing wooden bulkheads and so on, and secondly because they were 'shipbuilders' concerned with drawing out full-scale plans of the ship on the loft floor, preparing templates, marking off, fairing, erecting the steel members of the ship and preparing the ship for launching.

Demarcation once established tends to spread, and what was once primarily an issue between the shipwrights and the boilermakers is liable today to affect any or all of the many trades engaged in shipbuilding. There is room, of course, for a general division between the functions of shipwrights and those of other trades, and the existence of various trades is itself a recognition that some degree of specialisation has emerged. But the division between trades does not mean that there is no overlapping in their functions or attainments, and it is this which is liable to give rise to difficulty in practice. Each trade regards certain functions as being its particular right, but there are a great variety of tasks which can readily be undertaken by one or more of the fifty or so separate occupations which are recognised and which may devolve on one trade or another, partly as a matter of custom. Custom is not, however, inviolate, nor is it of much avail if constructional methods are changing or if one material replaces another in some use.

There is no limit to the variety of issues which may be raised as a demarcation dispute. Disputes may arise between plumbers, engineers and coppersmiths as to who should install particular kinds of piping, between shipwrights and joiners as to who should carry out particular operations, between joiners and upholsterers as to who should lay linoleum on particular types of surfaces, between woodworkers, sheet-metal workers and shipwrights as to who should drill holes in aluminium sheet and secure it to wood,[1] and in innumerable other ways.

The number of disputes arising is less than might be expected in the circumstances. In an area such as the Clyde, perhaps two dozen may arise in the course of a year. Most of these disputes, however, can be disposed of quickly on the spot. A system of arbitration dating from 1912, to which the boilermakers, however, are not parties, provides a procedure for dealing with demarcation disputes. In the event of a dispute the yard manager is entitled to give an interim decision as to which trade should carry out a particular task without prejudice to further negotiation. If this is accepted

---

[1] At Cammell Laird's 460 joiners went on strike for six months in 1955–6 over this issue.

by both parties to the dispute that is an end of the matter, but if one or both parties object to the decision the matter is taken from yard level to district level. The dispute is then examined further between representatives of the trades involved in the dispute (there may be more than two trades involved) with representatives of the employers in the district, but not of the yard concerned, participating. An agreement reached at this stage is binding for a year, and after that 3 months' notice must be given before it can be rescinded.

Since the Boilermakers' Society does not subscribe to the agreement[1] and even, as part of its bargaining attitude, refuses to acknowledge that there can be any question of demarcation between the boilermakers and other trades and unions, the procedure may have to be varied when disputes involve this Society. It is often possible for negotiations to pursue a similar course with the boilermakers sitting in a separate room rather than around the same table. Mr Hill, the Secretary of the Boilermakers, has been at pains to point out that in demarcation disputes the employers have in effect the casting vote; disputing unions each have three votes, and since these are almost bound to be cast on opposite sides, the three votes of the employers' representatives, even though they may be divided amongst the unions, must decide the issue. There is not, however, always uniformity in the system of negotiations adopted by the various branches of the Boilermakers' Society. At the one extreme the boilermakers may insist on settling a dispute directly with the opposing union (all too often the shipwrights), but in at least one district the boilermakers and the shipwrights have agreed to work together the 1912 procedure, and this is all to the good.

Considering the thorny nature of demarcation problems, the frequency with which they arise and inter-union rivalries involved, it can be said that the procedure for dealing with demarcation disputes works fairly well. That is not to say, however, that it is operated as effectively as it ought to be or that it would not have been better if the Boilermakers' Society had acknowledged its industrial responsibilities in the matter by formally adhering to the 1912 agreement.[2] And it must be recognised that the procedure adopted is a system of dealing with disputes as they arise, not a means to prevent disputes arising, except in so far as negotiation gradually results in the building of a system of case law widely accepted by the different shipyard trades. In settling demarcation disputes little attention is likely to be paid to which trade is best suited to the work in question, partly because both trades are likely to be able to carry it out in most instances, or to whether demarcation is really necessary. When some new issue is raised the ultimate decision may be a compromise in which work is shared between trades or started by one

---

[1] The shipwrights gave notice that they wished to withdraw from the agreement in 1958, presumably to be on a more equal footing with the boilermakers.

[2] See the *Report of the* 1957 *Court of Inquiry, op. cit.*

and finished by another. More often, the basis for decision is likely to be that of precedent, reference being made to what the practice has been in the yard in which the dispute has arisen, or in other yards where similar difficulties have been met. Sometimes the interpretation of written agreements previously entered into will be in question; sometimes the difficulty will bear little resemblance to other cases that have arisen. But the agreements reached are essentially local in application; it is a question of shipyard practice rather than of district practice and even less of national practice. Thus there is no reason to expect uniformity in demarcation decisions and different practices are followed in different yards.

It is important to emphasise that demarcation disputes are disputes between trades as to who shall carry out some operation; the disputes are not between management and labour. Management, however, cannot dissociate itself from the various issues raised, though it will not wish to become involved as a protagonist, for a dispute may threaten the whole system of yard organisation and production planning carefully built up over the years to meet modern conditions. But it will often feel powerless to influence the ultimate settlement in one direction or another for few managements would dare to reject a demarcation decision, once arrived at, on the ground that it did not fit in with yard practice, actual or intended, even if they were not already bound by the accepted procedure; and in all but a few key instances it is of greater importance to prevent a stoppage than press for what on paper seems to be the ideal solution. As a result efficiency is bound to suffer in a number of ways.

One consequence of demarcation is that shipyard labour cannot readily be diverted from one task to another. As we have indicated demarcation disputes arise because in a number of cases such a transfer is technically feasible, but with rigid demarcation practices management is prevented from taking advantage of interchangeability. An illustration occurred when an attempt in John Brown's shipyard to employ temporarily redundant riveters in the plating shed in 1956 largely failed because the platers were not prepared to have them as assistants.[1] Riveting is now largely superseded by welding, but some riveters must be retained in order to carry out the small amount of riveting that remains in new construction and to cater for repair work.[2] If they are to be retained on the establishment of one firm other work will have to be found for them when little or no riveting is being carried out. The alternative is for them to move from firm to firm following whatever work is available, or even in the last resort if work cannot be found to accept unemployment.

---

[1] For two versions of this episode see the evidence given to the 1957 Court of Inquiry.

[2] For new construction the percentage of riveters amongst the black squad has fallen from 30–40 per cent to 1 per cent and the percentage of welders increased from about 1 per cent to 20–25 per cent.

British shipbuilders frequently contrast the inflexibility of their labour forces with those of Continental countries. In Dutch shipyards, for example, there would be no obstacle to Dutch workers transferring from any occupations in which there was insufficient work available to other occupations for which there was a demand, and provided the workers had the requisite skill there would be no objection to woodworkers working metal or vice versa. The extent of interchangeability possible on technical grounds of skills and accomplishments is probably quite great. In the metalworking trades, for example, the basic training undergone in apprenticeship is practically the same for all trades; it is only at a late stage in training that specialisation is followed. Thus the simpler operations carried out by the various trades could probably be carried out by any one of them without much difficulty.

On occasions, there would be a considerable saving in construction costs if one trade were permitted to perform operations outside its demarcated function. In the fitting of a portlight, for example, a succession of trades are required to carry out a task which could equally well be carried out by one skilled man. A shipwright is required to mark the position for the light, a burner to cut the opening, a caulker to dress the opening, a driller to drill and fit the frame, a brass finisher to fit the hinged glass frame, a driller to fit the deadlight, and finally a joiner or a driller to fit the deadlight hook to the linings of the steel deck-head.[1] In the fixing of a door-stop a similar sequence of tradesmen is required; a joiner is needed to mark off the position of the stop and a driller to drill the hole and they are followed by a caulker, a mechanic to fit the bolt and a painter to touch up the job. In repair work, the removal of a forced draught fan on a T 2 tanker requires a plater to open up the air casings, fitters to break the couplings and draw the fan runner, fitters' labourers to lift the motor and electricians to deal with the motor when it comes out. Yet the whole operation could be equally well done by an electrician. In all these instances the various foremen of the trades concerned will be in the offing, summoning the members of the various trades as required.

In isolated instances such a chain of operations can be very costly; in a sequence of work it will be less so. But if maximum efficiency is to be obtained, very close managerial supervision will have to be given in order to prevent as little time being lost passing from one job to another as possible. In shipbuilding the Adam Smith argument of saving time in passing from one job to another by specialisation may work in reverse when the jobs lie far apart. These instances, and others like them, striking as they are, are not, however, characteristic of the work of building a ship. The main bulk of the work can be readily apportioned between the respective trades and carried

[1] It is not to be assumed that this is universal practice; different trades are likely to be involved in some part of the operations in different yards.

out without interruption or waiting for the services of some other body of men. A plater marking the plates preparatory to processing, a welder operating an automatic welding machine, a shipwright working in the loft and so on are likely to be able to pursue their work without waiting on any other trade.

Any change, however, in even these defined trades may bring the threat of dispute. Prefabrication, for example, means that much of the work of erection will be carried out in welding bays; work of fairing that would have been carried out by the shipwright on the berth may be incorporated in the work of platers building a large section; a clear-cut division with one technique of construction may thus become blurred as methods change and consequently become a potential source of dispute. It was a change of this kind that underlay the demarcation dispute at Stephen's shipyard in 1957, though the immediate cause was the failure to observe an agreement.

Each change in production methods must be examined by management with an eye to the possibility that it will cause demarcation disputes. If it seems probable that difficulty will be experienced, it is more than likely that some alternative method will be used. Management has great experience in negotiating these pitfalls, but they are an unnecessary obstacle to the introduction of new methods and materials, and on occasion they have brought the whole industry into disrepute, as an unfinished ship which could not be completed owing to a demarcation dispute has sailed to some foreign port for finishing touches.

It is hardly possible to estimate what the cost of the demarcation problem is to the shipbuilding industry. Strikes over demarcation issues can be exceedingly costly to the shipyards involved, but the whole of the strikes in the industry from 1950 to 1956, whether due to demarcation disputes or not, averaged a loss of only one man-day per year for those employed in the industry, and this can hardly have increased labour costs by more than $\frac{1}{2}$ per cent. Inefficient use of labour directly consequent on demarcation practices of the kind cited above is, perhaps, of greater consequence, but it varies a great deal from shipyard to shipyard and some shipyards appear to be comparatively untroubled by it. On the other hand, the indirect consequence of the whole demarcation issue can be much more telling. The distraction to management, the restraints that are imposed on the introduction of new methods of production, the irritation engendered by a constant source of friction—these are the most serious costs of demarcation which, in all their ramifications, contrive to retard industrial progress and prevent an improvement in productivity. But irrespective of demarcation troubles a few shipyards in the country have achieved a standard of productivity comparable with the best in the world, and it would be as wrong to assume that demarcation was the main reason for the failure of the others to

165

attain comparable standards as it would be to assume that other shipyards in other countries untroubled by demarcation issues invariably achieve higher standards of productivity than British yards. The cost of demarcation to the British industry should not be exaggerated; it is not, as one witness to the Committee on Industry and Trade reporting in 1928 stated, 'the greatest deterrent in British industry . . . the greatest thing you have to face in ship-building'. The most severe effects may be felt in ship-repairing, but in new building it was suggested in the *Industrial Survey of the South-west of Scotland* (1932) that 'in a well managed yard inefficiency due to rigid demarcation might be of the order of less than 5 per cent of the wages bill', and this estimate, while it can scarcely have been founded on a detailed investigation, probably puts the cost in its right perspective.

What are the prospects for eliminating the demarcation problem? The length of time for which the problem has existed indicates how intractable it is. Its historical origins can be traced, but the causes underlying it are complex and have changed over the years. We have stressed that the disputes occur between unions, and in many instances a demarcation dispute is a reflection of inter-union rivalries and a struggle for power. It is this aspect of demarcation disputes that has led some observers to conclude that if there were only one union representing the men in shipbuilding demarcation disputes would not arise. This is probably an unduly simplified picture of the problem. It is true that instances can be given where demarcation disputes would not have arisen if the unions had been differently constituted. The dispute at Cammell Laird's in 1955–6 is a case in point; on the Clyde the drillers and shipwrights are in the same union and would not have been brought into conflict. It is also true that on the Continent, where demarcation problems do not arise, shipbuilding workers are generally organised on an industrial basis rather than by a large number of craft unions covering other industries as well as shipbuilding, although union organisation is not without its complications in other ways. Exceptionally, in Denmark shipbuilding workers are organised on a craft basis, welders, carpenters, etc., being members of their respective unions, though all of them are members of the central Danish organisation for metalworkers. Craft distinctions are not followed in Holland, but there are three unions, the Roman Catholic Union, the Christian Union and the Socialist Union, matched by a somewhat similar division in the organisation of employers. Until recently these unions formed virtually one union, but co-operation has deteriorated of late. In Germany, Sweden and Norway one trade union represents the workers in the industry, while in Japan organisation is on a yard basis with some affiliation to the two national unions. It would be a mistake, however, to assume that if union organisation could be simplified in this country it would necessarily result in a suppression of demarcation incidents. Demarcation disputes, for example, arise *within* the United Society of Boilermakers, Shipbuilders and Structural Workers; the dispute between platers and riveters mentioned above is only one instance of what is a fairly common occurrence. Nor would a universal union solve those problems that arise when a particular job has become so simplified that it could equally well be done by an unskilled as a skilled man. In this case, however, the issue is likely to be one of the amount of dilution agreed between unions and employers and not primarily an inter-union dispute.

It is frequently claimed by the unions that demarcation is neither more nor less than a recognition that division of labour is the best means of achieving high output. There is a considerable element of truth in this, but at the same time it must be recognised that the subdivision into crafts and skills can be overdone. The comparative freedom of the Royal Dockyards from demarcation disputes has been attributed to the fact that there has been less specialisation by the labour force. The shipwrights in the dockyards fashioned iron and steel quite soon after the introduction of iron warships with the aid of semi-skilled men. There emerged 'broadly a three-fold grading of industrial employees in the dockyards as labourers, skilled labourers, and mechanics; and a considerable degree of interchangeability is achieved since the scope of the various trades is made as wide as possible, e.g. in the case of shipwrights, while skilled labourers are interchangeable to a greater degree than any class of mechanics'.[1]

The dockyards were fortunate in the evolution of their labour organisation along these lines, but it is one thing to recognise that a new system of labour grading might serve to eliminate most demarcation disputes and quite another to superimpose it on a much more diversified system of labour organisation. It is not just the opposition of the unions that would be encountered in any attempt to reduce the number of subdivisions between crafts, though it is obvious that the unions have no direct incentive to reduce their numbers or organise the craft divisions along simpler and perhaps more rational lines; it is a question first and foremost of creating conditions conducive to greater uniformity. This means, for example, that the opportunities of all skilled workers to achieve a given level of earnings must be about the same; there can be little hope of obtaining interchangeability between various crafts if one craft is consistently paid more than another, for there would be clear advantage for the higher paid craft to exclude other crafts from carrying out their particular type of work. It is also likely to mean that the resistance to interchangeability of work of any craft which considers that its employment possibilities are likely to be better than those of other crafts will have to be broken down. The first of these conditions simply

[1] Committee on Industry and Trade, *Survey of Metal Industries*, 1928, p. 394.

167

does not hold. In spite of the principle of uniform time-rates there is much greater opportunity for some crafts, particularly the black squads, to earn more than other crafts, such as shipwrights or the finishing trades, though their training and skill may not be superior in any way to other crafts. There is, in the greater earnings of welders than many other crafts at the present time, an economic reason why platers engaged on assembly of large sections are not allowed under the demarcation rules to make the tack welds that serve to hold steel members together in the course of assembly, before they are finally welded into position, though they have the requisite skill and knowledge; if ever tack welding became a generally accepted accomplishment of other trades, the essentially semi-skilled nature of most welding operations would be exposed and the carefully guarded monopoly of the welders broken down. And the resistance of platers to use of riveters in the platers' shop may also be understood in terms of the protection of a monopoly position, though it is generally admitted that the riveters may not be sufficiently skilled to do more than act as platers' helpers.

Thus it is difficult to see how the demarcation issue can be resolved without some attempt to even up the earnings opportunities of different trades. In this connection it may be pointed out that there is very little difference in the take-home pay of Continental shipyard workers engaged on different kinds of work, and, moreover, that this greater equality extends to the divisions between skilled, semi-skilled and unskilled work.

It must also be recognised that one of the underlying causes of the demarcation issue is that of security. It is true that there has been only a little unemployment in the industry since 1939, but so long as there are doubts in the minds of the union leaders as to the continuation of high employment in the industry, it will seem advantageous to each of them to secure as much of the available work for his members as possible and to protect them against redundancy by resisting dilution and insisting that incomers should be dismissed first in the event of a reduction in employment. And to the remaining squad leaders contracting for various parts of the vessel, the demarcation issue will seem to be one of assuring their independence and economic well-being rather than one of maintaining restrictive practices.

It should now be clear that there are a large number of obstacles in the way of eliminating the demarcation problem. It can be argued that the problem is so complicated that any attempt to solve it would be likely to involve no less than a major overhaul of divisions between crafts and skills, of systems of wage payments, of conditions of employment and recruitment of labour in the shipbuilding industry—to say nothing of the trade-union structure—and that increased provision against the risk of unemployment, should demand fail in the future, would also be required.

This would obviously be a large task which would be rendered more difficult by the many sectional interests and trade unions involved. A major reorganisation of this scope is hardly likely to be entered on voluntarily by either the Shipbuilding Employers' Federation or the unions involved. It would almost certainly require some outside body, perhaps even a Royal Commission, to prepare any scheme which would hold out the possibility of acceptance by both parties in the industry.

It is doubtful if demarcation is really so serious a problem as to need such heroic measures. It is a constant drag and source of irritation in the shipyards, but it is no more important in governing costs than many other factors; bad time-keeping, excessive tea breaks, late starting and early stopping, faulty organisation of work and labour are probably much greater sources of inefficiency. There can be no doubt also that inability to obtain steel in sufficient quantities, or the rate of technical progress, have been more potent influences on the United Kingdom competitive position.

If it is difficult to justify the grand approach to the demarcation problem, what can be done? The answer is probably not much more than is already being done. The Employers' Federation will certainly continue to raise the matter with unions and will no doubt remain anxious when wage negotiations arise to trade increases against undertakings about demarcation and other restrictionist influences. But this is something the unions are not prepared to do. And it is something that the Confederation of Shipbuilding and Engineering Unions is unable to do with its present constitution. Thus, so far all attempts to link demarcation to wage settlements have ended in failure. In this respect history repeated itself in 1957. The first major attempt to regulate demarcation by agreement with unions in 1926 likewise was not successful. The celebrated 'Joint Inquiry,' conducted by the Employers' Federation and union representatives into the state of the industry at that time, resulted in the employers making the following widely quoted recommendations.

(a) That in operations to commence and complete which two or more classes of workmen are under present conditions customary, there shall be freedom for one class of workmen to complete the work when it is within their competence to do it.

(b) That work which is not an essential and distinctive part of the work of any one class, although it may be incidental or ancillary to one or more crafts, may be performed by any one who is competent to do it.

(c) That when there is a definite shortage of any class of craftsmen, craftsmen of another class competent to do the work may be employed without prejudice to the work being regarded as an essential and distinctive part of the work of the first craft, and, if the rates of the two crafts are different, the higher rate will be paid.

Acceptance of these proposals by the unions acting in conjunction would have resolved the most frustrating aspects of demarcation, always provided, of course, that the acceptance could have been carried beyond the conference room to shipbuilding yards, but it was not to be. The 21 shipbuilding unions of the country were prepared to accept the recommendations of the joint inquiry only subject to the proviso 'that the vexed question of demarcation between union and union . . . should be negotiated between the employers and the individual unions concerned'.[1]

In this decision the deciding voice was a handful of the boilermakers' union; of some 50,000–60,000 members the votes of four or five thousand determined the issue; it is said the well-organised districts of Southampton gently tipped the balance against industrial compromise, and decided what would be the rule in the major shipbuilding centres. Yet in the last resort the decision may have been wise, for it is by no means clear that the unions would have been in a position to enforce any agreement that might have been arrived at. In the same way the Confederation was unable to meet the employers over the question of demarcation in 1957, though the executives of the affiliated unions were prepared to agree in exchange for a wage offer that they would hold special conferences to discuss, and where possible resolve, the difficulties referred to at the hearings before the Court of Inquiry. Few meetings, however, appear to have been held, and so far as demarcation is concerned it seems likely that shipyard action will have to continue to be directed to reducing the seriousness of demarcation disputes on an individual basis while looking to union leaders and the Trade Union Congress, which has powers to intervene in inter-union disputes when the livelihood of non-participants is threatened, to create a better basis for industrial co-operation.

This means that shipyard management will have to continue to take care to avoid situations in which a demarcation dispute is likely to emerge, while endeavouring to obtain the maximum amount of flexibility within the shipyard. As we have noted, shipyard practice varies in relation to demarcation, and there is no doubt that it is a more troublesome matter in some shipyards than in others; equally there is no doubt that it can be minimised by improving labour relations generally within the shipyard.

It is sometimes thought that labour relations in the shipyards and demarcation in particular will be improved only when the present wave of prosperity recedes and the employers are placed in a strong position to dictate terms to unions faced with the risk of unemployment amongst their members. As we have seen, this very fear is itself a cause of labour difficulties within the industry. In times of depression the unions may be cowed, but lasting settlement depends on the reaching of agreements between the two parties when both are in a position of strength and neither feels that an agreement is being forced upon it. It is possible that in less prosperous conditions earnings of the various trades would show less inequality, and that in consequence a new system of apprenticeship of a more universal nature could

---

[1] *Shipbuilding and Shipping Record*, 30 September 1926, p. 354.

be instituted which would provide for greater interchangeability. But the fact remains that the main hope of improving labour relations and, for that matter, efficiency generally lies in prosperity, not in depression.

IV

We have already shown that demarcation cannot be considered without reference to the wages structure of the industry. The system and structure of wage payments in the industry are much more complex than might have been expected under the operation of National Uniform Plain Time-Rates which have been negotiated for skilled and unskilled workers since 1930. Shipbuilding labour is predominantly skilled. The early techniques of shipbuilding called for time-served men in great numbers, and semi-skilled men were employed mainly as helpers to the skilled men or in ancillary operations e.g. as cranemen or drivers, although women were employed on production in small numbers and made excellent welders during the war and were again employed in this capacity in one shipyard in 1957, they are generally engaged in the shipyards only as french polishers or upholsterers, apart from clerical or administrative posts.

The uniform time-rates adopted in 1930 were increased by bonuses both before and during the war and these were consolidated in 1950 into new work plain time-rates for skilled men of 120s. per week and for unskilled men of 100s. per week. Since 1950 various advances have been made for skilled workers and incorporated in the inclusive time-rates which became 181s. 6d. in May 1957. For unskilled workers the corresponding figure at that date was 151s. 6d. National negotiations determine time-rates, not earnings, and the latter are determined in relation to the national time-rates by local negotiations.

The general tendency of unskilled wages to increase relatively to those of skilled wages is very evident in the industry. In 1906 unskilled wages amounted to about 50–55 per cent of skilled weekly rates and earnings of the unskilled to about 60 per cent of skilled earnings. In 1950 these percentages had risen to 84 and 80 per cent respectively. Recently there has been a tendency for proportionately higher increases to be given to skilled than to unskilled workers in the industry, but this has not affected the closing of the earnings differential between the groups to any significant extent. The long-term relative decline in the remuneration of skilled workers probably reflects some lessening of their responsibilities and an improvement in the facilities available for their work, though it is unlikely that this is more than a partial explanation of the movement.

Time-rates account for only part of the earnings of workers in the shipbuilding industry. Over 80 per cent of the workers in the industry are on some

171

sort of incentive payment.[1] One of the oldest systems of piece-work adopted in the industry was simply to subcontract a particular part of the construction of a ship to a squad leader. Part of the shell plating, framing or riveting, in typical examples, were put out at a price agreed by the management with the squad leader as a result of hard bargaining. Both sides to the agreement were knowledgeable as to what was a reasonable price in the circumstances. At the end of each week the squad leader would draw to account and he would pay his helpers, generally in the local pub, what he considered to be due to them for their efforts of the preceding week. In this way the earnings of the squad reflected its efficiency and the payments to the workers, if they were fortunate in their leader, something of their merits.

On the Clyde the contract system is still quite common and perhaps one-third of platers may be employed in this manner, although the system has been greatly modified in a number of ways. Riveting, also, may still be carried out by semi-independent squads consisting of three men—riveter, holder-on and rivet boy—but the price is likely to be fixed either by rate-fixing methods or by reference to existing piece-rate lists with individual bargaining playing a secondary role.

The shareout between the members of the squad may also have become formalised. In one yard, for example, the custom in 1955 was for the earnings of the rivet boy to be paid by the riveter, though the shipyard also paid him $1s.$ $5\frac{2}{16}d.$[2] per hour, representing increases in time-rates which had occurred since 1950. The earnings of the squad remaining after deduction of the payment made to the rivet boy were then divided equally between the riveter and the holder-on. A piece-rate list drawn up in 1896 for the Clyde and redetermined in 1926 might still, after extensive modifications as a result of later wage negotiations, have been used to fix riveting prices as late as 1954 when it was cancelled; and even so might continue to serve as a guide to pricing.

The caulkers' price list in use on the Clyde is of even earlier origin and was first in use in 1889. It is still in use, though it has had to be brought up-to-date by a series of percentage increases and a deduction to allow for the use of pneumatic tools, as the list was originally based on the use of hand tools. Not all types of operation can be priced from the list since new tasks have been introduced connected, for example, with the preparation of plates for welding, but with this proviso the rate of payment of a caulker depends in its essentials on an agreement reached more than half a century ago.

Efforts to accommodate new methods of work to methods of payment

[1] E. G. J. C. Knowles and D. J. Robertson, *Bulletin of the Oxford University Institute of Statistics*, November-December, 1951.

[2] On the Clyde fractions of a penny are measured in sixteenths.

fixed long ago are likely to be progressively more difficult. In the shipyard studied by Mr Robertson many platers were employed on individual work and not in the traditional squads. Consequently their work was rate-fixed and not determined by a price list. Nevertheless, older systems of payment were still evident in the fact that the platers' earnings were subject to a deduction for helpers. Platers in the frame squad, on the other hand, still operated in squads and were paid according to a price list based on a mid-ship frame, and the prices were fixed with the squad leader. A deduction of 9d. an hour was made from the earnings of these platers and paid to the platers' helpers. The earnings of the latter were made up by the shipyard, though they may also have been further supplemented by additional payments out of the pockets of the platers, presumably as an incentive to efficiency. These payments, though no concern of the shipyard, are recognised by the Inland Revenue as deductions from the platers' earnings for tax payments. What remains to the platers after deducting the money paid to their helpers is equally divided between them by agreement of the association of 'framers' on Clydeside.

The foregoing account illustrates the extreme complexity that is likely to emerge from attempting to adapt traditional methods of payment and ancient piece-work price lists to the requirements of modern industry. Where new trades have been introduced there is a greater opportunity to establish a clean edge and to attempt to fix piece-rates on a more scientific basis. This is true for welding, which is a comparatively new trade in the shipyards and lends itself to a more uniform assessment of the work involved in carrying out particular operations.

Various attempts have been made to put payments for welding operators on a quasi-scientific basis. Mr D. M. Kerr,[1] for example, divides the time necessary to carry out a weld between the time actually depositing the metal and the time carrying out auxiliary operations. The deposition rate of arc-welding is affected by a number of variables such as the volume of metal to be deposited in the joint, the position of the weld, the type of electrode used and the welding current. The weight of metal deposited per unit length of weld can be established by experiment, using experienced welders on test-pieces incorporating various types of joints and welded in various positions. Similarly, the effect of varying the types of electrode involved and the welding current may be established and verified.

The basic data once assembled may have to be applied to work which differs in some measure from test conditions. One of the main difficulties is likely to be variations in the widths of the gaps between the various pieces of metal which have to be joined. Quite a small variation can have a very marked

[1] See D. M. Kerr, 'Factors in production control of arc welding', *Transactions of the Institute of Welding*, February, 1948.

effect on the weight of metal which is required to be deposited and increase both the number of welders required and the cost of the operation very considerably. In fixing rates in practice, such deviations have to be allowed for by adjusting piece-rates to take account of the greater weight of deposition required owing to inaccuracies in preparation.

It is also necessary, of course, to take into account the time spent by welders in supplementary operations such as collecting electrodes, and removing slag from joints, and some time has to be allowed for recovery from fatigue.

On the whole, it may be said that for the bulk of the metal-working operations carried out in a shipyard, some basis can be established for payment by results, though changes in methods of work and improvements in technique require periodic modifications to the established norms. Where individual operators are concerned the application of piece-work payments will present the least difficulty. A large number of operations, however, are not carried out by individuals but by teams. Among the metal trades, for instance, the erection of sub-units is likely to require a team of men not all necessarily of the same trade, and the unit of output is likely to be the finished construction rather than a length of weld, a number of holes drilled or rivets inserted. Since time-rate earnings are much less than earnings on piece-rate, some system of additional payment has to be devised. This may take the form of a lieu rate designed either to bring time earnings up to a piece-rate level without necessarily being linked in any way to the rate of working or of a lieu rate granted on the explicit or implicit understanding that a piece-rate level of working is to be carried out. Such payments may be appropriate when made to individuals or groups who have little or no control over their rate of working, but if they extend beyond this there is the danger that the whole system of piece-rate working will be brought into disrepute.

The difficulty of linking output to wage payments is most evident in the case of the finishing trades who may be employed on a great variety of work carried out in varying conditions. Characteristically before the war, the finishing trades were paid time-rates. But efforts were made during the war to extend systems of payment by results to these trades under the pressure of the Ministry of Labour in the person of Mr Bevin. One system that has been tried for finishing trades involves the estimation of the number of hours that are required to carry out certain tasks and the assessment of bonus payments in terms of the hours saved.

It is probably best in these instances to take fairly large units of output for the calculation of bonuses. Thus typically the whole of the electric wiring of a ship or a substantial part of it might be considered as the job for which a bonus would be paid, or the whole of the furniture to be installed in a number of cabins. The time required (the number of man-hours) to do the work is assessed and the bonus paid depends on the relation of this figure to the man-hours actually taken for the operation. In practice the scheme is arranged to make it possible to earn in normal circumstances a substantial bonus, which might amount to one-third in a particular case. As part of the mechanics of the scheme the number of hours estimated to be needed is increased by a third and the number of hours actually taken is compared with this figure and payment made on the basis of hours saved. If the number of hours taken is the same as was estimated before the total was increased by one-third, a bonus of a third is payable. Other differences are paid for in proportion. The addition of one-third to the hours calculated to be required is a complication, but it is probably necessary to avoid the possibility that otherwise the stipulated number of hours would, on occasion, be exceeded, with the implication that the bonus should be negative. Even with the addition of one-third to the estimated man-hours required it may still happen that the stipulated time is exceeded in unusual circumstances, either because the tempo of work has been very slow or because the man-hour content of the work has been inaccurately assessed.

The assessment of the man-hours required may be arrived at either on the basis of time study when some new job is being considered for inclusion in a bonus system of payment or, when the scheme has been in operation for some time, on the basis of results actually achieved. Estimating the man-hour content of various jobs is likely to call for considerable skill and experience and specialist estimators are required.

The schemes themselves also require a good deal of care in their administration. Complaints may arise for a number of reasons, because, for instance, the man-hour content of the job has been inaccurately assessed, or because the bonus which is declared week by week has failed to come up to expectations, or because there have been interruptions to production due to disturbances outside the workers' control. Some form of consultative arrangements are necessary in order to ensure the smooth working of a bonus scheme which may be somewhat remote from the individual worker, particularly if it is operated on a team basis or embraces the whole of the workers in a particular shop and has a duration of a number of weeks before it is worked off and final payment made.

Bonus arrangements of this kind are not popular in all the shipyards partly because of their complexity and partly because they are not thought to have a great deal of effect on productivity. It is sometimes thought, for example, that paying a low bonus for one week, even if it reflects a drop in effort in that week and is likely to be made up in subsequent work, will have a more damaging effect on labour relations than a bonus which is more constant. There may be a temptation on the part of management, therefore, to smooth bonus payments week by week, thus reducing the connection between effort and payment. This is likely to be all the stronger in some weeks when a low rate of production has been due to some fault in organisation or a hitch in the flow of materials or in the completion of some preliminary work; in such cases the declared bonus may have to be made up to some reasonable amount. When this happens, inevitably doubts are felt about the working of the scheme because it cannot be made entirely cut and dried.

It is noticeable that the national wage agreements concluded by the industry have tended on the whole to weaken the sphere of influence of bonus payments based on output. Thus national wage increases have been drawn up in such a way as not to increase the earnings of employees engaged on piece-work, lieu rates, contract work, incentive or bonus schemes, or any other system of payment by results, by more than the flat-rate increases granted to the general classes of skilled, semi-skilled and unskilled workers. In the shipyard studied by Mr Robertson, for example, the bonus was in effect paid only on the rate of earning in 1950, subsequent increases being paid on the time worked and not on the time worked plus the time saved. In effect, in this case, the rate of bonus characteristic of the scheme had been progressively reduced, and if the process continued far enough bonus payments would cease to have any marked effect on the pay packet. Nevertheless, the fact that national agreements have been applied on time-rates does not necessarily mean that the remuneration of bonus workers falls relatively to that of time workers. There is in practice a great deal of flexibility in the application of a national wage increase within the different districts and shipyards, and other advances tend to be given to bonus workers in order to enable them to maintain their relative position.

One reason for this is that bonus payments are frequently regarded by management as means to attract workers to their yards. That those shipyards that are willing and able to attract workers to their yards by offering higher rates of wages than their competitors are contributing to the most efficient use of labour is a thesis which can easily be defended on general economic grounds. But national or local agreements on wages negotiated by employers through their established associations are expected to be fairly rigorously observed by those who are parties to the agreement, and shipyards are not likely, therefore, to depart from agreed wage-rates by paying higher time-rates than the average. Bonus payments, however, do represent a means to increase wage payments in a less obvious manner, and competition by shipyards for the available labour supply is likely to take the form of offering higher bonuses than are paid in other establishments. Thus, bonus payments tend to be regarded as a means to attract workers rather than as a means to increase output and productivity, and consequently may fail in their primary purpose.

The administrative complexities of payment-by-results schemes are one of their disadvantages in the eyes of management. Specially trained staff are required to deal with them and some increase in overheads results. Yet the cost of administration cannot be judged solely in relation to wage problems. One of the advantages of payment-by-results schemes is that it brings to the eyes of management every stoppage or impediment arising in the course of production which prevents those paid by results from earning their full bonus. If a welder is held up because work for him is not immediately available he will report it to the foreman so that his earnings will not suffer. If he finds that inaccurate workmanship results in a greater than normal quantity of metal having to be deposited, the matter will again be drawn to the attention of the foreman so that appropriate adjustments can be made in his rate of pay. And not only will such matters be brought to the attention of management but, at least as important, they will be brought to attention as soon as they occur so that remedial action can be taken while the difficulty is fresh in everybody's mind and the facts can be established.

Payment-by-results schemes are also a stimulus to management in other ways, for they lay emphasis on the cost elements of carrying out particular operations and so point the way to improvements.

The integration of the operation of payment-by-results schemes into an effective scheme of costing and budgetary control is not easy. It might be expected, for instance, that the mass of wage information accumulated in the working of such schemes would form the basis for estimating the cost of construction of ships for which tenders have been invited. This does not, however, appear to be the general rule. The very mass of detail accumulated often appears to defeat its use in estimating. The practice of many shipyards in preparing estimates of the cost of ships for which they tender is to use only a limited amount of detailed information. In estimating the labour costs of constructing the hull of a ship, for example, the starting point is likely to be quite simply the weight of metal which is expected to be incorporated in the hull. This is then multiplied by an appropriate coefficient for its labour content, probably determined from the past record of building a ship or ships of similar construction. Often no attempt is made to estimate costs in any greater detail than this. Estimating for furnishing may be equally rough and ready, largely based on relations established in the construction of previous ships. If a shipyard is fortunate such methods may give an accuracy of 1 or 2 per cent of total costs, but sometimes the error is much greater. As a few shipyards have learned, however, there is certainly scope for more detailed cost estimating when the detailed cost information available from payment-by-results schemes can be handled easily by cost-estimating departments. The need for close cost-estimating is not obviated by the insertion in a contract for the purchase of a ship of a ladder clause providing for price adjustment if production costs increase, for many of these clauses provide only for adjustment in relation to the movements of certain costs such as the price of steel or changes in wage-rates.

We have already noted that uniform time-rates have been established by agreement for skilled, semi-skilled and unskilled workers. Though such uniformity does not correspond to the supply and demand position for different types of labour at any given time it is not necessarily inconsistent with the long-term supply of labour of different trades to the shipyards. All trades are required to undergo a 5-year period of apprenticeship. There is thus no difference in the cost to the worker of training for different trades. For the 'ironworking' trades much of the initial training given is on the same basis with the different trades of shipwrights, platers, drillers, caulkers, riveters and welders specialising later in different processes. It is only towards the end of their apprenticeship that they become specialists in any true sense and take the union card of a particular trade. And even at a later stage it is possible for platers, caulkers, welders and riveters, who are members of different sections of the United Society of Boilermakers, to exchange their cards once for some other ironworking trade. If entry to all trades were unrestricted it might be expected that wages would broadly reflect the net advantages of the different ironworking trades, and since the size of the pay packet probably ranks high in relation to comparative advantages of the various occupations, no great difference between wages in the various occupations might result.

An examination of detailed figures of earnings, however, throws doubt on the extent to which this occurs. Table 19 shows the earnings of some skilled trades which were ascertained from a survey made on the Clyde during November 1957. It is compiled on the basis of a 44-hour week, and while it includes payments under incentive schemes and various forms of bonus it does not include overtime payments. To this extent it is not fully representative of the earnings of the various trades; riveters, for example, may have difficulty in getting work from time to time and their average earnings in and out of employment may be reduced below those of other trades in keen demand; but the table probably represents fairly well the earnings of the trades in relation to their hours of work.

Some interesting comparisons arise from the table. Welders are by far the highest paid of all trades (if allowance is made for the uncertainty of employment in riveting work), although, as has been observed, their work in many Continental shipyards is regarded as semi-skilled. Some of the older welders are employed on tack-welding, which keeps them in the yards doing a light job at a correspondingly reduced rate of earning. This throws an interesting light on the management complaint that production is slowed down because platers or other metal trades are not allowed to tack-weld.

More adequate pension arrangements might solve the difficulty. Platers engaged on squad work may earn about as much as welders, but the bulk of platers engaged in other ways earn appreciably less, and the same is true of the other trades concerned with metalworking.

The most striking difference in the table, however, is not so much these differences as the much lower earnings of the trades that are not organised by the boilermakers. First, the shipwrights are paid well below the squad platers although their work is certainly comparable in or out of the loft, and secondly, the finishing trades generally—the joiners, plumbers and electricians —who are as likely to be engaged in other industries as in shipbuilding, and

Table 19.—*An indication of hourly earnings on the Clyde in November 1957**

	Average Earnings
Skilled Workers	
Welders	7s. 0d.
Riveters	7s. 0d.
Caulkers, burners, platers, blacksmiths	6s. 0d. to 6s. 3d.
Shipwrights	5s. 6d. to 6s. 0d.
Electricians, plumbers, joiners, engineers	5s. 0d. to 5s. 6d.
Semi-skilled	
Stagers, redleaders	4s. 6d. to 4s. 9d.

* The estimates are on the basis of a 44-hour week and exclude overtime.

the engineers are paid at much lower rates than the black squads. Some of these differences can be explained in terms of better working conditions, but the bulk of the difference must surely reflect the comparative supply and demand for the various types of labour.

The welders, however, have been particularly adept at maintaining a tight hold on available labour by restrictive practices. By trade-union agreements welders limit their earnings to a maximum hourly figure, even though it would be well within the powers of many of them to exceed this figure. Indeed, it is not unheard of for a welder to have earned his maximum in 4 days' work and to continue to work unpaid for the remainder of the week, rather than be paid and face a union inquiry and the imposition of a fine, or let down the management by taking time off. There can be little doubt that welders are overpaid in relation to their work and accomplishments. Large numbers have been trained since welding was first introduced into the shipyards, but there is a considerable demand for their services, and with a strong union behind them they have been able to resist a cut in piece-work payments which would have been justified with the introduction of new machines, electrodes and other equipment. When agreements to limit earnings are abandoned, as has happened on the north-east coast, welders have little difficulty in earning as much as 10s. per hour. This is a very high rate of pay for work which is not highly skilled, but the output of a shipyard is closely geared to the efforts of the welders, and when this is taken into account high rates of pay may appear to be vindicated. On the Clyde, where restrictions on earnings have not been lifted, it is as much the low rate of working of welders as their high rate of pay that disturbs employers. Even so, piecemeal relaxation of restriction is not without its difficulties. Occasionally it happens that welders in a shipyard may decide to raise their permitted ceiling earnings (though they are likely to demand higher rates of pay first), and while such a procedure is welcomed in the shipyard in which it occurs it can raise considerable difficulties for other yards where similar action has not been taken. For a time they lose their welders to yards where by agreement between the *men* higher earnings are now possible, only to be faced with a demand for higher rates of pay without a corresponding rise in output, in order to secure their men back again. Such difficulties, however, are almost unavoidable when the demand for labour exceeds the available supply and the upward creep of wages from one shipyard to the next goes at a rate of perhaps 2 per cent per annum above the negotiated improvements in national rates. It is a movement that employers can do little to subdue even by collective action, for the opportunity to lever the remuneration of one or another trade upwards by a small amount on the basis of some traditional differential is always present. In this the United Kingdom is not necessarily worse placed than other countries, but she is more prone to restrictive action to enforce wage claims.

It is frequently stated that United Kingdom shipyard workers are less ready to adopt new methods of work than those abroad and do so only at a price. There is some truth in this. Generally, where there is the alternative of hand or machine work, machine work is more highly paid. While the employers may resent having to pay more because methods have improved, the tendency is to be welcomed. A new method of working does enhance the earning power of labour, and it is this that makes it worth while to change to new methods of working. In this respect at least there is an encouragement to labour to adopt new ideas, and hope that new methods will eventually be welcomed from the workers' side.

It will be clear from the foregoing that there is great complexity in the wage structure of the shipbuilding industry and apparent irrationality in many instances. Inevitably this complicates relations within the industry. There might be something to be said for a reversion to a straight system of time payments if the unions were willing to agree to incentive bonuses being removed. Bonus payments are the common fare of shipyards in the European centres of production, though not in Japan, but few regard them as very satisfactory ways of raising output. In one shipyard, that of Akers at Oslo, the experiment of reverting to time-rates is being made. It remains to be seen whether the experiment will be successful, and if so whether it could be applied in the different conditions ruling in British shipyards in order to develop a more interchangeable and adaptable labour force with its eyes fixed more on productivity and less on differentials.

CHAPTER 13

The Industry Abroad

The United Kingdom's most important competitors are first Japan (which produced nearly 2½ million g.r.t. in 1957), second Germany (1½ million g.r.t. in 1958), and third Sweden and the Netherlands (¾ and ½ million g.r.t. respectively). The output of Japan has increased by leaps and bounds from 150,000 g.r.t. in 1949 to 600,000 g.r.t. in 1952, 1¾ million g.r.t. in 1956 and nearly 2½ million g.r.t. in 1957. Germany, Sweden and the Netherlands have also been increasing their output but more slowly. In these countries available manpower has been limited; in Japan it has not. There are a number of other shipbuilding countries which, while of smaller importance than the foregoing or less well placed competitively, produce as much as Japan between them. These include the United States, which has produced ¾ million g.r.t. of merchant shipping in a good peacetime year, Italy and France with an output around 200,000–300,000 g.r.t. per annum until 1957, when they produced over 400,000 g.r.t., Norway and Denmark with an output of about 200,000 g.r.t., and Belgium and Spain producing about 100,000 g.r.t. of shipping per annum. Italy and France can be described as uncompetitive without subsidy payments except when demand is very high, though the future evolution of costs could alter the situation; the United States also is uncompetitive, though as we shall see competition from that country is effective in an indirect form; but the other countries with a large industry stand as competitors with the United Kingdom on any count and invite close attention.

JAPAN

The full force of Japanese competition is comparatively recent; 600,000 g.r.t. were produced in 1919 and over 300,000 g.r.t. in 1939, but for most of the inter-war period Japan was a comparatively minor producer of merchant tonnage as she had been before the First World War. When shipbuilding was recommenced after the Second World War output was rapidly increased, but until about 1954, demand for Japanese-produced ships was insufficient fully to employ her available capacity and costs were high, so that the industry remained in the background. The decisive change in Japanese fortunes must be put down to three factors: the tremendous increase in tanker orders in 1955 and 1956, secondly, state aid to the Japanese shipyards so that they could reorganise their yards and overcome foreign competitive

182

advantages, and thirdly, the determination with which the shipyards have seized their opportunities.

In 1957 no fewer than ten shipyards produced over 100,000 g.r.t. including four in the Mitsubishi group, one of which produced over 200,000 g.r.t. with the launch of twelve ships, and the shipyard of National Bulk Carriers, which is United States owned and also launched over 200,000 g.r.t.[1] Five other shipyards made up the bulk of the remaining output with launchings of some 50,000–100,000 g.r.t. The larger companies with one or two exceptions combine marine engineering with shipbuilding in the same establishment.

The increase in output between 1952 and 1957 was not due to the establishment of new companies but to a larger output from existing yards, and so far as ocean-going ships of over 2000 g.r.t. are concerned, it is broadly true to say that doubling the number of ships trebled the tonnage produced, as the slips were used for larger cargo ships and, more particularly, for tankers. Thus the Japanese have become specialists in the production of large ships mainly of simple construction, but they have earned the distinction of launching some of the largest super-tankers in the world, including the *Universe Apollo* of 104,000 d.w.t., by far the largest ship launched in 1958, and at that time the world's biggest tanker; and they have also produced some of the largest diesel engines to be made.

It is very noticeable that the individual shipyards have programmes providing for the construction of a sequence of similar vessels. In 1956 six tankers of 20,500 g.r.t. (not always with the same engines) were launched from the Nagasaki shipyards of Mitsubishi Shipbuilding and Engineering Co., and two tankers of 26,000 g.r.t. The Hiroshima yard of the same company launched six cargo ships of 7800 g.r.t., all for the Liberian flag, and there were a number of sister ships giving fair runs launched from other yards in the same year.

The frequency of batch production probably owes something to the government supervision that has been exercised over the industry as part of a programme of giving subsidies to stimulate output and arranging for the placing of home orders in order to build up the domestic fleet. Subsidies for export included the allocation of sugar import licences to shipbuilders, which could be sold for a profit, averaging 5 per cent on the price of export ships. Builders did not hesitate to quote cut-rate prices in order to secure foreign orders, and at times sold at a loss. At the same time credit was allowed by shipbuilders to encourage export sales on the basis of loans made to them by the Import-Export Bank at 4 per cent per annum—less than half the commercial bank rate. For the domestic market 65 per cent of the value of

---

[1] See above, p. 36.

the ships was lent on the average at low rates of interest by the Development Bank or subsidies were paid to bring interest rates down to the Development Bank level.[1]

The policy of promoting output by subsidies would have failed if it had not been backed up by a decisive effort to bring down costs. Cheap labour is not enough in the modern world to ensure competitive shipbuilding costs; capital equipment which is not overwhelmingly expensive in the European centres of shipbuilding production boosts output per man, and helps to offset higher wages; new techniques improve the quality of ships, and production planning cuts costs still further. If the Japanese industry was to compete it had to meet foreign competition on its own ground, and that meant, as in other centres, that welding had to replace riveting, and that prefabrication was as indispensable as the cranes and buildings to enable it to go forward. By mid-1956 the industry had spent some £23 million since 1950 on rationalisation, one-quarter of which had gone to the improvement of prefabrication and welding techniques. Over this period capital expenditure was probably at least on a par with that being carried on in United Kingdom yards. The money was well spent, costs began to come down and according to the Japanese Shipbuilders' Association by 1955 prices were down to 86 per cent of 1951, in spite of the fact that steel prices had risen by 8 per cent.[2] The change from riveting to almost universal welding was doubly fortunate in this respect, for it was even more important to save steel in Japanese yards, where steel was, in conditions of scarcity, exceptionally dear and needed in large quantities for super-tankers, than in the United Kingdom where it was the cheapest in the world.

Expenditure on the stocks was matched by expenditure on welding equipment, diesel and turbine boiler manufacturing equipment, new assembly shops and transportation facilities, and as a result some of the Japanese shipyards now rank amongst the most efficient in the world. In the Harima shipyard, for example, there is an assembly area between the berths with a sliding roof through which various sections can be lifted directly to the slips. Clamping jigs operated by compressed air are used to assist welding and various devices are used to increase the amount of downhand welding. Nearly three-quarters of the welding is carried out in assembly shops and lifts up to 80 tons can be made. The organisation is good enough for a berth cycle of 6–7 months to be maintained for 40,000 d.w.t. tankers.[3]

Good organisation is matched by skilled workmen. There is general agreement amongst shipbuilders in Europe that the quality of the welding

---

[1] *The Times*, 17 October 1956.   [2] *Ibid.*

[3] See the report in the *Journal of Commerce, Shipbuilding and Engineering Edition*, 21 February 1957, of a lecture given to the Liverpool and District Branch of the Institute of Welding by R. Ibson.

carried out in Japanese yards is first-class, and although some criticisms of the quality of machinery are to be heard, this is not true for the products of a leading European engine-builder with licences in Japan. Payment is mainly on a time-rate basis with some periodic bonus payments. Overtime, whether in the daytime or at night, is paid for at the rate of 25 per cent. With overtime payments, efficiency pay and dependants' allowances ordinary workers were earning about £26 a month (basic £18 10s. 0d.), and staff members about £28 (basic about £22 10s. 0d.) in 1956, while working hours appear to have been about 42 per week, without overtime. While this adequately represents the earnings of labour, it does not necessarily represent the full cost to the employer, for in Japan employers are not free to discharge permanent workers, and workers temporarily laid off receive 60 per cent of normal wages. This occurred, for example, in the summer of 1954 when work could not be found for all the 100,000 workers employed in the industry.[1]

The number of men in the industry has remained largely unchanged in spite of the rapid increase in output which has taken place and productivity has greatly increased. In 1949 a medium-speed 10,000 t. cargo vessel required 1,015,000 man-hours, but only 600,000 in 1955. Since then there has been a further reduction. Between 1949 and 1956 the number of man-hours required for the steelwork of a 38,600 d.w.t. tanker in the Kawasaki shipyard fell by about two-thirds.[1]

In 1957 there can be little doubt that productivity in some of the best Japanese shipyards was close to Swedish standards, but more generally perhaps 50 per cent more men were required than with the most efficient forms of organisation. But a high proportion of clerical and administrative workers seem to have been required to reach these standards, and some 20 per cent of workers were employed in this way.

On the technical and managerial side standards appear to be high, with a large number of graduates entering the industry, who are keenly interested in theoretical problems, hydrodynamic research (with the use of well-equipped tanks) and developments in other countries.[2]

GERMANY

Like Japan shipbuilding in Germany was not recommenced on any appreciable scale until 1949–50. Output increased rapidly, and by 1953 the highest pre-war output of merchant ships was overtaken and left far behind. Some of the shipyards were badly damaged and the equipment of others had been surrendered in reparations, but the setback to the industry has generally been overestimated, and it was possible to bring a number of shipyards

[1] See *Lloyds' List*, 'Labour Position in Japan', January 1957, p. 8.　　　[2] Ibson, *loc. cit.*

185

speedily into production when new construction of large ships was permitted. As time went on more shipyards were brought into commission; A/G Weser at Bremen launched 71,000 t. of shipping in 1953, and by means of a loan of £1 million the former Blohm and Voss shipyard was restored to production in 1954, under the name of Steinwerder Industrie, to receive an order from Norway. The main assistance required to put the German shipbuilding industry on its feet was the payment of subsidies and the provision of cheap loans to shipowners in order to provide them with the means to place orders and reactivate the shipyards. Credits were provided by the Federal Republic, the coastal Länder, banking interests, the E.C.A. and by the use of counterpart funds. In the middle of 1953, shipowning companies were financing substantial proportions of their capital requirements by these means. Federal loans were granted for up to 40 per cent of aggregate building costs with a life of 16 years, and bearing only 4 per cent interest. Special income-tax provisions were also a means for encouraging the provision of capital. The governing regulations varied from time to time, but their substance was that lenders investing in the shipbuilding industry could claim such investments as costs to be set against income tax up to certain limits.

These measures sufficed to get capital to flow again into the shipping and shipbuilding industries, and as orders were placed and production expanded, the shipyards were once again enabled to stand on their own feet. The capital stringency has left its mark, however, on the organisation as well as the conduct of most shipyards. Although it was possible for a 1953 visitor to the Hamburg shipyard of Deutsche Werft to declare that there was no establishment in Europe or the United Kingdom to compete with it in facilities and general organisation,[1] a policy of make-do-and-mend and cautious spending on capital equipment was more characteristic of the investment programmes of many yards.

About 80 per cent of the total output of new ships is produced by eight shipyards: Deutsche Werft at Hamburg, A/G Weser at Bremen and Bremerhaven, Kieler Howaldtswerke at Kiel, Howaldtswerke at Hamburg, Lübecker Flender-Werke at Lübeck, Nordseewerke at Emden, and Bremer Vulcan at Bremen. Stülcken Sohn at Hamburg is the last family business remaining of any size; other shipyards are either State-owned—Kieler Howaldtswerke and Deutsche Werft—or part of large combines. Howaldtswerke (Hamburg), previously state-owned, was sold to three private companies (Dortmunder Huetten Union, Deutsche Bank and Siemens Schuckert) in October 1958.

As in other European countries the main difficulty in expanding output has been getting more labour into the shipyards. When the shipyards were starting operations it was frequently said by foreign observers that two and

---

[1] *The Glasgow Herald Trade Review*, January 1954, p. 140.

three shifts were being worked. This was not, however, a clear description of the arrangement common in 1957 when three-shift working on a very limited scale might be employed to overcome an acute bottleneck and two-shift working involved the employment of no more than 20–25 per cent of the labour force on a partial overlapping second shift. In one respect the German worker contrasts favourably with his opposite number in the United Kingdom: he is an excellent time-keeper, more prone to start work a little before time than after the signal has gone. He may be a less skilled man, however, than the United Kingdom craftsman, and his training takes only three years against the five common in the United Kingdom, but it is a moot point whether the United Kingdom training period is longer than is needed to learn all that is required for most shipyard occupations.

Like the Japanese shipyards, German shipyards have concentrated on the production of simple cargo vessels and tankers. For the most part these have been of small and medium size; in 1958 11 ships over 20,000 g.r.t. were launched against 10 in the United Kingdom, 21 in the United States and 40 in Japan. Much of the tonnage built has been for export orders, including a large batch of factory trawlers for Russia. Apart from this Kieler Howaldts-werke A/G and Bremer Vulcan have been conspicuous in the production of standard ships, and repeat ships have been common in other yards. Orders have not always flowed too freely; in 1954–5 orders were difficult to get and for a time fixed prices were given. As so often happens in such circumstances costs increased as the market improved, and the financial results were not always satisfactory. In order to sell ships at this period it was also necessary for German shipyards to be able to arrange favourable terms of payment, and to ease the financial position the steel industry was approached to give a £4 rebate per ton of steel used for export orders. When the flow of orders was resumed, however, prospects greatly improved, there was no steel shortage to hold back output and the shipyards could be operated at a greatly enlarged peak capacity.

Parallel with the increase in the output of new ships the shipyards have been able to make a greater contribution to repair. The speed with which new ships can be constructed (6 months from keel laying to delivery in many cases) is matched by corresponding performance with repairs and, with the construction of new floating docks, the German shipbuilders are able to offer reliable service.

It is more unusual for German firms to have associated marine-engineering works than in this country. Deutsche Werft does not construct its own engines although it caters for repairs; Kieler Howaldtswerke and Howaldts-werker Hamburg, on the other hand, construct some engines for outsiders in addition to those needed for their own use. But the bulk of German engines are built by specialist producers. And in this respect a contrast may be noted in the evolution of the German and the United Kingdom industries, with the former emerging more as constructors in steel than builders of a complete ship.

SWEDEN

The three best-known shipyards in Sweden are Götaverken and Eriksberg at Gothenburg and Kockums at Malmö. They have launched over 100,000 g.r.t. of merchant ships year after year as well as carrying out repair and naval work and constructing engines. In 1958, Uddevallavarvet at Uddevalla also launched 100,000 g.r.t. and Oresundsvarvet, a subsidiary of the Gotaverken yard has launched 50,000 g.r.t. There are also three other yards launching significant amounts of tonnage. By common consent, Swedish shipbuilding can be described as the most efficient in the world and as such it merits special study.

Yet it can be said at once that there is nothing visibly very special about the Swedish yards, unless it be the fine office blocks of recent construction and interesting architectural features which tend to dominate the yards themselves. The yards are not particularly spacious, nor is the equipment used in them vastly different from that used in any other yards; the distinctive features of the yard are to be sought in other places, mainly in the application of managerial skill to the job of running a shipyard.

The Eriksberg shipyard can be described as cramped by desirable standards of space. The main portion of the yard stands between the cliff and the river, and the length of the berths is determined by the point at which the cliff rises and cannot be pushed back farther by blasting operations; this limits the largest size of tankers that can be built to 34,000 d.w.t. It would be pointless and fabulously expensive to attempt to alter yard facilities in order to enable the largest size of tanker to be built, and if the market for super-tankers develops it may be expected that the yard will establish a suitable berth down the river where adequate sites can be found, and bring the hulls up stream for outfitting and the installation of machinery. The neighbouring yard at Götaverken has already decided to take this course, although it can handle vessels up to 45,000 d.w.t. Kockums also, while giving the impression of greater space than the existing Götaverken yards, is not without problems in providing sufficient ground for its requirements, and it has been necessary to reclaim ground from the sea in order to carry out the most recent modernisation of facilities. It will be seen from the foregoing that the Swedish yards have not been at an advantage in having particularly favourable shipbuilding locations. Nor for that matter is the climate particularly helpful to ship construction.

All the Swedish yards have spent comparatively freely in improving their facilities, and the general impression of the yards is that there has been a steady succession of improvements in layout and in facilities almost from one year to the next. Old buildings have been demolished and new ones erected in their place, so that in the past ten years the shipyards have virtually been made new. Even so there is nothing very startling in the equipment used or the facilities available, nothing that could not be seen in many other yards on the Continent or in Britain. The welding bays and prefabrication shops are spacious, but not more so than in other yards and not spacious enough to meet all requirements,[1] the cranes are no larger than those used elsewhere and the characteristic weight of section lifted on to the berths is little if any greater than that common in other shipyards—up to 50 tons with a lift of 30 tons much more usual. Thus it can be said that the £¾ million or so invested on the average each year by the large shipyards in Sweden has done no more than provide up-to-date production facilities which offer little advantage at the present time over those installed by shipyards in the other countries and which, in some respects, are inferior to those in use in Japan. The design of the new shipyard being constructed in 1959 at Arendal by Götaverken, at a cost of £10 million, does represent however, a radical departure in shipbuilding techniques and equipment. From the steel stock-yard to the fabrication hall, plates will flow along a moving belt through the various processing departments. Prefabricated sections of up to 200 tons will be constructed and when they are completed they will be attached to the main body of the ship. As each new section is attached the latter will be propelled by hydraulic rams towards the foot of the dry dock from which the completed ship will be floated with its engine installed almost ready for its trial trip. Twenty weeks is expected to suffice for a 40,000 d.w.t. ship to reach this stage.

There is evidence that productivity has been increasing steadily over the years. Figures of the tonnage of ships produced at the Eriksberg yard can be set against the number of men employed since 1913, and although this no doubt presents a very misleading picture of the growth of output per man, it appears that there was a considerable improvement in performance by the 1920's from the early beginnings of the yard, and that in the inter-war period the foundations were laid for further improvement so that at the end of the thirties 20 g.r.t. of shipping (with its engines) might be produced per man, while by 1956 this had probably increased to 30 or more g.r.t. per man.

It is as difficult to attribute this high productivity of Swedish yards to the individual efforts of workmen as it is to the equipment mustered by the yards. The Swedish workman is no more inclined to start on time than his United Kingdom counterpart; his tea-breaks can be as extended; and he

---

[1] In 1957, some welded prefabrication work had to be done in the open for example.

applies himself to his work with no more evidence of vigour or purpose than would be seen in a British shipyard. Nor is he as comprehensively trained as craftsmen in this country. Three years' training is required in order to be a skilled mechanic, but a shipyard worker may be trained within the yard in a matter of months rather than years, without a period of apprenticeship. About only one-third of the labour force would properly be regarded as skilled by United Kingdom standards, but this does not mean that Swedish shipyards are at any considerable advantage financially in substituting dilutee labour for skilled labour, as the difference in pay between skilled and unskilled workers is rather small. The ease with which labour can be trained and the fact that there is no gulf between skilled and unskilled workers is one reason why Swedish workers are willing to accept new methods of working readily and why there is very little trace of demarcation, although it does occasionally arise in such practices as electricians being obliged to leave the insertion of certain types of screws to joiners. This, however, is a recent development. For the most part working conditions are good with attractive canteens provided, changing and washing facilities of a high order and three weeks' paid holiday.

Since neither equipment nor the quality of the labour force is unduly different from what is available elsewhere, it is natural to seek part of the explanation of the success of Swedish shipbuilding in the quality of management. On this score there can be little doubt; there is a very high standard of organisation and skill in shipyard management, and there is a relentless search for ways and means of carrying out work more economically. First and foremost the Swedish manager is a production engineer, and to increase productivity is every bit as important to him as to launch a fine vessel is to a naval architect. And with this attitude goes the conviction from experience that the opportunities for cost reduction will be every bit as great in the future as they have been in the past and no effort is spared to bring them about. In the Arendal yard, for example, it is expected that output per man will rise by 50 per cent compared with previous methods of construction. By British standards Swedish organisation is top heavy; a ratio between administrative personnel and operatives of 1–5 seems excessive; and Swedish management itself sometimes fears that administration is getting too cumbersome. But if an increase in managerial staff is the price of high productivity there can be no doubt that in cost saving it is well worth while.

Skilful management is evident in a number of other directions: in the selection of ships most suitable for the facilities of the yards; in the production of sequences of vessels of similar construction with consequent savings in production costs; in a readiness to move elsewhere if the size of ship outgrows a shipyard's berths; and in shrewd and careful purchases of bought-in materials and components. It is to management more than any other single factor that the present success of Swedish shipbuilding is due.

THE NETHERLANDS

The Dutch industry is composed of one large builder of new ships, the Nederlandsche Dok and Scheepsbouw, half a dozen other shipyards producing between 25,000 and 50,000 g.r.t. of shipping per annum, most of which cater for repair work in addition, and a large number of other producers ranging from those building one or two ships of 2000 or 3000 tons in a year to others launching a handful of small ships or even a single coaster. Of the total output the smaller shipyards account for perhaps one-third, whereas, as we have seen, the proportion is much less in the United Kingdom.

The organisation of the production of the small coasters contrasts vividly with that of the vast accumulation of capital and the large number of men that are necessary to launch super-tankers, and it is interesting that the shipwrights breaking off the cultivation of their fields to build a wooden ship on the river banks of Britain more than a century and a half ago have their modern counterpart on the canals of Holland. There are twenty-two shipbuilding yards on the narrow Winschoterdiep between Groningen and Sappemier.[1] There is a strong community spirit in these areas, and in hard times all will band together to ensure that an order for a ship will not be lost for want of the resources to build it, so that these Dutch builders are amongst the most competitive in the world.

The larger Dutch yards are also competitive and they have been very profitable. Much of what has been earned has been ploughed back into the business, and when this has been insufficient to allow plans to go ahead money has been raised on the market. The Nederlandsche Dok and Scheepsbouw Co., for example, has been spending the equivalent of £1 million per annum on reconstructing, improving and extending its facilities.[2] This must surely be one of the most spacious yards in the world with its fine roadways and clean layout. It is also one of the most progressive without yet having reached the highest standards of productivity.

On the new building side the yard has concentrated on producing tankers, with some cargo vessels from time to time; some naval work is undertaken but passenger ships are no longer constructed, with a resultant lightening of the load on management, which is free to concentrate on getting the maximum number of ships down the slips. Repair work is probably rather less important than new construction, but a large number of men are engaged on this work, for which fine graving docks are available. The largest of these is 800 ft. long 120 ft. wide and 28 ft. deep, so that very large ships can be accommodated, and all are equipped with modern facilities, ranging from a

---

[1] J. W. F. Werumens Buning, 'Delivery vans of the North Sea', *Progress*, Winter 1956–7, p.237.
[2] See the various balance sheets published since 1951 in English translation.

miniature engine room for servicing the ships, to washing and changing rooms for the men, built into the sides of the dock.

For Dutch shipyards, repair is probably more profitable than new building. In 1957, it was necessary to book months ahead to secure a place for overhaul in Dutch ship-repairing establishments which draw, not only from the thousands of ships calling at the ports of Rotterdam and Amsterdam, but from more distant ports, including a large number of ships from the United Kingdom. The Wilton-Fijenoord yard at Schiedam is equipped both for repair work and new building; the latter takes place in the graving docks, so that additional repair facilities could be made available if it were desired. There is an engine works which like most of the rest of the works is of recent construction, and it is large enough as well as diversified enough to cater for the construction of most types of engine, including Doxford, M.A.N., Sulzer and Pametrada designs as well as repair work of all kinds.

The Rotterdam Dry Dock Co. is another Dutch shipyard combining repair with new building; it also undertakes a considerable amount of engineering work of various kinds, including the manufacture of oil-refinery equipment and repairs to ships' engines, but not the construction of new engines. The company specialises in the production of crankshafts formed from a solid bar by means of a hydraulic press, and these are supplied in standard sizes to firms all over Holland and as far afield as Italy and Sweden, even though they are of great weight. In spite of the considerable first cost of the machinery required to do the job, the work is highly profitable and is an interesting example of what can be done by specialisation in engine building.

One of the main difficulties of the Dutch shipyards in 1957 was to obtain an adequate supply of labour of all kinds. Wages are closely regulated between the government and the trade unions and employers' associations. Periodic wage negotiations take place, but when the demand for labour generally exceeded the supply of labour at the wage-rates fixed, it was necessary to see that employers conformed to the terms of the agreements and did not pay wages and allowances in excess of the agreed rates. At the same time it appears that the movement of workers between firms to posts of the same grade (but not to a higher grade) is strongly discouraged in order to prevent poaching. It was interesting to find in shipbuilding that comparatively low wage-rates, which make it possible to earn profits high enough to reconstruct and expand the shipyards, are an obstacle to the recruitment of sufficient workers to man the yards nearer to full-capacity working, not only in the Netherlands but in other countries as well. Some yards have found it possible to import and employ foreign workers, but shortage of housing was an obstacle, and it was not always possible for firms to construct the dwellings needed to house workers near to the shipyards. Shortage of manpower is one reason why the Netherlands' shipbuilders have been opposed to the establishment of a new shipyard, the Verolme shipyard, in part extending and incorporating existing shipyards on the Island of Rosenburg, at an estimated cost of £20 million.

Increasing efforts are being made to train new workers in the industry. Boys may be given 2 or 3 years' instruction in schools attached to some of the shipyards, probably combined with instruction elsewhere, but the number catered for is not sufficient to hold out any promise of a large increase in the skilled labour force available in the yards in the near future. There is no opposition from the trade unions to the interchange of skilled men between different occupations, and if the management of a shipyard thought it desirable that a man with the requisite skill should be transferred from joinery work to sheet-metal work, or to any other occupation within his capabilities, they would be able to effect the change without provoking a strike or disturbing labour relations. This was a considerable advantage in early post-war years when the yards were sometimes held up for the delivery of a particular material, perhaps steel, and were able to transfer steelworkers to other jobs that they could not normally have undertaken. If a change in the composition of the labour force is necessary on a more permanent basis the training necessary to fit a worker for a new trade may be given in the shipyard school, if one exists.

Partly because of the difficulty of getting an adequate number of shipyard workers but also for other reasons an opportunity has been taken in the rebuilding of the larger shipyards to make employment as agreeable as possible. Admirable changing rooms and shower facilities are provided. Canteen arrangements are good and enlivened by simple but effective means of decoration. The Dutch shipyards are seeking in the provision of such facilities to bring shipyard conditions into line with, if not in advance of, the change in social outlook that is taking place in Holland. Some shipyard managers with many years' experience in the industry contrast the toughness of hard-drinking shipyard workers with the more responsible and materially better-off worker of today. It is not that the men have changed so much as the environment, physical and mental, and the shipyards are anxious that they should play their part in these changes which they judge to be for the better.

OTHER EUROPEAN PRODUCERS

The attitude of the Dutch to working conditions is common to all the Scandinavian yards. Apart from Sweden there are shipbuilding industries in Denmark and in Norway. The Danish industry is small but it is distinguished in including the world's largest producer or licenser of any type of large marine engine—Burmeister & Wain. This company acquired the Danish manufacturing rights of the diesel engine from the inventor in 1898, and by 1904 the first ten Burmeister & Wain stationary diesel units had been built. The success of the diesel engine owed a great deal to the improvements effected in the design by one of the company's engineers, Ivor Knudsen, and in 1912 the world's first ocean-going motor ship *Selandia* set out on her maiden voyage from Copenhagen to Bangkok. Another motorship, the *Fionia*, was so revolutionary that she was bought on sight by the American Line in 1912, and Viscount Pirrie was quick to see the possibilities of the Burmeister & Wain engine.

The output of the Burmeister & Wain shipyard in Copenhagen has increased spectacularly to 80,000 g.r.t. in 1958, somewhat less than Odense Vaerft, but rather larger than the other Danish shipyards. It would be possible to increase output quite considerably in Denmark if orders were adequate. Even in 1957 it was still possible to attract additional workers from other occupations (shipyard workers from distant parts are prepared to get up at 4.00 a.m. in order to be at work by 6.30 a.m.), but output has exceeded the levels attained in 1938 and 1939 only in 1957. Additional capital investment may be needed if it is to expand. The extensive reconstruction of Burmeister & Wain's facilities is likely, however, to increase capacity. There is some second-shift working on repair work but it is rather small in relation to the whole labour force, affecting perhaps no more than 5–10 per cent of workers, and small numbers of men may be engaged on a night shift if this is necessary. There is an additional payment of about 10–15 per cent for shift work.

Both Denmark and Norway have experienced difficulty in getting the tempo of work up to pre-war levels. In both countries a deliberate policy of 'go slow' was introduced in order to frustrate the completion of new ships during the war. (The only ship to be completed in Denmark sank as a result of an explosion soon after leaving the shipyards.) The rate of working is now satisfactory, and output in Norway has climbed well above pre-war levels. Roughly a dozen shipyards build ocean-going tonnage, but the output of none of them is very large, about 50,000 g.r.t. a year being the highest rate of output attained from any one shipyard. The shipyards build almost exclusively for Norway, although an occasional foreign order is taken. The industry could be of great advantage to Norway, which until 1958 built only one-fifth of the total tonnage added to the Norwegian fleet (one of the largest in the world) each year, and to build more ships would be a considerable relief to the balance of payments. One of the difficulties of increasing output has been the familiar one of developing an adequate supply of labour in some of the main centres of shipbuilding. In part this is being combated by training schemes for apprentices, and the provision of hostels—Akers at Oslo, for example, have built magnificent accommodation for this purpose—but an attempt has also been made to get some of the hull fabrication done in areas where labour is more plentiful, leaving the assembly or finishing to be completed in the main yards.

Shipbuilding in all the above European countries is likely to be competitive, so long as demand does not fall below average levels, without the need for state intervention or subsidies. In France and Italy this has not been the case in post-war years, and both have experienced difficulty in getting orders to keep their yards employed. Italian output fell sharply in 1954 and 1955 for this reason, and many orders would not have been placed if it had not been for government subsidies made available under the Tambroni Law approved in the spring of 1954 and named after the then Minister of the Merchant Marine. This replaced and co-ordinated earlier measures and was designed to expand the merchant marine and bring the output of the shipyards nearer to capacity levels by giving subsidies for new construction. The proposals put forward in 1954 were for a subsidy of 27 per cent towards the cost of building cargo vessels and 21 per cent towards the cost of passenger liners. From the point of view of Italy's competitors this was slightly better than the act of 1938 which subsidised as much as 40 per cent of the cost of ships built in Italy.

It is, of course, easy to condemn the practice of foreign governments in giving subsidies to shipping or shipbuilding; there was all too much of it in the inter-war period. But at the same time it is as well to realise that the level of costs in any country reflects not only its natural advantages or disadvantages for carrying on certain kinds of production but also more broadly the whole of the financial policies of the state. There is something inconsistent in reasoning which condemns a subsidy offered to a particular industry but condones a levelling of production costs by means of devaluation.

In 1954 the Italian yards were certainly at a disadvantage in a number of ways: the price of steel was high and the extra cost of raw materials in relation to the United Kingdom added 4–7 per cent to the cost of a ship; the yards were also burdened by being unable to dismiss redundant workers under labour regulations, besides being inefficient in the use of labour. But these are not necessarily good reasons for abandoning shipbuilding.

In spite of the fact that it has been difficult to employ the Italian yards at full capacity there are proposals to extend shipyard facilities. In 1957 a site was being cleared for a new shipyard north of Spezia, although this was expected to involve filling in about 2 million cubic metres of a bay and perhaps cutting a long tunnel to link up with the railway line. Even before starting work the company was in a position to receive a large number of orders. The Nederlandsche Dok and Scheepsbouw Co. is also interested in establishing operations in Italy. It is understood that their proposals are largely concerned with the repair of tankers coming round the foot of Italy in transit to and from the Suez Canal.

The combination of subsidies and favourable market conditions was such that Italian output was able to expand considerably. In 1956 over 350,000 g.r.t. of new ships were produced and output rose to 550,000 g.r.t. in 1958. Of the dozen or so shipyards launching ocean-going ships the Ansaldo Co. with three shipyards and an engine works is the most important, launching over 220,000 g.r.t. in 1958; it is followed by the Adriatico shipyards, which launched 115,000 g.r.t. in 1958; and a number of other yards produced much smaller tonnages.

There are about the same number of yards in France, of which the Penhoet-Loire group is the largest and the others much smaller. The French yards, like the Italian yards, continue to cater for the production of passenger liners, but again for a variety of reasons, including the over-valuation of the franc, have had to be subsidised in a number of ways.

There would be no shipbuilding output in the United States in normal circumstances without the payment of subsidies. Thus the output of the United States has in large measure depended on the amount of new shipbuilding that the Federal Government has been prepared to underwrite or the amount of protection that has been afforded to United States ships. There are a large number of devices that have been operated to give some preference to the American marine and American shipyards. On the shipbuilding side these range from the placing of government orders in United States yards to the provision of loans on generous terms and turn-in allowances on old vessels if the operator agrees to build a replacement vessel in a domestic yard.[1] A recent example of this kind of arrangement was the permission granted to Niarchos to remove some of his tankers building in the United States from the United States flag and so reap taxation concessions on condition that new orders were placed in United States yards.[2]

On the shipping side there is a long history of preference. The Cabotage restrictions date to almost the beginning of the United States as a sovereign nation; there have also been a number of provisions of long standing subsidising the operation of shipping as well as legislation to ensure that 50 per cent of United States aid shipments are shipped in American bottoms, and other forms of concealed subsidy.

These measures have not on the whole operated in such a way as greatly to increase the output of the United States shipbuilding industry. After a fall in 1946 and 1947 United States shipyards launched over 600,000 g.r.t. in 1949, and since then have built from 73,000 g.r.t., in 1955, to 730,000 g.r.t., in 1958. At times of keen demand for ships the reserve capacity of the

[1] The reader is referred to Wytze Gorter, *United States Merchant Marine Policies, Essays in International Finance*, no. 23, June 1955, Princeton University, and to the same author's *United States Shipping Policy*, 1956.

[2] *The Financial Times*, 22 January 1957.

United States shipyards is useful in relieving a shortage of shipping, and since maintaining shipyards in an operative condition well below full capacity is an expensive business, it is not certain that foreign shipbuilders have much to grumble about in American protective measures.

Indirectly the United States is potentially a much more serious competitor with European shipyards. The revival of Japanese shipbuilding owes something to United States influence, and United States interests have been instrumental in the establishment of a new shipyard in Formosa by the Ingall's Shipbuilding Corporation which it is expected will be competitive with the lowest cost producers in the world. The engines for the ships will be provided by the Westinghouse Corporation. In this way American technical skill and organisational genius will be combined with a plentiful supply of cheap labour and, in spite of the fact that the merchant output of United States shipyards is modest, technical development is on a grand scale. The development of the *Nautilus*, the building of subsequent submarines of the same pattern, experiments with various types of prime movers in war-built tonnage in order to evaluate the possibilities of gas-turbine and other types of engine, attempts to modify T 2 tankers by increasing their length in order to carry more cargo are only some of the ways in which the United States, well prompted by the Maritime Administration, is pushing on with technical developments in ship design.

With so much know-how behind them, United States business men, financing the construction of tankers in many parts of the globe for the use of extra-national shipping companies, are formidable competitors with United Kingdom shipping interests and directly and indirectly with United Kingdom shipbuilding, and they must be rated a greater challenge to United Kingdom maritime prosperity than the state-controlled infant industries of Spain or India feeling their way to economic independence.

CHAPTER 14

The Competitive Position

With a detailed picture of the United Kingdom industry and an outline of the main characteristics of the United Kingdom's competitors, it is possible to pass to an assessment of their comparative competitive strengths. Before doing so it may be useful briefly to review the main factors that influence the competitive position. Pride of place must, even in this era of highly organised production, be given to inventive genius. Far more has been done to reduce the cost of sea transport by technical progress than by increased productivity in the shipyards, and far more remains to be done by man's inventiveness than by shipyard organisation, however imperfect that may be. The United Kingdom shipbuilding industry would have been in a vastly different position if the patent of Herbert Akroyd Stewart had been developed into the first practical diesel engine. But, having said this and implied its warning in the conduct of research and in its application, it is as well to remember that technique is free to all in a way that shipyard organisation is not, and that in the last resort it is economic factors—sales and marketing—that decide the day.

In the last resort what determines where ships are produced is where costs are lowest, or where orders can be attracted by favour, custom or subvention, or where delivery can be made speedily to take advantage of a transient situation. But in attempting to assess the competitive position of the main producers in the industry over a longish period of time, it is useful to approach the question by looking at the cost structure.

For the United Kingdom industry in 1954, Table 20 gives an impression of the relative importance of the various kinds of costs. The cost pattern shown in the table relates to the whole of the output of the shipbuilding and ship-repairing industry; it does not include the marine-engineering industry except in so far as shipbuilding establishments[1] bought in engines and other equipment from marine establishments and installed them themselves.

Although the table does not represent any one side of the activities of shipbuilders, but presents a composite picture of the whole industry (including the naval dockyards), it is of value in pointing to some of the factors that influence the competitive position. It is customary in all economic writings on the subject to refer to shipbuilding as an assembly industry with the implication that it has little influence over its own costs beyond that exercised

[1] For the purpose of the Census the marine-engineering and shipbuilding businesses of firms that combine these activities are regarded as taking place in separate establishments.

by buying carefully and well. There is a good deal that is misleading in this view. It is by no means unusual for any industry to buy in 50 per cent of the value of the raw materials or semi-finished products that it transforms into what for it is a finished product; indeed, this is the characteristic pattern when establishments and not whole industries or the gross national product are considered. But to call the shipbuilding industry an assembly industry is also to belittle the amount of processing that is called for in working the steel or constructing engines, and unjustifiably to suggest that it is in the main an unskilled work of connecting one component to another.

Table 20.—*Costs elements in shipbuilding and ship-repairing as shown in the* 1954 *Census of Production*

		£ million		Percentages
Gross output		311		100
Work on materials given out		34		11
Cost of materials		136		43
of which:	Iron & steel	30·8	9·7	
	Other metals & alloys	2·8	0·9	
	Paints and compositions	2·0	0·6	
	Timber	6·4	2·0	
	Marine machinery and associated equipment	39·1	12·4	
	Radio equipment	0·3	0·1	
	Other purchases (errors and omissions)	54·5	17·2	
Net output		141		46
of which:	Wages	108	35	
	Overheads and profits	33	11	

This is not to say, however, that the purchasing department of a ship-yard does not exercise an important influence on costs, although in the United Kingdom the opportunities for shrewd buying are less than they were 25 years ago. Much the most important single material used in ship-building and ship-repairing is steel, but there is very little that an individual buyer can do to keep down the price of this, since costs are determined by the pricing policy followed by the whole of the steel industry. The opportunities to purchase well are restricted to ensuring that the right sizes of plates and structural parts are available in order to minimise waste, and that steel requiring the minimum amount of preparation in the way of rolling and rust removal is obtained from suppliers. In times of acute shortage of steel, however, it is not price or quality that is at stake so much as delivery. Some of the shrewdest bits of buying have been to secure marginal quantities of steel from various sources, including foreign sources, to prevent hold-ups and increase the loading of an individual yard nearer to capacity without cavilling at a price much in excess of what is normally paid.[1]

The next most important item to steel in bought-in materials is usually timber, but none of the items specified in the table is as important as the bought-in machinery included in the purchases of the shipbuilding and repairing industry or the miscellaneous collection of other purchases, including textile materials, plastics, refrigerating equipment and many other articles that go to the making of the ship.

The importance of subcontracting to specialists working on the finishing of the ship can also be seen from the item 'work on materials given out'. It is important to keep a careful watch on these items, for although there are few forms of even specialist construction that cannot be undertaken in a shipyard (they can often be done as cheap as or more cheaply than by outsiders), it is necessary to look to continuity in employment as an important element in costs and to balance a yard's productive facilities with the type of work it is called upon to undertake.

The table we have been discussing shows that, for the Census data, wages accounted for 35 per cent of the gross output of the industry. The importance of shipyard wages as an element in costs varies considerably according to the class of work that is undertaken. It is more important in repair work than it is in new construction, more important in the cost of highly finished ships, such as passenger liners, than in simple types, and less important in the construction of large tankers than in smaller vessels. Similarly, the proportion of total costs represented by material purchases, and particularly steel, varies with the class of work, whether it is repair or new construction of various types. It follows from this that, apart from other considerations, countries with low wages will be able to carry on repair work comparatively cheaply, while countries with low steel costs and high rates of wages might be best advised to concentrate on the production of large tankers. In practice, as we saw in the last chapter, extreme specialisation on one or the other of these kinds of work does not take place along country divisions for a variety of reasons, and there are types of ships which are produced in all shipbuilding countries of the world, ranging from simple cargo vessels to tankers of very considerable size.

In order, therefore, more readily to compare the competitive advantages of shipbuilding countries, it may be least misleading to think in terms of the typical breakdown of costs involved in the construction of a cargo vessel. This pattern will not be followed in all shipbuilding countries, but it enables

---

[1] Bartram's yard, for example, have cited 'sweeteners' of foreign steel as being a factor contributing to their high productivity. See the *Shipbuilding and Shipping Record*, 3 January 1957, p. 25.

a rough comparison to be made of the various factors affecting the competitive ability of the leading producers.

Steel accounts for 17 per cent of the cost of this vessel. With a large tanker the percentage would be appreciably higher, perhaps 20–25 per cent, depending on size and whether the steel was bought at high or low prices. Until 1958, the relative cheapness of United Kingdom steel gave an appreciable cost advantage to United Kingdom shipbuilders in the post-war period, though as we have indicated it would have been more advantageous for them to have had unlimited supplies of steel on less favourable terms. Not all shipbuilding steel was more expensive than that supplied to United Kingdom shipbuilders by the steel industry, even in conditions of scarcity. The small steel-producing industry in Denmark operating with scrap was able to turn

Table 21.—*Analysis of construction costs of a* 10,000 *d.w.t. cargo vessel*
Percentages, January, 1957

	Material cost	Labour cost	Overhead charges	TOTAL
Steel work	17	8	—	25
Deck machinery and equipment	9	1	—	10
Ship outfitting	6	6	—	12
Main and auxiliary engine-room machinery	23	10	—	33
Total	55	25	20	100

Source: *Shipping World,* 16 January 1957

out steel of the highest quality at least as cheaply as the United Kingdom industry, and perhaps with some advantage on the Danish side. All other countries in Europe, Japan and the United States were, however, forced to pay more for shipbuilding steel, and the scarcer steel became, the more they had to pay, for Continental producers have not followed the United Kingdom practice of attempting to stabilise the price of steel irrespective of the level of demand.

When steel was scarce it probably cost more in Sweden than in other countries. In the summer of 1957 Swedish shipbuilders stated they were sometimes paying as much as £65 per t., though this may have exaggerated the average competitive disadvantage they were labouring under at the time. But the system of differential prices for home consumption and export sales meant that in 1955 steel plates were costing free on board roughly one-fifth more than the delivered price in this country, and in 1951, when shipbuilding steel was acutely scarce, Swedish shipbuilders are reputed to have told their customers that if they wished their ships to be completed quickly, they would have to be prepared to pay for steel as much as £80 per t., and it is scarcely surprising that owners felt at the time that this was well worth while. Steel costs in Japan were also higher than in the United Kingdom, though the price charged to shipbuilders depended on the extent to which it was thought desirable to subsidise the cost of building ships. In 1950 steel was supplied to the shipyards at about £18 per t.,[1] but by mid-1956 it had risen to over £50 per t. and in 1957 steel imported from the United States bearing a freight charge of £14 per t.[2] may have cost getting on for £60. In Germany ship-building steel was being supplied to the yards at about £50 per t. in June 1957, a price that the industry was well able to pay, but in 1956 a system of differential charging was in use, in which the steelworks were supplying steel at 550 M. per t. (roughly £47) rather than the 840 M. per t. (£72)[3] that was the world-market price at that time. The Dutch shipyards appeared to be more favourably placed in June 1957 with steel costing around £45 per t. for normal delivery, although £65 per t. might have to be paid for special steel needed for ship-repair work. About half the steel used came from Dutch sources with some sections being imported from the United Kingdom in exchange for ingots, and other supplies being drawn from Continental steelworks.

A great deal has been said by Continental shipbuilders about the competitive advantage that cheaper steel conferred on United Kingdom producers. In fact the advantage has been somewhat overrated. If, for some large size of tanker, steel costs amounted to about 20–25 per cent of total costs, to take an extreme example, buying steel at about £40 per t. in June 1957, rather than £65 per t., would have enabled United Kingdom shipbuilders to cut their costs below their competitors by as much as 10 per cent, but for smaller vessels and a more usual differential on steel prices of 25 per cent the advantage would not have been more than 5 per cent. By 1959, however, steel prices had turned full circle. Far from the United Kingdom charging more for the steel it exported than for deliveries at home, Continental producers were charging less for exports than the home price and undercutting United Kingdom supplies. If anything the United Kingdom industry was operating at a disadvantage.

Comparison of shipbuilding wages amongst the main shipbuilding producers is fraught with statistical difficulties. Wage-rates cannot be used, for a proportion of labour costs is made up of overtime earnings and other payments and the ratio between the two varies from country to country, and according to the amount of overtime that is carried out from time to time, as well as with the incidence of shift-working. Moreover, in order to obtain a

---

[1] *Shipbuilding and Shipping Record,* 11 June 1951.
[2] See *The Financial Times,* 3 October 1957.
[3] See *The Financial Times,* 9 October 1956, p. 7.

comparison of labour costs to the employer, it is necessary to take into account social security contributions that have to be paid in consequence of employing a workman. This is not, however, the whole story, for it is common practice for employers voluntarily to provide additional benefits to their workmen over and above those required by law; these may include subsidised meals, the provision of changing rooms, sports facilities, and subsidiary insurances of a variety of kinds. In so far as these become part and parcel of the conditions of employment or the wage bargains struck with the unions, and cannot be easily withdrawn, they must be regarded as part of the costs of employing labour and brought into the comparison of labour costs between countries.

As a result of a number of discussions with shipbuilders on the Continent in June 1957, an attempt has been made to obtain a comparative picture of labour costs in certain countries, but the discussion that follows is somewhat impressionistic and should be regarded as giving no more than a very rough indication of the orders of magnitude involved. In the Netherlands, where 48 hours per week was worked with no great amount of overtime, hourly earnings appeared to be around 1·75 guilders per hour; over and above this, however, 40 per cent was paid in obligatory social security charges, including holiday payments, so that hourly labour costs amounted to about 2·5 guilders, or about 4s. 8d. Overtime payments are an additional 25 per cent on weekdays, 50 per cent after 5 o'clock on Saturdays, and double time on Sundays. Workers on second shifts (a small proportion) are paid an additional 25 per cent.

In Germany average hourly earnings, including overtime, appeared to be about 2·50 M. for skilled workers and about 10–15 per cent less for the unskilled, say about 3s. 9d. per man on the average; social security charges, including paid holidays, were assessed at about 20 per cent of earnings by the International Labour Office[1] in 1956, so that the equivalent cost is about 4s. 6d. Swedish workers were paid about 5·50 kröner an hour for a working week, including a small amount of overtime (which is not allowed by government legislation to exceed 200 hours per year), of about 50 hours. Overtime is paid at the rate of 25 per cent for the first two hours in the week and at 50 per cent thereafter with 100 per cent on Sundays. Social security charges can be put at about 10 per cent, so that the cost of an hour's labour to employers was in the region of 6·00 kröner, or roughly 8s. 4d. In Norway average earnings for skilled and unskilled men amounted to about 5s. 6d., excluding overtime and shift working. A 44-hour week is usual, with time and a half for overtime, except on Saturday afternoons and Sundays, when it is double time. Social security charges including voluntary expenditure add about

---

[1] *Social Aspects of European Economic Co-operation*, p. 33. I.L.O., Geneva, 1956.

15 per cent to labour costs, bringing the total to about 6s. 4d. In Denmark earnings are about the same, averaging about 5·7 kröner in Copenhagen and 4·8 kröner in the provinces, say 5·2 kröner or roughly 5s. 6d., and social security charges also bring the figure up to about 6s. 4d. per hour.

Against these figures United Kingdom shipbuilding workers were earning about 5s. 6d. and allowing for social security charges cost the employer about 6s. It must be emphasised again that the above figures are no more than a guide to comparative labour costs in some of the main European centres of shipbuilding, and it is with this in mind that the following broad generalisations are made. The cost of an hour's labour to an employer in June 1957 was least in Germany and the Netherlands, where it was only about 75–80 per cent of the United Kingdom level. In Denmark and Norway, on the other hand, it was slightly greater than in the United Kingdom, perhaps 5 per cent greater, while in Sweden it was about 40 per cent greater. Earnings in Japan, however, are much smaller than in any of these countries. Without attempting any precise estimate it may be said that the earnings of a Japanese workman in the shipbuilding industry are of the order of half that of a United Kingdom workman and about one-third that of a Swedish workman. Finally, it may be noted that the United States workman is paid 2½ times the Swedish rate, more than 3½ times the United Kingdom rate, and 7 times the Japanese rate.

The effect of these differences on the cost of shipbuilding in the various countries depends on the weighting that is assigned to labour costs in the selling price of a ship. If labour costs are taken to represent one-quarter of the selling price in the United Kingdom, we can say that, if Swedish rates of wages had to be paid, the cost of a ship would be increased by 10 per cent; if United States rates had to be paid, costs would be put up by 60 per cent; while if wages were down to the level of the Japanese worker, costs would be reduced by around 12½ per cent.

The United States yards, we have already stated, cannot compete in normal circumstances without subsidies. Even allowing for the fact that it was estimated by the Federal Maritime Board in 1954 that British yards required nearly a fifth more man-hours of direct labour than American yards,[1] it is hardly surprising that United States shipyards are unable to compete in world markets. Nearer home, in Sweden, hourly earnings, while not approaching United States levels, are substantially greater than those in the United Kingdom, while steel, as we have seen, is often more expensive. How is it that the Swedish yards, nevertheless, have been able to compete with the United Kingdom? The answer lies, of course, in high productivity. It may be estimated, albeit with great reservation, that output per man in Swedish

---

[1] See Wytze Gorter, op. cit. p. 3.

yards is something like half as great again as in United Kingdom shipyards. This is sufficient to offset the higher wages that are paid and, moreover, it probably has the indirect effect that capital equipment is used more intensively, thus spreading overheads and offsetting the disadvantage of high steel prices.

The low rate of wages in Japan is not matched by any corresponding disadvantage on the side of labour productivity—at least in relation to the United Kingdom. Output per man in some Japanese yards is said to be comparable with that of Swedish yards, though the average is appreciably worse. There is no reason to believe, however, that Japanese yards are more prodigal of manpower than United Kingdom yards—perhaps the reverse. Broadly speaking, therefore, it may be said that in relation to the United Kingdom, the higher cost of steel and other bought-in materials to Japanese yards in 1957 was about balanced by lower wages. In relation to Japanese and European shipyards it can be argued that the Dutch yards are in the most promising position from the competitive point of view. Their steel costs have been among the lowest in Europe, and in the future they should certainly not be at any disadvantage on this score; wages are lower than elsewhere in Europe, and not so vastly different from those paid to Japanese workers; the larger yards are very well equipped and in an excellent position to cater for remunerative repair work in times of boom or to keep going by this means if orders should be difficult to get in times of slump. Finally, they are well managed, and although productivity is not yet on the Swedish plane there is no reason why it should not become so.

Germany also is in a favourable position on the ground of wage-rates and is plentifully supplied with steel, but the equipment of many yards is still in need of modernisation and productivity does not approach the highest standards.

At the level of demand ruling in 1955 and 1956 it has been possible for the United Kingdom, Germany, the Netherlands, the Scandinavian countries and Japan to operate their industries at a high level of profit. Their costs are sufficiently in line one with another for orders to be spread amongst their shipyards when demand is keen. This does not mean that they have all been quoting the same prices for similar ships at different times. Table 22, compiled from data given in *The Financial Times*, illustrates this point.[1]

In 1954 orders were hard to get, and the Japanese, anxious to get into the export market, quoted low prices. As the market improved prices were increased until in mid-1956, when orders were flowing freely, the Japanese price was increased above that quoted for the United Kingdom, although it was below that charged by Western Germany. By March 1957, however,

[1] 9 March 1957. The figures appear to have been lifted out of an article in the *Shipping World* 16 January 1957. See the proceedings of the Court of Inquiry in 1957.

the United Kingdom quotation had gone up to about £86 per t. At this time about the same price per ton as for the cargo vessel was being quoted for 20,000 d.w.t. tankers in the United Kingdom and in Germany, while Scandinavian yards were quoting £80–85 per t.; French prices were within the upper limit of the range, Japanese prices £85–90 per t. and Italian prices £95 per t. without the subsidy. By the end of 1958, the position had again changed. Japanese prices had been drastically reduced in order to obtain new orders. The cost of a 46,000 d.w.t. tanker which might have been £80 per ton when new orders rocketed in 1957 had fallen to about £55 per ton.[1]

Table 22.—*Price (in pounds) per ton for* 11,000 *d.w.t. dry-cargo ship*

	1954	1955	1956 mid-year
		£	
W. Germany	71	75	91
Japan	63	71	86
United Kingdom	66	70	78

Three observations may be made on these figures assembled in *The Financial Times*. First, the fact that different quotations were made by yards in different countries probably illustrates as much the imperfections of the market as any differences in cost; secondly, there is scope for quite marked movements of prices in a downward direction when the market is tight; the contribution to overheads and profits, often nominally recorded at 20 per cent of the price of a ship, can very well be halved if orders are hard to get, or even eliminated if the yard must be kept going at all costs; thirdly, the delivery dates that the various yards were able to offer had an important relation to the price they were able to get on the market; the sooner delivery can be made, the more likely is an owner to be ready to pay a higher price, if freights are high.

There is no need to elaborate the first conclusion; we have already discussed the spheres of influence of the various shipbuilding countries and their need to secure a share, sometimes a substantial share, of export markets. With a larger protected market, in this sense, than other countries the United Kingdom is at an advantage and has not felt such acute anxiety to obtain orders as the Japanese yards have on occasion.

On the second point it is worth pointing out that shipbuilding is becoming increasingly capitalised and the proportion of overhead to prime costs is growing. This is evident in a rather unexpected way from the data supplied by *Fairplay* to the Maritime Transport Committee of the O.E.E.C.

There has been, of course, no change in the specification of the Fairplay

---

[1] See *The Financial Times*, 29 October 1959.

ship over the period for which the figures have been compiled. The total cost is arrived at by asking a shipbuilder what it would cost to build such a ship, allowing on his estimate a reasonable profit. In the details of the index only two items are given for the cost of the ship, the price of steel and hourly earnings, which we may assume to cover 20 and 25 per cent respectively of the cost of the ship, leaving the remaining 55 per cent to cover the cost of other bought-in raw materials and fittings as well as overheads and profits. Since hourly wage-rates have little more than doubled during the post-war

Table 23.—*Cost of building* 9500 *ton 'Fairplay' basis ship* (9500 *d.w.t.*, 5300 *g.r.t.*, 3200 *n.r.t.*, 12 *knots*)*

	Average hourly rates	Index	Price of steel plates per ton £ s. d.	Index	New ship per dwt.t. £ s. d.	Index
1945	28·5	100	16 3 0	100	26 0 0	100
1946	29·3	103	16 19 7	105	28 0 0	108
1947	33·5	117	17 4 6	107	31 10 0	121
1948	35·8	126	18 3 0	112	37 0 0	142
1949	36·5	128	18 11 6	115	40 0 0	154
1950	36·6	128	20 14 6	128	42 0 0	162
1951	39·4	138	20 14 6	128	46 5 0	178
1952	43·0	151	25 6 6	157	58 0 0	223
1953	46·1	162	29 14 0	184	65 5 0	251
1954	48·6	170	30 6 6	188	65 5 0	251
1955	52·9	185	31 1 6	193	65 15 0	253
1956	58·0	203	33 1 6	204	72 10 0	278
1957	58·0	203	39 2 0	242	79 0 0	304
1958	62·0	217	42 12 0	264	83 15 0	322
1959	63·5	223	42 2 0	262	84 5 0	324

* The figures relate to January of each year except that hourly earnings from 1947 to 1956 relate to April.

period and steel has increased in price by only 1½ times, while the price of a ship has trebled, it appears to follow that other costs must have increased by over 3 times. It is difficult to believe that bought-in raw materials and fittings have increased by so much more than the price of steel and labour that they can account for all of this increase, and it appears likely that there must have been a rise in overheads included in the figures by the shipbuilder preparing the Fairplay estimate. It is perhaps unreasonable to belabour the figures or to attempt to read more from them than they are intended to convey; yet there is little in them to suggest that productivity has been rising as a result of the improvement in yard facilities that has given rise to the increase in overhead charges. Such advantages as have been reaped arise not so much from an improvement in output per man, of which there is scant evidence, but in the building of better ships—a point we have already made but which cannot be reflected in the cost of construction of a ship of unchanged specification.

There is one other point that is worth touching on before concluding our survey of the competitive position of the various countries building ships, and that is the time taken to construct ships. We have already noted that speedy delivery is an attraction to shipowners when freights are high, and at times orders have been lost to the United Kingdom because delivery times were longer than those offered by other countries. Speedy construction, while

Table 24.— *Construction times (in months) for certain types of vessels* (1952–6)*

	Material being worked or on the stocks	Fitting out	Total
Passenger and Passenger cargo vessels	16	7½	23½
Tankers	14½	5½	20
Cargo liners	13½	5	18½
Cargo tramp	10½	4	14½

* From J. R. Parkinson 'United Kingdom shipbuilding times', *Scottish Journal of Political Economy,* June 1957, p. 149.

not necessarily a means of increasing output when order books are full, is nevertheless a means of reducing costs to which too little attention is paid in the United Kingdom. Ships undoubtedly take longer to build in the United Kingdom than in other countries.

Figures given in Table 24 have been compiled by dividing the tonnage of vessels under construction, but not fitting out, by the total of the tonnage launched each year to give the first column; and by dividing the tonnage of vessels fitting out by the tonnage completed each year to give the second column. The third column is the sum of the first two. All the basic figures are given in *Lloyd's Register Shipbuilding Returns*, issued quarterly.

The figures arrived at in this way probably exaggerate the time taken to launch the ship (but not to finish it), because as soon as any work is commenced on a ship, the whole tonnage of the ship is shown under construction, not just the equivalent tonnage of the work that has been carried out; thus if one of the keel-plates is fabricated in a plater's shop and laid down 3 months later on the ship, to be followed 3 months later again by active construction, the ship will be shown as having been under construction for 6 months, although during this period practically no work was done on it.

Nevertheless, there can be no doubt that ships take much longer to construct in the United Kingdom than other countries, and that this effectively increases the price of the ship. In Japan the shipyards are organised to maintain a berth cycle of 6–7 months, even for 40,000 d.w.t. tankers; in Holland tankers of 20,000 or 32,000 d.w.t. are commonly launched in 6 months and fitted out in 3 months; in Germany even better launching times are attained, with ships taking no more than 3 months on the berth and 3 months to complete in some yards; and in Sweden very little, if any, more time is needed in total than in Germany. A sample analysis by Dr G. A. Theel[1] of the time taken to complete various types of vessels in the United Kingdom and in other countries in the period 1951–5 showed the same picture. From keel-laying to completion the United Kingdom times for the construction of a 32,000 d.w.t. tanker varied from 517 to 930 days, with an average of 808 days, compared with 204 days for an isolated tanker in a Swedish shipyard, 307 days in Western Germany and 414 days in Italy. For a 10,000 d.w.t. motor tanker the comparison was also strikingly adverse to the United Kingdom, which took an average of 509 days against 227 days in Western Germany and 200 days in Sweden. Indeed, there were instances of ships in these categories taking longer to complete after launching in the United Kingdom than to build in their entirety in other countries. It is not possible to explain such extreme differences on the grounds that United Kingdom shipbuilders, having relatively more berths and less steel than their competitors, laid the keel well before they were ready to begin active construction. Nor, on the other hand, can the remarkably good times achieved by foreign shipbuilders be explained on the grounds that they produce most of the ship in assembly sheds before erection on the berth in the way that enabled United States yards to build ships in less than a week during the war, since, in fact, their practice in this matter is not vastly different from that of United Kingdom shipyards.

Speedy construction is a sign of good organisation and good management, and the time needed to complete a ship, without having to have recourse to expedients to accelerate construction, is a good indicator of a shipyard's efficiency. Quite apart from this, however, it makes for a cheaper article. If it can be assumed, for example, that construction is evenly spread over time in all cases, a tanker taking 808 days to complete in the United Kingdom will cost the equivalent of its value in interest charges over 404 days against 102 days for a tanker taking 204 days to construct in Sweden. Thus in broad terms, interest charges (and, for that matter, insurance charges) will have to be borne over an additional 302 days for a tanker constructed in the United Kingdom compared with one constructed in Sweden. It is difficult

---

[1] *Weltwirtschaftdienst*, April 1952, p. 212.

to know what the appropriate interest rate would be for money borrowed to finance tanker construction. But it may be proper to reckon the cost in terms of what shipowners would expect to earn on the capital tied up in vessels in progress if they had this capital liberated for other uses; and on this basis at current rates of taxation the appropriate rate would be 15–20 per cent rather than the rate of 5–7 per cent which might normally be paid on bank credits. Thus, in the example given above, the greater time for the construction of the tanker in two different centres may increase the equivalent cost of the tanker by at least 12 per cent.

This is not, however, the whole story. When there is surplus building capacity, shipowners will frequently require speedy delivery of a ship in order to take advantage of a sudden, and perhaps temporary, increase in freights above ruling levels. In these conditions there is a strong incentive to place orders where quick delivery can be given.

V
CONCLUSIONS

E.S.U.K

CHAPTER 15

Efficiency and Prospects

We have now surveyed the more important aspects of shipbuilding economics and are in a position to draw the threads together and assess the efficiency of the industry and review its prospects.

Efficiency must be assessed in relation to a number of factors: the progress that has been made in adapting the industry to modern conditions; the state of the industry in other countries; and so far as can be seen, the improvements that can be made on the basis of existing knowledge in ship design, in shipyard processes and managerial organisation.

The progress made since the end of the war is at one and the same time encouraging and disappointing: encouraging because the industry has shown resilience in emerging from the prolonged period of depression that it went through in the thirties, and disappointing because the pace of modernisation has been too slow and the fruits of it uncertain. The industry undoubtedly suffered from too gloomy a view being taken of its prospects in the immediate post-war period. This affected it in two ways. First, too little priority was given to securing steel supplies, and too little priority was given to the investment of the comparatively small sums that the industry needed; there can be no doubt that the industry suffered from a policy that gave encouragement to the investment of huge sums in motor-car production and oil refineries and little help to shipbuilding, although it was a ready source of foreign exchange; but if it was right to spend large sums on the reconstruction of the Dutch shipyards, on improvements to the Swedish yards and on German shipyards, it would have been no less right to have pushed the reconstruction of British shipyards forward as a matter of economic policy. Secondly, the combined effects of market forebodings and restrictions on the means to increase output reacted on initiative—already at a low ebb—and resulted in complete failure to exploit what proved, for many years, to be a large and growing market. While German output doubled between 1952 (it was then $\frac{1}{2}$ million g.r.t.) and 1956 and Japanese output trebled to touch $1\frac{1}{2}$ million g.t. in 1956 and increased to little short of $2\frac{1}{2}$ million g.t. in 1957, United Kingdom output increased by only a small percentage.

Part of the explanation of this must lie in the structure of the industry. Family concerns must be expected to expand with an eye to the risks involved when a comfortable living is to be had from existing levels of output and taxation discourages further profit making; and at the other extreme companies with a wide spread of interests appear to have neglected the profitable

213

opportunities existing in shipbuilding as well as in newer industries. In some ways it is a pity that there was no serious threat to the competitive position of existing shipbuilding companies from new arrivals on the scene in this country.

The reconstruction of shipyards has taken place in two stages. The first stage involved adaptation of yard facilities for welding and prefabrication, but while some firms invested large sums in this direction at an early stage a number lagged behind and began programmes of capital investment ten years after the end of the war, which most desirably would have been completed some years before. A second stage of shipyard alterations became necessary in 1957: the enlargement of existing berths and modifications to other facilities needed to build the very large tankers of 60,000–100,000 d.w.t. that were being ordered in increasing quantities; at the same time the need for new repair facilities and dry docks became increasingly apparent.

The sums involved in creating new facilities on the scale now envisaged are very large. If Dutch experience is any guide, a large shipyard producing perhaps 100,000 g.r.t. of shipping a year and carrying out a large volume of repair work may need to spend up to £1 million per annum for many years on end, and this is in line with the cost of some schemes now in hand. While it is not beyond the means of shipbuilding companies to provide the funds they need from reserves and undistributed profits, or to raise them on the market, there is a need to ensure that capital is used economically, that there is not over-investment in relation to the likely flow of new orders and that the fixed capital is not unnecessarily exposed to risk. In this respect double-shift working would be valuable wherever it can be put into practice, not only in reducing the amount of capital needed and so providing an opportunity for workers to increase their remuneration on second-shift working but also in reducing the amount of capital which is at risk.

In this connection it is also reasonable to ask whether there are not too many firms in the industry. It is difficult to be dogmatic on this point. In so far as net output per man is any guide to the efficiency of firms this appears to be higher in smaller rather than in larger firms, and it is interesting that two firms in the industry reputed to be highly efficient both produce no more than 30,000–40,000 t. of shipping per annum. On this scale of output rather more than 30 shipyards producing ocean-going ships does not appear unreasonable. It may be noted, however, that the Swedish yards, catering likewise for simple cargo vessels or tankers, have a very high output per man, although they launch more than 100,000 g.r.t. per year. On this scale of output half the number of shipyards in the country would suffice for present output levels, and there might be advantages in having a smaller number of firms if greater co-ordination of industrial policies became feasible in consequence.

At present there is too little specialisation in the industry. The number and tonnage of passenger liners launched each year is much smaller than the importance attached to this work would suggest; the average tonnage launched in the period 1952–6 was only 100,000 t. per annum. This is no more than could be handled by one specialist shipyard, and it is difficult to see why so many shipyards should be equipped for passenger-liner work unless the facilities they require can in some way be regarded as essential for naval work, which on the face of it seems unlikely. It is sometimes argued that to have only one passenger-liner producing company would be to rob the liner operators of the benefits of competitive tenders and designs. One solution might be for passenger-liner operating companies to control their own shipyard, but even if this is not feasible prices are at least as likely to be reduced by greater specialisation and greater continuity of passenger-liner work as they are to be increased by monopolistic tendencies, and although comparatively few shipbuilders in other countries build passenger liners it is still possible to obtain competitive tenders from overseas producers.

The benefit to existing shipbuilders of not feeling that on grounds of prestige they had to cater for passenger-liner work would be considerable, for they would be free to direct their attention to other things. Those yards on the Continent which have ceased to build passenger liners and decided to concentrate on cargo ships have invariably found that their task has been much simplified, that productivity has risen, and that financially they have benefited. In order to encourage one shipyard to concentrate largely on passenger liners it would probably be desirable for shipowners to attempt to draw up a common programme in order to ensure continuity of employment for the specialist yard. In view of the higher labour content of passenger-liner work and the amount of unemployment in Northern Ireland a case could be made for the concentration of passenger-liner production at Belfast.

Quite apart from passenger liners there is a much more general need for standardisation and specialisation. Standardisation of tankers would make an appreciable inroad into costs. Runs of ten to twenty tankers from the same (large) shipyard might well reduce shipyard costs per tanker by 10–15 per cent. Again, if standardisation is to be brought about there is a need for shipowners and shipbuilders to get together in their common interest of promoting maximum efficiency. Given this essential prerequisite certainly half and not inconceivably three-quarters of the tonnage of ships produced in United Kingdom shipyards could be divided into recognisably standard types distributed amongst shipbuilders according to their facilities. And from this beginning further savings from the standardisation of components might emerge, since the shipbuilding industry buys in large quantities. So far as standardisation is concerned other countries, mainly Sweden and Japan, are much more alive to the economies of longer runs and this gives them some competitive advantage.

What has been said about standardisation of ships applies in equal measure to engines; large reductions in costs can be made by producing batches of engines in appropriately laid out workshops instead of attempting to produce a medley of engines of different types and sizes in the same shop and passing indifferently from one to another in order to engine all the ships launched from the parent shipyard. This practice must also be seen in relation to the constant development of new and improved types of prime mover and the capital expenditure that is involved. 'In short, can the small-scale non-specialist engineering shop stand up to the large concentration of technical knowledge and capital that modern industry is developing?'[1]

By the time that present investment plans are completed it will be true to say that the capital equipment of United Kingdom shipyards will stand comparison with that in use by her competitors. As it is, there are many shipyards in the United Kingdom which, without being in advance of their leading overseas competitors, are, to say the least, at no great disadvantage in respect of capital equipment, and the increased tempo of investment now planned should mean that a number of shipyards will be rather better equipped in a few years' time than either Continental or Japanese rivals. This is encouraging, but by itself it will not be enough to re-establish United Kingdom supremacy. Good capital equipment is as necessary for shipbuilding as for any other industry, but the first requirements are good organisation and good planning. With these, results can be achieved with even mediocre equipment; without them the most advanced equipment will not suffice to attain high production standards.

Organisation has been, and continues to be, one of the weakest links in United Kingdom shipbuilding. In comparison with Swedish shipyards and others elsewhere productivity is low. Greater specialisation would help to remedy this and would simplify the organisational problem, but it is not the whole story; for high standards of productivity to be achieved a patient, thorough and repeated overhaul of all processes is necessary until the best and most economical methods of working are arrived at. If this is to be done with success new norms will have to be established and standards gradually raised to what has already been achieved or seems capable of achievement.

There can be no doubt that the relations between unions and employers at the present time are not conducive to improvements in productivity. It is all too true that the unions evince no interest in increasing output or productivity and that restrictive practices are a considerable hindrance to the efficient and smooth running of shipyards and ship-repairing firms. Yet productivity is far below the highest standards in many yards and low

[1] Sir Donald Anderson, speaking to the Scottish Section of the Institute of Marine Engineers, February 1957.

productivity is a serious handicap to the payment of higher wages. If Swedish workers produced no more than their British counterparts (whatever the reasons for this may be) they could not be paid almost half as much again. More serious, in the next few years there is the possibility that shipyard workers will be unemployed on an appreciable scale. If, as seems likely, orders continue to be few and far between, as they were in the first half of 1959, and United Kingdom shipyards continue to find difficulty in increasing output per man sufficiently to stave off foreign competition, some contraction in output will be inevitable.

This is what is so disappointing in the shipbuilding industry; with reasonable capital equipment, with great experience, with technological skill and scientific research, with men devoted to the industry and the most skilled shipbuilding workers in any country, productivity is far below what has been shown to be possible by overseas performance. Yet, paradoxically, it is in this conclusion that the shipbuilding industry's prospects lie. For there can be no doubt that the United Kingdom is as well placed to produce ships as any other country. The price of steel is likely to be no higher and may even continue to be lower than its costs to overseas competitors; wages are lower than wages in some countries and not so vastly different from what is paid in Germany, the Netherlands or Japan that the difference will not be narrowed to manageable dimensions as time goes on or offset in other ways. Technically there may be spectacular changes with the use of atomic energy in which the United Kingdom could be well placed to lead. And it would be wrong to underrate the qualities of the leaders in the industry who with increasing determination and doggedness are preparing the way for new advances by reconstructing their yards.

But the modernisation of an old industry with a century of history behind it, is not an easy task. And no-one can yet feel confident that shipbuilding can succeed in escaping from its past and regain in a modern setting those qualities of technical excellence combined with productive efficiency and cheapness that made the United Kingdom the shipyard of the world.

217

INDEX

For EU product safety concerns, contact us at Calle de José Abascal, 56–1°,
28003 Madrid, Spain or eugpsr@cambridge.org.

www.ingramcontent.com/pod-product-compliance
Ingram Content Group UK Ltd.
Pitfield, Milton Keynes, MK11 3LW, UK
UKHW042212180425
457623UK00011B/182